Competitive MINDSTORMS™: A Complete Guide to Robotic Sumo Using LEGO® MINDSTORMS™

DAVID J. PERDUE

Apress®

Competitive MINDSTORMS: A Complete Guide to Robotic Sumo Using LEGO® MINDSTORMS
Copyright © 2004 by David J. Perdue

All rights reserved. No part of this work may be reproduced or transmitted in any form or by any means, electronic or mechanical, including photocopying, recording, or by any information storage or retrieval system, without the prior written permission of the copyright owner and the publisher.

ISBN (pbk): 1-59059-375-8

Printed and bound in the United States of America 9 8 7 6 5 4 3 2 1

Trademarked names may appear in this book. Rather than use a trademark symbol with every occurrence of a trademarked name, we use the names only in an editorial fashion and to the benefit of the trademark owner, with no intention of infringement of the trademark.

Lead Editor: Dan Appleman
Technical Reviewer: Jona Jeffords
Editorial Board: Steve Anglin, Ewan Buckingham, Dan Appleman, Gary Cornell, Tony Davis, Chris Mills, Steve Rycroft, Dominic Shakeshaft, Jim Sumser, Karen Watterson, Gavin Wray, John Zukowski
Project Manager: Kylie Johnston
Copy Edit Manager: Nicole LeClerc
Copy Editor: Marilyn Smith
Production Manager: Kari Brooks
Production Editor: Janet Vail
Compositor: Diana Van Winkle, Van Winkle Design Group
Proofreader: Lori Bring
Indexer: Kevin Broccoli
Cover Designer: Kurt Krames
Manufacturing Manager: Tom Debolski

Distributed to the book trade in the United States by Springer-Verlag New York, Inc., 175 Fifth Avenue, New York, NY 10010 and outside the United States by Springer-Verlag GmbH & Co. KG, Tiergartenstr. 17, 69112 Heidelberg, Germany.

In the United States: phone 1-800-SPRINGER, e-mail orders@springer-ny.com, or visit http://www.springer-ny.com. Outside the United States: fax +49 6221 345229, e-mail orders@springer.de, or visit http://www.springer.de.

For information on translations, please contact Apress directly at 2560 Ninth Street, Suite 219, Berkeley, CA 94710. Phone 510-549-5930, fax 510-549-5939, e-mail info@apress.com, or visit http://www.apress.com.

The information in this book is distributed on an "as is" basis, without warranty. Although every precaution has been taken in the preparation of this work, neither the author(s) nor Apress shall have any liability to any person or entity with respect to any loss or damage caused or alleged to be caused directly or indirectly by the information contained in this work.

The source code for this book is available to readers at http://www.apress.com in the Downloads section.

For Jay and Mary Jo Perdue

Contents at a Glance

Contents

Part Two
The First Approach:
The Small-and-Fast Strategy

Part Five
Getting Involved in a
Robotic Sumo Event 293

Foreword

WHEN DAVID CONTACTED ME to ask about writing the foreword for his MINDSTORMS book, my first thought was, "Another book about LEGO robotics—is there still something to write about it?" In fact, the shelves of the bookstores now offer a wide selection of books about building robots with the LEGO MINDSTORMS system. Many of them are actually very good books, which cover the matter quite deeply and exhaustively.

However, a few lines below in his e-mail, David explained to me that the book was to deal exclusively with robotic sumo. That raised my interest and made me feel suddenly excited, because I love sumo. I strongly believe that building a robot to attend a sumo contest is one of the best experiences for hobby robotics fans, because it's both extremely instructive and a lot of fun!

Let me clarify my thought. Generally speaking, attending a contest is a very good way to learn about robotics. First of all, the contest helps the builder to keep focused on a specific goal. In fact, many beginners get lost in simply deciding what to build—either getting quickly bored by too simple projects or frustrated by too complex ones.

In the second place, the rules of the tournament state very precisely what is allowed and what is not, providing a context to the designer's choices and narrowing the possibilities. The beginner is guided to build something that complies with some technical specifications, while the expert gets challenged to find creative solutions without infringing the rules.

Finally, during the progress of the contest, the builder has the invaluable opportunity to compare his own technical choices and programming strategies with his competitors' ones. There's always something to learn, something that makes you say "I didn't think of that." Even when you win, you should study carefully the defeated robots, because you will surely find nice ideas to store in your knowledge base for future uses.

Robotic sumo in particular is definitely my favorite kind of competition. If you've never attended one, forget any impression you might have received by some TV shows, where crazy machines try to destroy each other. As David clearly explains in the first chapter, those are not robots, but rather remote-controlled vehicles. In true robotic sumo tournaments, violence is forbidden, with pushing being the only action allowed against the opponent. More important, during each match, the robot is under sole control of its own program, and human intervention is not possible. That forces the designer to try to forecast any possible situations, find a way to recognize them, and trigger the proper behavior.

The rules are basically very simple (the first robot to exit the field within a give time loses); however, as in the most important board games, a simple set of rules generates a huge number of situations and endless complexity for the competitors. A good sumo robot is a well-balanced mixture of structure and strategy. It will require its designer to have clear ideas of what he wants from his robot, and both good building and programming skills to implement them. A robot will not benefit from sophisticated software if it loses pieces every time the opponent just touches it. On the other hand, being rock-solid will not take it very far if it's so dumb as to be at the mercy of the other robot in the field.

Sumo teaches not to bite off more than you can chew. In other words, don't approach complex strategies if you are not sure you can make them work. Start with simple behaviors and architectures that work, and build on top of them as you get more and more confident with the matter. Simple things just have fewer ways to go wrong!

When I started organizing and attending sumo contests with the other friends of the LEGO club I'm part of, it was not uncommon to see robots committing "suicide." Robotics and sumo were both new experiences for all of us, and the temptation to write some very "clever" piece of software was hard, if not impossible, to resist, especially for those of us with a solid programming background. The result in most of the matches was that the robots were not able to properly recognize all of the different situations and behaved in many absurd—and often comical—ways. Thus, we came to the conclusion that when developing a sumo robot, the first test it had to pass was what we called "the brick test"; that is, the robot had to survive for a given time when fighting against a totally passive opponent like a brick or a very heavy book! This seems like a joke, but it's a crucial test. When your robot is able to safely run along the field, find a book placed somewhere inside that field, and push it out, things are going well.

Finally, I want to reveal to you what makes sumo so special to me: the fact there's no winning strategy. Don't misunderstand me; you must have a strategy, because if you don't have one, you're doomed to failure. David points out this very well, and he's perfectly right. There isn't a specific strategy that is better than any other possible strategy. Your robot can be slow and powerful, or lightweight and quick; it can rely on mass and grip, or on momentum; it might be designed to attack, or to defend itself when attacked. Whichever solution you choose, whatever experience you might have, you're not guaranteed to win. There is always the possibility that a particular robot will beat your robot, even if the latter was, on average, the weakest of the tournament and yours was one of the strongest. In fact, the transitive property doesn't apply to robotic sumo: if A beats B, and B beats C, there's no certainty that A beats C. The result of a match is difficult to predict by simply knowing the contenders, and every tournament has its surprises and its outsiders. This is what makes sumo so exciting!

You are now in good hands. David knows the matter very well, and he will guide you through all the secrets of robotic sumo with a steady hand. His writing is very clear, pleasant, and well organized, and I'm sure that this book will give you a solid basis and will trigger your creativity, making you a fearful sumo robot builder.

Hope to meet you at the next tournament!

—Mario Ferrari
Co-author of *Building Robots with
LEGO MINDSTORMS* and
LEGO MINDSTORMS Masterpieces

About the Author

 **David J. Perdue**, like many others, played with LEGO sets as a young child. However, LEGO MINDSTORMS became David's main hobby when he picked up a LEGO MINDSTORMS Robotics Invention System. Immediately, he saw that he had a natural talent with the set. He purchased thousands of pieces, spent countless hours building and programming, and devoured thousands of pages of documentation to learn as much as he could. After passing the beginner stage, David let loose his imagination and won three Special Mention awards for his creations from the LEGO MINDSTORMS web site within a period of less than six months. He then went on to become a devout LEGO computer-aided design (CAD) fan, and uses the system to document his creations. David currently resides in Elgin, Texas, where he builds, writes, programs, and updates his web site at www.davidjperdue.com.

About the
Technical Reviewer

Jona Jeffords founded the LEGO Robotics Group of Ann Arbor (LRGoAA) in the summer of 2001 and has hosted five sumo events, as well as several other events based on challenges including stair climbing, line following, item gathering, soccer, trash collection, and king of the hill. He believes that absolutely anyone can build a successful robot given the right tools, learn something, and enjoy mastering the challenge of sumo. Information about Jona and LRGoAA can be found at www.24tooth.com.

Acknowledgments

WITHOUT THE ENTIRE LEGO community, this book would not have been possible. For many years now, thousands of LEGO fans have tirelessly documented and explained everything there is to explain about LEGO, shared creations, made web sites for fans to share their creations, encouraged each other, and so much more. It was through their efforts that I was able to learn much of what I know about LEGO MINDSTORMS. Unfortunately, I can't write down the name of every single LEGO fan. So instead I'll say, "Thank you LEGO fans one and all!"

The images for this book played a huge role, and were made possible by the LEGO computer-aided design (CAD) system known as LDraw, which was designed by the late James Jessiman, to whom I extend a special thanks for his hard work and CAD system of outstanding quality. In the past several years, LEGO CAD has become increasingly popular and has gained many supporters, who have also tirelessly documented (and even written entire books) carefully explaining LEGO CAD. It was through one of these books, *LEGO Software Power Tools*, by Kevin L. Clague and Miguel Agullo, that I learned how to "LDraw." Thank you guys for such an instructive, imaginative, and fun-to-work-through book! I'd also like to give an additional thanks to Kevin Clague for his LEGO CAD programs LSynth and LPub, which I used (with other programs) to generate the images for this book. There are so many supporters and individuals who have contributed to LDraw and LEGO CAD in general, once again, I unfortunately can't list all the names. Here's a big thank you to LDraw and LEGO CAD fans everywhere!

I would like to thank Apress for giving me the opportunity to write this book and for being such a great publisher. From my Project Manager, Kylie Johnston, to my Product Manager, Julie Miller, the entire Apress staff has been friendly and competent. A special thanks goes to my Lead Editor, Dan Appleman, who himself is a published author of many books. He was always encouraging, and his comments and suggestions at the beginning of the project were extremely helpful. Dan, thanks so much for your help and encouragement.

Another special thanks goes to my technical reviewer Jona Jeffords. He carefully and systematically read the text, built and tested all the sumo-bots, and offered his suggestions and ideas. I'm convinced that there are few people as knowledgeable and passionate about LEGO MINDSTORMS robotic sumo as Jona. I'd also like to thank Mario Ferrari for writing the foreword—it was the greatest honor to have you do this, Mario.

A *special* thanks goes to my family. Thanks go to my older brother—Christopher—and younger sisters—Stephanie, Tiffany, and Jessica—for giving up their computer time because "David needed the computer," and especially for understanding when I finally took one of the family computers into my room (sorry about that!). Thanks go to my mother, Mary Jo, for being my homeschool teacher all the way from kindergarten to high school—you taught me everything I know. Thanks go to my father, Jay, for reading over every single page of the entire manuscript, despite never having had anything to do with MINDSTORMS or robotic sumo or programming. He carefully read over the entire book, offered his (much-wanted) suggestions, and stayed up past midnight helping me make corrections. If it weren't for my parents and their encouragement and help, this book wouldn't exist.

Lastly, but most important, my thanks go to my Father in heaven for giving me this opportunity. If there was one thing that got me through this whole project, it was the fact that I knew He was there, that writing this book was His will for me, and that He was always there to help me. And He did help me—all the time. I would like to give all honor to Him. He gave me everything I needed—the materials, knowledge, and endurance—showed me the right path, and I just followed that path. Thank you so much, Father—this book was a lot of fun to write.

Introduction

FOR MANY YEARS, the LEGO Company has been releasing products of top-notch quality and ingenuity. But there is one aspect of the company's products that sets them apart from many others: the potential for more than one creation. You get more than one function, ability, or purpose in the same LEGO set. While many other toys and games allow very finite possibilities, or even worse, only one function, LEGO products have almost always had just one constraint: your imagination.

Despite this trademark ingenuity in all their products, one LEGO set has stood out in the crowd of official releases: the MINDSTORMS Robotics Invention System (RIS). The current version of the set (2.0) boasts 718 parts; a thick idea book known as the *Constructopedia*; and fascinating robotics-related parts such as an IR transmitter, a microcomputer called the RCX (Robotics Command System), and so much more. But this set is far from an ordinary LEGO toy. Indeed, calling it a *toy* is debatable. With the almost perfect balance of the amount and types of pieces in the set, the number of crazy contraptions you can invent is mind-boggling. MINDSTORMS fans are always on the lookout for new and amazing projects they can build.

When some people were watching shows like Robotica, Battlebots, and Robot Wars, they wondered, "Can I build a robot like that, too?" The book *Robot Riots*—a guide to fighting robots—talks a bit about the cost: "…building your own bot will cost you anywhere from $750 (a conservative estimate for a very rudimentary rookie robot) to upwards of $40,000 (for a souped-up super heavyweight)." The cost of a good fighting robot is *$40,000?* Isn't there a better way to join in on the fun?

Others watching those robot competitions must have been wondering something similar: "Can I build a *LEGO MINDSTORMS* robot like that?"

Yes, building fighting MINDSTORMS robots is a completely achievable goal. And it's a lot cheaper, too, considering the cost of an RIS set is $200. With a price tag like that, along with its great potential and ease of use, the RIS makes building fighting robots something that not just MINDSTORMS or robotics fans can do, but something *everyone* can do.

This idea of fighting LEGO MINDSTORMS robots stirred much interest and eventually took on the form of LEGO MINDSTORMS robotic sumo. The game of robotic sumo is an engaging section of the many classes of functionality of the RIS. With a unique blend of different tasks that must be accomplished, it is a very entertaining undertaking. That is why so many different LEGO user groups have organized events in which MINDSTORMS fans meet and bring their own robots to "fight." In reality, these robots do not fight. Robotic sumo is about pushing and strategy, not violent fighting actions. In the game, the robotic opponents are placed within a large ring encircled by a thick line. The goal for the robot is to be the first to push its opponent outside the limits of the line.

What This Book Covers

This book is divided into five parts. Part One is dedicated to describing the concept of robotic sumo and how to conceive a robot—that is, sumo-bot—for the competition.

The next three parts of the book contain seven projects, which are intended to teach you the three different methods of approaching robotic sumo. The small-and-fast strategy is covered in Part Two, the M-class (medium class) strategy is discussed in Part Three, and the "big-bot" approach (big-sumo strategy) is detailed in Part Four. In each of these parts are building instructions for the sumo-bots and their programs. You'll also find detailed discussions of LEGO pieces, building methodology, and the implemented strategies and programming techniques.

All of the programs presented in this book are available for download from the Downloads section of the Apress web site (www.apress.com). Also available at the Downloads section of the Apress web site are two bonus chapters for additional sumo-bots, one of which belongs to the small-and-fast strategy and the other of which belongs to the M-class strategy.

The book concludes with Part Five, which discusses participating in a robotic sumo event, organizing your own event, and more. After all, to play robotic sumo, you need more than one bot! You could build more than one sumo-bot yourself and stage them against each other, but part of the purpose of robotic sumo is to test your strategies, skills, and ideas against someone else's. Summed up, robotic sumo is about conceiving (and then testing!) ideas and solutions to make your little fighter better than the opposing one.

Robotic sumo is not *all* about ideas and the like, though. It's about fun, too. That's exactly what the LEGO Company intended. The very name LEGO is a Danish contraction for the phrase "play well." You must remember that, when attending a robotic sumo event, having fun *is* the ultimate goal. The goal of this book is to help you to play well. It teaches you how to make, program, optimize, strategize, and plan LEGO MINDSTORMS sumo-bots, *and* more. Whether you win or lose in an event, being part of the action is what matters most of all. But you should try your best to make your sumo-bot a champion. You never know—your very own sumo-bot just might earn you first place!

About the Building Instructions in This Book

Within the building instructions for the sumo-bots in this book are two types of images: *construction images* and *part list images*. There is also one image, which always precedes the building instructions, called the *bill of materials*.

- The construction images show the actual construction with the pieces for each step, along with any other pieces added in previous steps.

- The part list images show you which pieces you'll need, how many you'll need of each piece, and the color of each piece. The number with an *x* by the pieces in the part lists designates the quantity, and the large letter(s) by the pieces is an abbreviation for the color of the piece. Also, the LEGO pieces known as *axles* have an additional number directly above and to the far-right side of the piece, which designates their size. For instance, a #5 axle will have the number *5*, and a #8 axle will have the number *8*.

- A bill of materials is like a super-size part list image. It shows all the parts you will need for a given project, and also includes color abbreviations, axle numbers, and so on.

Some colors are not designated with an abbreviation in the part list images and bill of materials, as it is very easy to determine those colors from looking at the pieces themselves. For example, any piece in black or white does not have a color abbreviation. However, many pieces do have color abbreviations. The following is a list of all the abbreviations for colors used in this book:

COLOR ABBREVIATION	FULL COLOR NAME
Y	Yellow
R	Red
B	Blue
G	Green
Ppl	Purple
DC	Dark Cyan
TO	Transparent Orange
TLG	Transparent Light Green

So, to successfully follow the building instructions in a given project, first look at the bill of materials to familiarize yourself with the required pieces. Then, once you've actually started construction, gather the pieces shown in the part list for that step and position them as shown in the construction image.

Lastly, in the construction of the sumo-bots in this book, you'll need to occasionally create two subassemblies that are identical, except that the orientation of the pieces on one of them is reversed—that is, it is a mirror subassembly. Rather than wasting paper by adding all the nearly identical steps for the mirror subassemblies in this book, you can follow the building instructions for the other subassembly and switch the orientation of the pieces while you're building, to construct the mirror subassembly. However, if you would rather follow the mirror subassembly's actual building instructions, you can download them from the Downloads section of the Apress web site (www.apress.com).

The Companion Web Site

I have created a special companion web site for this book, where you can find updates, detailed contact information for contacting me, an FAQ, and much more interesting and useful material related to this book and robotic sumo. I've also included the building instructions for the mirror subassemblies on this site (the same instructions that are downloadable from the Apress web site). The web address for the companion web site is www.davidjperdue.com/competitivemindstorms.

Part One

The Concept of LEGO MINDSTORMS Robotic Sumo

CHAPTER 1

Introduction to LEGO MINDSTORMS Robotic Sumo

You MAY HAVE SEEN fighting robots on TV shows, and your head may be filled with images of mechanical monsters equipped with spinning blades and flamethrowers. Amidst showers of sparks, screaming fans, and an energetic host who keeps shouting something, it's obvious the show's purpose is to impress you with "deadly robot warriors." Indeed, the robot's goal usually appears to be to tear the opposing robot to shreds. So, these robots are monstrous, lethal, ferocious machines whose sole purpose in life is to destroy, right? Wrong.

In robotic contests, sometimes the two adversaries are trying to win points by accomplishing various goals; other times, they are trying to shove each other into a hole in the ground; and on some occasions, they are placed on a raised platform, and their goal is to be the first to push their opponent off that platform. The latter scenario is what *robotic sumo* is all about.

In the literal sense, robotic sumo is played on a platform—called an *arena*—which is outlined with a thick line, and the goal is to push the other robot out of bounds. In the more abstract sense, robotic sumo is not a game about turning the opponent into junkyard material, but a game of strategy and skills.

This book will demystify the process of making a robot with which to participate in a robotic sumo event—a *sumo-bot*. But we're not going to be looking at just any sumo-bots in this book; we're going to be looking at LEGO MINDSTORMS sumo-bots. When the worlds of MINDSTORMS and robotic sumo collide, the result is more than amazing. By building and programming the sumo-bots described in this book, and understanding how their design and construction was planned, you will become a robotic sumo expert. This chapter will get you started by explaining the basic concepts of robotic sumo and sumo-bot construction.

Can You Build a Sumo-Bot?

On the TV shows featuring fighting robots, we all see those guys who walk around and get to show off their robots. People say, "Wow! He designed a *robot*. He must be a rocket scientist or something." I'm sorry to disappoint any fans or aggravate any of those "rocket scientists," but the simple fact is that those "robots" on TV aren't really robots at all. A robot is a contraption that's completely autonomous, which means it's capable of making its own decisions. The machines on TV are controlled by humans via huge remote controllers, so they are *not* autonomous. The robots described in this book really *are* robots.

The RCX, the microcomputer that comes with every LEGO MINDSTORMS Robotics Invention System (RIS), is the brains of these robots (see Figure 1-1). You can program it to perform a wide variety of actions and make its own decisions. It is even capable or some artificial intelligence. The RCX is also one of the largest and most expensive LEGO pieces ever made. With a retail price of $120, this is not an easily borrowed LEGO brick.

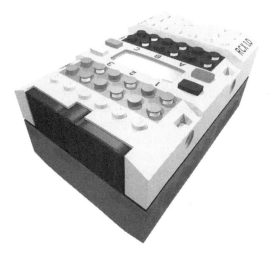

Figure 1-1. The RCX: The brains of your robot

Taking a huge box of LEGO pieces, building a robot from the ground up, and then programming it sounds like a daunting task. If someone asked you if you could build a LEGO sumo-bot, could you? With a bit of experience using the RIS, guidance from the *Constructopedia* included in the RIS, and maybe some help from friends, chances are you could probably make a decent one. On the other hand, any LEGO MINDSTORMS fan can make a little sumo-bot that has two wheels and goes. It's making a *good* sumo-bot that can be difficult.

On the side of the RIS box is a paragraph defining the purpose and philosophy of LEGO MINDSTORMS:

> *The philosophy behind LEGO MINDSTORMS is to not only allow you to under-stand technology but to also become a creative master of it. This happens when you design, construct, and program your own intelligent inventions.*

This is not only true of LEGO MINDSTORMS—it also applies to robotic sumo. You must become a creative master of it by designing, constructing, and programming sumo-bots. The first step toward your "creative mastership" of robotic sumo is to fully understand how robotic sumo is played.

How Is Robotic Sumo Played?

What happens in robotic sumo isn't much like the robotic mayhem portrayed on TV shows. First, robotic sumo events usually don't take place in surroundings such as those seen in "warrior robot" TV shows. Instead, you'll find them in a variety of other places—some you can probably guess, others might surprise you. For instance, you can find robotic sumo events in someone's living room, the middle of a RadioShack, and at scientifically or technically inclined museums.

There's a lot of variety in where a robotic sumo event can be held. Likewise, there's variety in how a robotic sumo event is operated. However, it's not difficult to describe a basic LEGO MINDSTORMS robotic sumo event. First, two sumo-bots are placed—usually facing in opposite directions—in the arena and are started either remotely or with a flick of a bumper or a switch mounted on the sumo-bots. At this point, a *round* has been initiated. A round will usually last for a period of about 3 minutes, and the *host* or *judge* will keep track of the time. Within this round are *bouts*. Each time one of the sumo-bots is defeated, it's set back up to start another bout. This continues until the time period for the round has run out.

The arena in which the sumo-bots "play" is circular and measures usually between 3 and 5 feet in diameter. The thick line encircling the arena is for the sumo-bots. Once they've detected the line, they know they've reached the outermost part of the arena and need to turn around. The size of this line can vary greatly, but it will often be about 2 inches thick. When both sumo-bots are moving around on the arena, they must take great care not to accidentally go over this line and off the arena, because this ends the bout and gives the victory to the sumo-bot still on the arena.

We hope that most of the sumo-bots' time won't be spent in accidentally falling *off* the arena, but maneuvering *on* the arena. They will scurry all over the surface, reverse or turn around each time they detect the outer line, bump into each other, and possibly use sumo-bot searching techniques until one or both of them gives its opponent a good, direct hit.

Offensive and defensive mechanisms and subassemblies then come into use, and it becomes a matter of pushing, escaping, or smartness—whether in the construction or programming. Once the unfortunate one has been pushed off the arena, the victorious sumo-bot is awarded his hard-earned point(s), and the two bots are set back up for another bout, if their 3-minute round hasn't run out.

How many rounds a sumo-bot will go through and how long an event will take depend on two factors: the number of people participating and the rules. Obviously, an event with a lot of people will take longer than an event with only a handful of people. However, you could have a rule for a small event that states that every sumo-bot goes through 10 rounds, which makes for a long event.

As you can see from this description, robotic sumo is a harmless game. But it isn't a predictable, easy, or simple game. Robotic sumo relies heavily on strategy, and there's a lot more to it than there seems at first glance. You'll see this for yourself as you work through the rest of the book. And just one object—something you can't really touch but can only see—controls all the aspects of robotic sumo we have just discussed, as well as many others I haven't yet mentioned. That object is a *rule set*.

A rule set is a compilation of all the rules for an event, and every aspect of the event revolves around that rule set. This is why, in order to participate in robotic sumo correctly and efficiently, you must thoroughly know the rule set for the event in which you are participating. In addition, you must also have a sound knowledge of the tools— what you'll use to build and program your sumo-bot. The materials that you are *allowed* to use in your sumo-bot's construction are nearly as important. Let's take a look at some common rules first, and then we'll cover building and programming tools.

What Are the Rules of the Game?

The first thing you should know is that there isn't a robotic sumo organization that dictates a set of rules for everyone to follow. However, several basic rules apply to all robotic sumo events because they represent robotic sumo itself. Also, some rules vary from event to event and person to person, and sometimes there are variations to the game itself.

The Basic Rules

In order to have a law-abiding, decent sumo-bot with good survival capabilities in most rule sets, the sumo-bot must

- Comply with rules on weight

- Comply with rules on width

- Not intentionally damage or harm the opposing sumo-bot in any way

- Not drop any pieces intentionally on the playing ground

- Have an efficient, sturdy, and well-attached line detecting mechanism for "seeing" the line around the perimeter of the arena

Let's take a closer look at each of these basic rules and how they affect your sumo-bot's design.

Weight and Width

First, weight can be a factor. Some rules state that your sumo-bot may weigh up to 2 pounds. As you will see later in this book, weight and brute force do not always matter the most. Sometimes, going with a slightly lighter sumo-bot is better.

Similar to the weight rule—similar because it will affect the size of your sumo-bot—is the maximum width rule. The width is measured in *studs*, a basic measuring and LEGO term. A stud is the round "button" on a brick that has "LEGO" inscribed on its top. The studs system easily shows the measurements of a brick or model. For an example, if you have a 2x4 brick, this means the brick is two studs wide and four studs long. The first number in a measurement (2 in this example) is the width, and the second (4 in this example) is the length.

Having a maximum of 30 studs wide is one example of a sumo-bot width rule. This rule is designed to prevent those participants with a large inventory from making a giant sumo-bot capable of sweeping the competition off the board!

Intentional Harm

Robotic sumo is a noviolent sport—violent behavior or intentional abuse of the other sumo-bot is always forbidden. Hurting the other competitor's sumo-bot or actually breaking or ruining (melting?) its pieces is just not part of the robotic sumo game.

But what happens if a sumo-bot gets flipped over or stops working? If a sumo-bot is overturned or somehow no longer functional, the other (functional) participant is declared winner of that bout. You can come to two conclusions from this statement. First, you can use this to your advantage and design a sumo-bot that relies on a strategy that will flip the opponent. Second, you must be careful to protect your sumo-bot from getting flipped. Both of these ideas will be discussed and put into practice later in the book.

Loss of Pieces

Something that is inevitable in a game such as robotic sumo is pieces falling off. It *will* happen. To deal with this, rule sets often have a rule that addresses this specific situation. Basically, if a piece or pieces are dropped during play in the ring, those objects will be immediately removed by those running the event. This means that your sumo-bot cannot drop pieces during the game! (So much for that LEGO land mine idea.)

Sometimes a sumo-bot will crash into another one at high speed and send a piece flying—whether from itself or the competitor. When this happens, you might say, "Hey! I couldn't help it!" Don't worry; you won't get thrown out of the competition if your sumo-bot accidentally loses a piece somewhere on the arena. Cases such as this just confirm the great unwritten MINDSTORMS building rule: Make your robot as robust and break-free as possible. After all, if you place a sumo-bot that can fall apart easily into the ring, it will! Once it gets slammed, pieces will start falling off, and that is definitely *not* good.

Line Detection

The line that encircles the arena is an extremely important element. It must be very "seeable" for the LEGO MINDSTORMS light sensor, because if it isn't, there are going to be a lot of sumo-bots blundering off the playing area.

Often, the line will be black, and the surface of the arena will be white or vice versa. The line itself should be at least several inches thick to give the sumo-bots time to slow down and turn around once they see it. The LEGO light sensor (see Figure 1-2) must be attached very sturdily to your sumo-bot and will often be in the very front for early detection. You will see and build examples of light sensor attachments later in this book.

Figure 1-2. The light sensor: The eyes of your robot

A Common Rule Set

The following list contains a sample of a few rules from a common and basic rule set. This is not a full rule set (which can be rather long); its purpose is to help you get an idea of what can be expected from a full rule set.

- The sumo-bot must be built within the limits of *one* RIS, *one* LEGO MINDSTORMS expansion pack of your choice, and *no more than* 100 bulk bricks.

- The sumo-bot may use up to two output ports on the RCX.

- The sumo-bot may use up to three input ports.

- The sumo-bot may be up to 30 studs wide.

- The sumo-bot may *not* use any custom sensors.

- The sumo-bot may use *only* normal alkaline or rechargeable batteries. Any other battery setups are *not* allowed.

- Rounds will be exactly 3 minutes long.

- The sumo-bots will play in a white, circular arena, 4 feet in diameter, outlined with a 2-inch-thick black line.

These rules are typical of all rule sets. You must look at *all* the rules in a competition very carefully before designing your sumo-bot, paying special attention to the details.

Chapter 11 of this book will provide a more detailed discussion of rules. In that chapter, you will see a full rule set, get some ideas for making your own set of rules, and learn how to check your own rule sets for loopholes.

Now that you have seen some rules, let's examine the tools.

Introduction to LEGO MINDSTORMS Robotic Sumo

What Are the Tools for Building and Programming a Sumo-Bot?

When it comes to building your sumo-bot, you can choose from a wide range of pieces and programming languages. Although some are better than others, there is no one perfect programming language or set (the RIS comes pretty close though!). To give you a better idea of what is available, what works well with LEGO MINDSTORMS robotic sumo, and what is used in this book, I've listed a few of the possibilities in this section. Let's begin with the building side, and then look at programming in the LEGO MINDSTORMS world.

Building Tools

When you are building a sumo-bot, think carefully about what pieces you choose. The pieces you use will directly affect your sumo-bot's performance. Your best bet is to use the famous LEGO MINDSTORMS RIS, which is certainly the most popular in its line of products (see Figure 1-3). This set includes the bright-yellow RCX, with the distinctive "beep-beep" sound it plays on activation. Using other sets with their own LEGO micro-processors, such as the MicroScout, Scout, or CyberMaster is a possibility; however, the RCX delivers the most power and flexibility.

> **NOTE** *There is one central web site for the RIS and the other MINDSTORMS products, which include MicroScout and Scout:* www.legomindstorms.com. *The CyberMaster is out of production.*

This book is based on the RIS, and the sumo-bots I describe here do not use any LEGO microcomputer other than the RCX. But these sumo-bots are not just made out of pieces from the RIS. In some projects, I have used pieces that are not included in the RIS or are not included in sufficient quantity in the RIS. I'll provide the parts list, bill of materials, and information about where to get pieces that may not be included in the RIS where necessary to assist you with the construction of your sumo-bots.

> **NOTE** *There is a variant of robotic sumo called* mini-sumo, *in which—stated in MINDSTORMS terms—participants are limited to making their sumo-bots out of a single RIS set. You will see some examples of sumo-bots that can be considered mini-sumo-bots in Chapters 4 and 5.*

Figure 1-3. The RIS is the most powerful MINDSTORMS set.

Building Blocks

If you aren't going to be using only the RIS, what else will you need to make a sumo-bot? The truth is *any* LEGO piece will do, as long as it fits within the rules. If that piece helps you accomplish something you want your sumo-bot to do, if it makes your sumo-bot stronger, if it makes your sumo-bot just plain better, then by all means use it!

An example of a set you could buy to expand your inventory is one of the official LEGO MINDSTORMS Expansion Packs. As of this writing, there are currently five of them: RoboSports, Extreme Creatures, Exploration Mars, Ultimate Builders, and the Ultimate Accessories Set (if that can be counted as an Expansion Pack). Some of them are useful, while others are not quite so useful.

The RoboSports and Extreme Creatures Expansion Packs appear to be designed to appeal more to children, and they are also the least popular ones. The Exploration Mars Expansion Pack is, in my opinion, better than the RoboSports and Extreme Creatures Expansion Packs (if you don't need the extra motor RoboSports offers). Exploration Mars holds both useful and interesting pieces, including very long electrical wires, super-large plates, and extra gears and axles.

The more popular Ultimate Builders Expansion Pack and Ultimate Accessories Set work well for any MINDSTORMS builder and have a more "mature" feel. Ultimate Builders offers pneumatics, an extra motor, and many useful pieces. Ultimate Accessories provides a remote control, extra touch sensor, LEGO lamp, rotation sensor, and a handful of colorful and specialized building elements.

There are also many other types of pieces you could use as well, such as those from the TECHNIC line of products. The TECHNIC line works best with MINDSTORMS, as the pieces in the RIS set actually are TECHNIC pieces. There are large numbers of TECHNIC sets to choose from, although the smaller ones generally do not provide you with many useful pieces. Bulk bricks are also an option, as are pieces from theme sets (pirates, space, and so on). TECHNIC pieces remain the most useful, but you shouldn't limit yourself entirely to them.

The bottom line is that you should use whatever pieces are necessary to build your sumo-bot so it serves its purpose and you are pleased with the results. Don't be afraid to walk into a competition with a sumo-bot bearing a pirate sail. I've seen a space mini-fig (a small LEGO character that comes with a theme set) placed on top of a robot at a MINDSTORMS competition!

> **TIP** *A great place to look for MINDSTORMS pieces and sets (especially rare ones) on the Internet is BrickLink, at* www.bricklink.com. *Also be sure to look around on eBay for good deals.*

Navigational and Searching Mechanisms

When giving their robots navigational abilities, people will mount homemade electronic compasses, rotation sensors, and other amazing devices on their robots. Then they will load custom firmware into their RCX to complement these devices.

Unfortunately, just about any possible sensor or amazing contraption made for navigation you might place in your sumo-bot will not operate properly in robotic sumo. It simply will not work! This doesn't have anything to do with the quality of the device or software. The reason is that when a sumo-bot is hit by another sumo-bot (which *is* going to happen in robotic sumo), it confuses the internal software, and the sumo-bot is immediately lost.

Can you use custom (homemade) distance sensors (a sensor that can see if something is in front of it) to help your sumo-bot search for its opponent? Some events do not allow custom sensors, so they are not implemented in the sumo-bots described in this book. As an alternative, the light sensor can be used to detect the proximity of another object, to some extent. There are also other methods you can use to help find the opposing robot, one of which you'll see in a later chapter.

Programming Tools

The programming language included with the RIS—RCX Code—has been greatly improved since its first release. It is very capable of programming a sumo-bot efficiently and reliably. But the RCX Code language can be difficult to read with a large program, and people who are used to using textual programming languages can find it hard to work in this programming environment.

To program the sumo-bots described in this book, I have chosen the programming language NQC (for Not Quite C), which was created by Dave Baum. This is a very powerful textual language that is fairly easy to understand and learn. It is quite well known among the MINDSTORMS community, and many builders use this language to program all types of robots, including other LEGO microcomputers.

John Hansen is the maintainer of a great integrated development environment (IDE) known as Bricx Command Center (BricxCC), and this is currently the most popular way to program in NQC (see Figure 1-4). You can download the BricxCC program for free from `http://bricxcc.sourceforge.net/`.

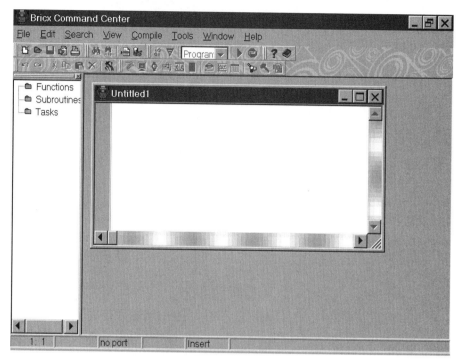

Figure 1-4. Bricx Command Center's main screen

NOTE *As of this writing, Dave Baum has recently turned over the maintenance of NQC to John Hansen. John has transferred the NQC web site to a new address, http://bricxcc.sourceforge.net/nqc/, and all future versions of NQC, as well as documentation and information, will be appearing at this web address as soon as the switch has been completed.*

A recent version of BricxCC, 3.3.7.6, now supports several different programming languages and all of the MINDSTORMS programmable bricks (and a few other LEGO programmable bricks as well). A window entitled "Searching for the brick" pops up (see Figure 1-5) before taking you to the main screen of BricxCC. In this window, you pick your microcomputer, programming language, and port for your IR tower. Thanks to John Hansen's hard work and continuing efforts, programming with NQC and many other languages is now very user-friendly.

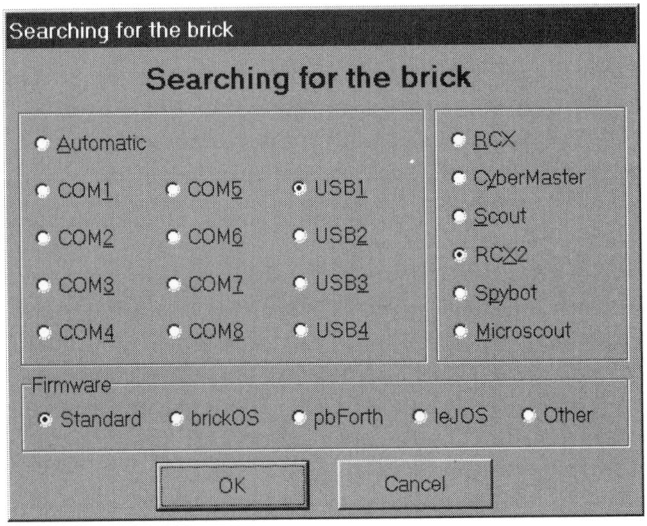

Figure 1-5. Searching for the Brick screen

As I mentioned, you are not limited to using only NQC or RCX Code to program your sumo-bots. If the rules for a particular event allow other programming languages, it might be a good idea to take advantage of this factor (yes, this is a factor in robotic sumo). What languages could you use? A great place to start is with those languages that BricxCC now supports. Let's go through these custom-firmware programming languages to see what they're about:

- **brickOS:** This language allows the user to program the RCX in the real-life programming language C. brickOS is renowned for its speedy execution of code.

- **pbForth:** This language is based on Forth, which is a well-known and veteran programming language. The name pbForth stands for Programmable Brick Forth. With its highly unique features and code structuring, this is a very powerful language with great potential.

- **leJOS:** This language is developed around Java. Besides the typical structure and heritage of Java, this language boasts numerous special features including navigational abilities, behavior controlling, and more.

> **NOTE** *In the past, brickOS, pbForth, and leJOS were difficult to set up and use. Now, using BricxCC version 3.3.7.6 and some downloadable all-in-one files that John Hansen has included on his web site, operating these languages is a breeze. The downloads, information, and John's e-mail address for support can be found on the BricxCC web site:* http://bricxcc.sourceforge.net/.

All three of these languages must be uploaded to the RCX in the form of custom firmware. Although none of them are used for the sumo-bots in this book, don't let that stop you from using any of them. If you already know how to program in one or more of these languages, or would like to eventually learn any of them, feel free to use that language for the sumo-bots described in this book and for other sumo-bots you design. It will most likely give your sumo-bot a fighting edge!

Robotic Sumo: A Game Within a Game

When some people look at robotic sumo, they might consider it just a game of robot A crashing into robot B and knocking him out of the ring. As I said earlier, while this might *seem* to be the case at first glance, it really isn't true. In reality, robotic sumo is a game *within* a game. There are other aspects to robotic sumo that are so important to the outcome that they become whole tasks themselves! Many of these go on behind the scenes before the competition even starts.

One of the first "games" inside robotic sumo you should consider is the process of picking a strategy for your sumo-bot (strategies are covered in the next chapter). Related to this is the building game—building a sumo-bot is indeed a whole game in itself. The design and construction of your sumo-bot will depend greatly on the strategy you have chosen.

Another unseen portion of robotic sumo is programming. *Definitely* unseen from the outside, it can easily be taken for granted. This was apparent at a MINDSTORMS event (sponsored by RoboLab) I recently attended. After the competition was over, one of the competitors, just for fun, placed his robot on the large track that had been built for the entries. The little bot was following a certain path and making interesting maneuvers once it saw a black line. It was going up and down an elevated portion, through a bumpy terrain section, and trying to ring bells. It was obvious to me that a great deal of thought went into the programming that led to such an impressive performance. Another guy watching this little robot picked it up and flipped up and down a movable attachment that held the light sensor. He looked at the creator and shouted above the din of the crowd, "I still really like this part!" The point is that you'll find it a lot easier to impress people with your robot than with your programming skills.

But don't ignore this important task! A sumo-bot with an empty RCX (no programming) would just sit in one place; it certainly wouldn't win any competitions. This is exactly why you must take the time to create *good* programming in order to make a *good* sumo-bot. As I have heard it said, a robot is only as good as its programming, and a program is only as good as the robot it is in.

These are all "games" within the game of robotic sumo that deserve your attention. Remember not to zone in on just "playing robotic sumo" and forget these important tasks. If you look at the whole picture, your sumo-bot's overall performance will be much better.

Conclusion

This chapter covered the basic concepts of LEGO MINDSTORMS robotic sumo. Understanding how everything works and why it works the way it does is important. Without a sound knowledge of these concepts, you can easily introduce errors into your sumo-bots that could hinder your progress in a robotic sumo event.

You must carefully plan the process of designing and constructing a sumo-bot to make sure that you've taken care of all the necessary tasks and that any mechanisms, parts, and subassemblies aren't in conflict with each other. Factors that influence how you make your sumo-bot are the rules for that event, your inventory, and the extent of your knowledge and experience.

Another factor that will affect your sumo-bot's design is the strategy you pick and use. The next chapter describes various sumo-bot strategies you can use in your sumo-bot, as well as the strategy of thinking about what your opponents might be planning for *their* sumo-bots. Turn the page to take the next step in this competitive journey!

CHAPTER 2

The Importance of a Battle Plan

IMAGINE A ROBOTIC sumo tournament in progress. One of the participants brings out his sumo-bot and places it in readiness. A spectator comes up to him and asks curiously, "So, what strategy are you using?" The sumo-bot's maker replies, "None. No strategy is my strategy." The spectator walks away, wondering exactly why he did this and if it was such a good idea. During the competition, the strategy-deficient sumo-bot comes up against a highly developed opponent with a particular tactic. In the ensuing combat, the latter participant completely defeats its opponent.

Why Do You Need a Strategy?

If you construct a sumo-bot without a strategy in mind and have it oppose one that does, almost always, the one lacking the strategy will lose. Why? Several reasons contribute to the answer:

- Your sumo-bot will often not know how to respond to the other sumo-bot's actions.

- Your sumo-bot will likely not be able to search for the opposing one.

- Your sumo-bot could miss opportunities to gain advantage over the opponent.

I cannot stress enough the importance of picking a strategy, and I cannot stress enough the importance of picking a strategy *before* you begin building a sumo-bot. Getting halfway through building before deciding on a particular strategy will result in an inept sumo-bot.

> **TIP** *Some rule sets allow you to modify your robot after the competition has started. For instance, if the rules state that there is a limit of 30 studs in width, this rule can be legally ignored once the event has started. As an example, the robot could run one or more motors to move mechanisms in different positions, making itself wider than 30 studs. If this rule is present at a competition, don't be afraid to use this to your advantage.*

A sumo-bot that has not been well planned and given a behavior or task will not survive long in a competition, especially when staged against a sumo-bot that does have a strategy. The story at the beginning of this chapter may be fictional, but the moral holds true. A sumo-bot that does nothing but run straight until it sees the line is not going to survive!

What Are the Different Approaches?

Now that we have discussed *why* you should have a strategy, let's begin examining the strategies you can choose for your sumo-bots. There are generally three different ways a builder can approach making a sumo-bot, each with its own subapproaches:

- **Small and fast:** This strategy is suitable for the mini-sumo game, but it's also appropriate for robotic sumo. Its high level of speed and maneuverability make it an excellent choice for many situations.

- **Medium-class (M-class):** This strategy compromises between speed and push, and it can take advantage of a great number of possible mechanical solutions and programming behaviors.

- **Big sumo:** This strategy goes all out on brute force and size, and when used carefully can wield satisfying results—and admirers!

Table 2-1 summarizes the strategies and their characteristics. You'll see sumo-bots built with each of these strategies in Parts Two, Three, and Four of this book.

Table 2-1. Main Sumo-Bot Strategies and Their Attributes

SUMO-BOT STRATEGY	LEVEL OF SPEED	LEVEL OF MECHANICAL COMPLEXITY	LEVEL OF PROGRAMMING CAPABILITIES
Small and fast	High	Low-Medium	Medium
M-class	Medium	Medium-High	High
Big sumo	Low	High	High

NOTE *Although all of these strategies use the RCX in this book, sumo-bots designed with the small and fast strategy have less room for sensors, motors, and so on than sumo-bots built with the other strategies. Therefore, their level of programming capabilities is generally lower than those built with the M-class and big sumo strategies.*

There is a possible fourth strategy: small and slow. When you're participating in a small event with a couple of close friends, using a strategy like this one is okay, as long as you know the other sumo-bots are using that same strategy. But, in most cases, you won't know the exact strategies your opponents are using.

The small and slow strategy obviously lacks an important property: *speed*. Generally speaking, the more speed your sumo-bot has, the better. Speed is important for finding the opponent first, being able to get away if necessary, and having momentum for a crash. Furthermore, when a small and slow sumo-bot is staged against, say, a big sumo-bot, the big one wins because it has more bulk and weight. Even though the small one has a low gear reduction, that doesn't offer an advantage because of its opponent's size. So when staged against a sumo-bot wielding another strategy, the sumo-bot using the small and slow approach is at a disadvantage.

For these reasons, I won't cover the small and slow strategy in this book. But keep in mind that if used carefully and in certain situations, the small and slow strategy can be fun to use and engaging to watch. And after you learn about the other three strategies, you'll find it easy to build small and slow sumo-bots as well.

Finding a Strategy to Suit Your Needs

"All right, that makes a lot of sense," you might be thinking right now, "but which strategy is best?" That's a good question. I will talk about which one is best in a moment. For now, let's talk about which one *you* should choose that will best suit *your* needs.

The most important factor for picking a strategy revolves around the rules for that particular event. Considering the rules, you need to eliminate those strategies you know will not work. Then you find your way to the one approach that you know would do well in that situation and develop it further by picking a substrategy.

The ultimate goal is to make a sumo-bot that works efficiently as possible under a given rule set. The other competitors have the same limitations, and your job is to make the *best* solutions within those limitations. For instance, if the contest had restraints keeping you from using more than two motors and two input ports, along with strict size restrictions, your best choice would be the small and fast strategy. This strategy would fit well within the size and the motor/sensor limitations.

Your inventory is also something that could affect your choice. Let's say that there is a robotic sumo event with very gracious rules that allow large sumo-bots. Unfortunately, you do not have enough pieces to build a large sumo-bot; you have only one RIS and a few other smaller TECHNIC sets. In this case, you would choose the M-class strategy. Using your available parts and the M-class strategy, you can build the biggest possible sumo-bot, and—in this specific case—the bigger you can make your sumo-bot, the better your chances.

Yet another factor is personal preference. You might like big sumo-bots, while someone else likes small ones. Does this make big sumo-bots necessarily better? No, not really. You should pick one you like to build, but keep in mind that it must abide by the rules and also do well in a particular competition. It would not make much sense to build a tiny sumo-bot for an event involving opponents of gigantic size.

Thinking Outside the Box: What Is Your Opponent Planning?

Let's talk about thinking outside the box—literally. While seriously concentrating on making a robust sumo-bot for yourself, don't forget about the rest of the world! Instead of just thinking about your sumo-bot, you must also think about *their* sumo-bots.

Try to imagine what plans other builders are devising, and then formulate ways to counteract them. For example, suppose that you think an opponent is planning to create a sumo-bot that can run itself underneath your sumo-bot with a slope. You should then plan a way to prevent the opponent from flipping your sumo-bot. Of course, you won't be able to think of every little thing your competition will be planning, and you cannot implement every single safety feature in your sumo-bot (especially smaller sumo-bots). But if you do implement various defensive features in your sumo-bot, they will greatly help its performance and survival capabilities.

However, don't get caught up in a mass of defensive mechanisms. Instead of concentrating *only* on protecting your robot, you should also equip your robot with gadgets and mechanisms to attack the other robot. Could the other robot be small? Make a big sumo-bot then! Is the other robot going to be medium sized? Give him a taste of his own bricks and make a medium-sized one yourself! How about making a claw to trip up the other robot? Be creative and try to think of ways that can help your sumo-bot be victorious. Robotic sumo really can be a game of wits sometimes! And to help you come up with ideas and tricks, throughout this book you'll be learning ways to attack and prevail over other sumo-bots.

The Perfect Sumo-Bot: Is it Achievable?

Earlier in this chapter, I said I would tell you which strategy is the perfect one. I will now keep my word. The answer is . . . none! One of the reasons that LEGO MINDSTORMS is so wonderful is its level of variety. The builder can do the same thing a number of different ways, and no one way is better than the others. All this is directly related to the *unachievable* perfect sumo-bot.

Now, there is the possibility of one sumo-bot being better than another one. You could spend an hour or two putting together a simple sumo-bot and hope it wins, or you could spend several weeks designing and building a super-sumo-bot. The choice is yours, but if you want to make a sumo-bot to be proud of, you'll take the latter option. You do not necessarily need to spend several weeks, but the time you invest in your creation will be returned in a formidable sumo-bot.

All in all, your goal as a robotic sumo competitor is to submit the best possible entry in an event. The perfect sumo-bot may not be achievable, but if you try to model one on the principles of perfection, it will be better than one modeled on the principles of "okayness." In other words, trying to make a perfect sumo-bot will yield a sumo-bot that is better than one put together without the intention of really winning a competition.

Conclusion

After having read through these first two chapters, you should have a grasp on the overall concept of LEGO MINDSTORMS robotic sumo. By now you should know

- What type of competition robotic sumo is

- What the basic rules for a contest are

- What tools can be used to build sumo-bots

- What tools can be used to program sumo-bots

- The importance of picking and using a strategy

- What a sumo-bot's possible strategies are

So now you know the secret to making a successful sumo-bot: pick and use a strategy, and spend plenty of time on building and programming. Now you're ready to move on to some real building, programming, and testing. In the next chapter, you'll learn how to construct the chassis for a very amusing sumo-bot: Zip-Bam-Bot. His name should tell you something about his strategy!

Part Two

The First Approach: The Small-and-Fast Strategy

CHAPTER 3

The Zip-Bam-Bot Chassis

ZIP-BAM-BOT is a practical member of the small-and-fast strategy and takes the strategy's meaning to the max. Because of its low amount of torque, it relies on momentum and speed to gain superiority over opposing sumo-bots. In this chapter, you will build the Zip-Bam-Bot chassis, which will be the cornerstone for the next two chapters. In each of those chapters, you will construct and attach various subassemblies, which will transform that sumo-bot into its own unique creation.

Because members of the small-and-fast strategy do not have any pushing ability, they must rely on hit-and-run or hit-and-hit-again tactics. All of the sumo-bots that you will build in Part Two of this book will work on some variation of these tactics. This will give you an introduction to designing, building, and programming sumo-bots. When we move onto the other strategies (M-class and big sumo), you'll see how other tactics and building materials come into play. Also, all of the sumo-bots described in Part Two can be built with just the RIS, so if you have only that set right now, you'll be able to build them.

Building the Zip-Bam-Bot Chassis

This chassis is a simple yet robust example of a mobile structure and also leaves room for add-ons. Although the chassis itself, shown in Figure 3-1, may not look like much, don't worry! Once you start adding subassemblies, the real character of Zip-Bam-Bot will emerge.

Figure 3-1. The finished Zip-Bam-Bot chassis

Bill of Materials for Zip-Bam-Bot

The only set you will need for this project is the RIS (practically any version will do). A list of the pieces you will need—the bill of materials—is shown in Figure 3-2. Onto the building now!

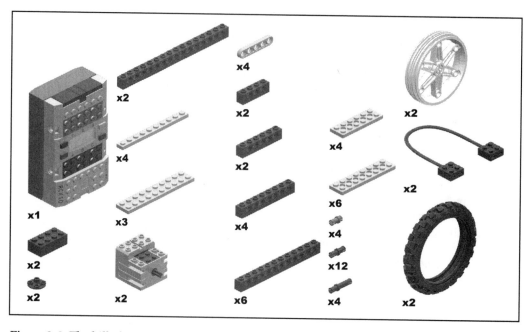

Figure 3-2. The bill of materials for Zip-Bam-Bot (xn represents the number of each type of piece)

Zip-Bam-Bot's Construction

Steps 1 and 2 begin the core base of the chassis. The base consists of two 2×10 *plates* and various black *beams,* and we also add four *friction pins* and four *long friction pins* to this base. Since beams can connect with a wide variety of pieces and have a lot of bulk and strength, they are perfect for chassis and most bases and core assemblies. And the pins help strengthen the robot (which I will discuss more as we go along) and also serve as a place for attaching beams.

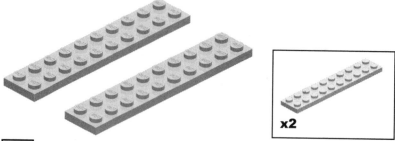

 Zip-Bam-Bot Chassis Step 1: *Lay down two 2x10 plates.*

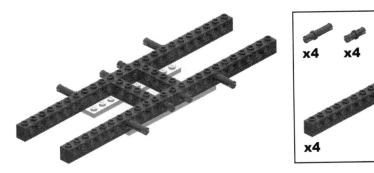

 Zip-Bam-Bot Chassis Step 2: *Add four 1x12 beams, two 1x4 beams, and snap eight pins into the beams.*

In step 3, you snap two 1x12 beams onto the pins you added in step 2. The long friction pins should still be sticking out one stud's space from the chassis.

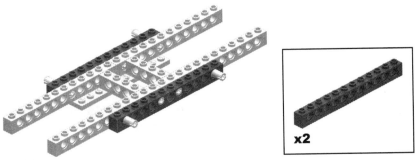

 Zip-Bam-Bot Chassis Step 3: *Add two 1x12 beams.*

Steps 4 and 5 attach the motors, their accompanying electrical wires, and various plates onto the beams. Remember to connect the wires to the motors *exactly* as shown. If the wires aren't connected correctly, the wheels will go in the wrong direction!

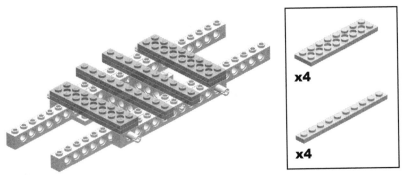

 Zip-Bam-Bot Chassis Step 4: *Place four 1x10 and 2x8 plates across beams.*

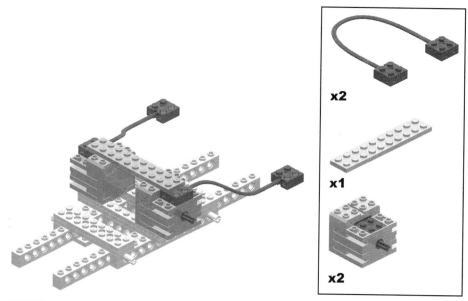

 Zip-Bam-Bot Chassis Step 5: *Position motors, electrical wires, and a plate onto base.*

Steps 6 and 7 build on top of the motors, finish the section that uses something called *bracing*, place the RCX on the chassis, attach the "loose wires" to the RCX, and bring more plates onto the scene. How bracing works, and the amazing strength it offers, will become visually obvious in a moment. The friction pins you add in step 6, and the friction pins from step 2, provide the proper means to do bracing. In step 7, you vertically connect four 1x8 beams onto the friction pins—*this* is bracing. Examine, and test, its incredible durability.

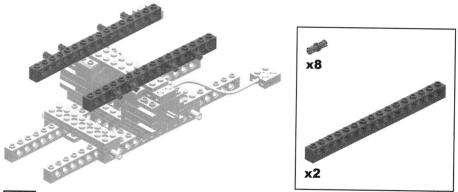

Zip-Bam-Bot Chassis Step 6: *Add two 1x16 beams and eight friction pins.*

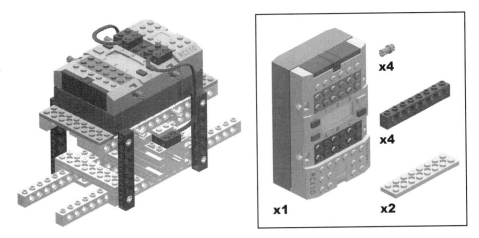

![hammer icon] ***Zip-Bam-Bot Chassis Step 7:*** *Brace chassis with four 1x8 beams, and place two 2x8 plates and the RCX with four 3/4 pins on the chassis.*

In step 8, you first firmly connect the RCX to the chassis, and then you add the wheels directly to the motors. Notice that you're attaching the RCX to the chassis with bracing as well. Using bracing, you can get an extremely strong connection, yet you can also easily take the RCX off of the robot by simply removing the vertical bracing pieces.

The wheel type used in this model is the largest in the RIS. Its technical name (but not necessarily official) is *81.6 x 15-mm motorcycle wheel*, but you can refer to it as just *motorcycle wheel*. Why use these particular wheels? One reason is that they actually help to make the robot go faster; this is due to their large size. Another reason is that they provide good traction when compared with the other types of wheels you could use.

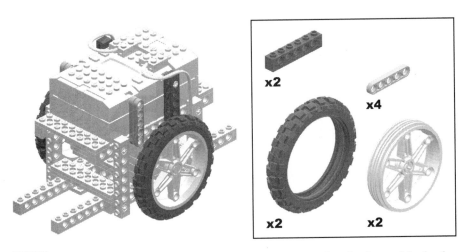

 Zip-Bam-Bot Chassis Step 8: *First brace RCX to chassis, then add wheels directly to motors.*

TIP *In this particular attachment of the RCX to the chassis, the RCX—without the bracing—doesn't really connect to the chassis at all. The very outer edges of the bottom of the RCX are smooth (and without the ability to connect), and you laid these on beams at the top of the chassis. Pushing the RCX directly into bricks is possible, but very difficult. That is why you attached the RCX with bracing. With the benefits of bracing, and the ease of connection, this method is one of the best for attaching the RCX to a chassis or structure.*

In steps 9 and 10, you finish off the front and back ends. For this robot, you need *skids* on the ends. Because the robot can (and will) tip to one end, you need something that will help reduce the friction; in other words, let's not have the robot dragging itself on the ground. A skid is specifically designed to solve that problem. It is a small, 2x2 plate, rounded on one side that the robot "skids" on, as opposed to just dragging itself on the ground. Technically, the robot is still dragging on the ground, but just not as much. Using skids results in less friction, because very little of the robot is in contact with the ground. So for Zip-Bam-Bot, you use two skids: one on each end.

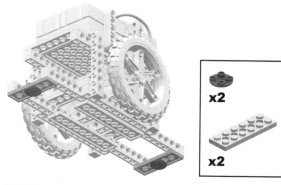

Zip-Bam-Bot Chassis Step 9: *Attach two 2x6 plates and two 2x2 skid plates to chassis.*

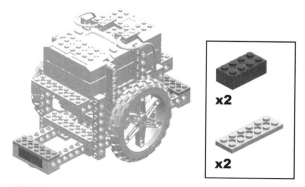

Zip-Bam-Bot Chassis Step 10: *Place two 2x4 bricks and two 2x6 plates onto chassis.*

You're finished! Your model should look like the one shown earlier in Figure 3-1, and it will be the basis for the next two chapters. If you would like to test the durability of this model, take off the RCX, and then drop the chassis from a height of about a foot and see if anything breaks off. Hopefully, nothing will.

> **TIP** *The position of the center of gravity (COG), or weight, is important in a sumo-bot. For the best results, it should be as close as possible to the axles giving mobility. In the chassis here, this is mainly the case. The RCX and motors are all in the center, which is where the driving wheels are positioned. Also, the front end of the chassis is a mirror image of the back end, which helps to make sure the weight is evenly distributed and the COG stays where it should be: in the center.*

Now that you've assembled the chassis, you're ready to do a little programming.

Programming the Zip-Bam-Bot Chassis

Before you start envisioning a super complex program to give Zip-Bam-Bot AI capabilities, I must mention something: You won't do any serious sumo-bot programming right now. You're just going to test the new Zip-Bam-Bot chassis a bit so you can see it in action. However, you will start writing and testing programs.

For those of you new to NQC, you might be wondering just how you're going to understand all the programs in this book. Don't worry; I'll explain all the code examples in this book. After working through some examples, you'll find it easy to program your own sumo-bots.

> **NOTE** *To find out more about NQC, check out the NQC Programmer's Guide that comes with BricxCC (see Chapter 1 for details on acquiring this programming IDE). For additional information and examples in NQC, see Dave Baum's book* Definitive Guide to LEGO MINDSTORMS *(Apress, 2002).*

Downloading Programs to the RCX

Even though programming can be complex, downloading a program to the RCX is easy and shouldn't take more than a few seconds. All of the programs in this book can be downloaded to the RCX in the same way. Here is the procedure for downloading your programs to your RCX using BricxCC:

> **NOTE** *The following procedure assumes that you have previously established a successful communication between your computer and RCX, using your IR tower, and uploaded the firmware to your RCX. Without the firmware, the RCX cannot accept user-made programs. So if you have not yet done this, you should first take some time to install the software that came with the RIS, follow the instructions for setting everything up and uploading the firmware to the RCX, and also possibly take a few tutorials to quickly familiarize yourself with the RIS.*

1. Plug in your serial tower or USB tower, and then open BricxCC (see Chapter 1 for details on acquiring this programming IDE). From here, you can compile and download all your NQC programs.

    > **CAUTION** *You might need to turn off your computer before you plug (and unplug) your tower. Some computers and electronic equipment have the ability to hotwire, but others do not. If you are not sure, be on the safe side and turn off your computer before plugging in or pulling out your tower.*

2. Open the File menu (at the top left of the window, in the menu bar) and select Open. Then choose the program you want to open for downloading. Figure 3-3 shows BricxCC with an open NQC file.

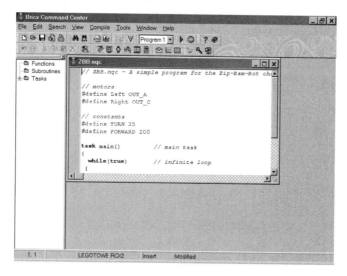

Figure 3-3. An open NQC file in BricxCC

> **NOTE** *You don't need to retype the programs in this book into BricxCC. All of the programs for this book are available from the Downloads section of the Apress web site (*www.apress.com*).*

3. Before you download a program to the RCX, you should compile it. Compiling checks the code for errors and converts the information into the proper byte codes. To compile the program, press F5 on your keyboard, choose the Compile option from the Compile menu on the menu bar, or click the Compile button, which is on the far left of the Compile toolbar, shown here.

4. Make sure you have your RCX on, facing towards your IR tower, and positioned within 4 to 6 inches of the tower. Then, to download the program, press F6 on your keyboard, choose the Download option from the Compile menu, or click the Download button, which is directly next to the Compile button on the Compile toolbar. You can change which slot you want the program to go into on the RCX (slots 1 through 5) by clicking the drop-down menu in the middle of the Compile toolbar and then selecting the slot you want to use.

5. After activating the download procedure, wait until the RCX emits a sound and BricxCC pops up a window telling you the program has been successfully compiled and uploaded. Click OK in the window or press Enter on your keyboard.

The program has been downloaded, and your robot is ready to go! To run the program, press the Run button on your RCX.

Programming the Chassis to Run Around

First, let's create a little program that will repeat a simple behavior infinitely. The behavior runs the robot forward for a few seconds, executes a turn, and makes the robot go forward again. The program is called ZBB.nqc, which stands for Zip-Bam-Bot.nqc. We'll begin by looking at the program and testing it out, and then we'll dig into the particulars. Listing 3-1 shows the ZBB.nqc program.

> **NOTE** *Remember that you can download all the programs presented in this book from the Downloads section of the Apress web site (*www.apress.com*).*

Listing 3-1. ZBB.nqc

```
// ZBB.nqc - A simple program for the Zip-Bam-Bot chassis

// motors
#define Left OUT_A
#define Right OUT_C

// constants
#define TURN 35
#define FORWARD 200

task main()        // main task
{
  while(true)      // infinite loop
  {
    OnFwd(Left+Right);    // turn on both motors forward
    Wait(FORWARD);        // wait two seconds
    Rev(Right);           // reverse right motor
    Wait(TURN);           // wait 0.35 seconds
    Fwd(Right);           // forward right motor
  }
}
```

A Quick Test of ZBB.nqc

Find a nice open space, such as in your kitchen or another room with a hard surface, and place the chassis in the middle of it. Using the process outlined in the previous section, open, compile, and download ZBB.nqc to your RCX, and then press the Run button on your RCX. Be ready to redirect your sumo-bot if it starts going in a wrong direction. It could crash into a wall and get stuck, since it can't detect it.

When you ran the program, did Zip-Bam-Bot run forward, turn right, and then run forward again? Did it keep on doing it? If it did, then the program worked correctly. If it did not, check the orientation of the wires to see if they are connected properly. The wires should be facing toward the LCD on the RCX and toward the back of the robot on the motors.

> **NOTE** *You can start and stop all programs by pressing the Run button on the RCX. Also, you can toggle through the five program slots on the RCX by pressing its Prgm button. Later in this chapter, you'll be downloading multiple programs to the RCX, and you'll need to use the Prgm button to switch between programs.*

This is all pretty simple, but it lays the foundation for more advanced creations. With the addition of a sensor or two, bricks, beams, and more, a simple chassis can easily turn into a highly interesting mechanical marvel. Now let's take a closer look at the NQC program powering this little bot.

Understanding ZBB.nqc

Notice that the first line of the ZBB.nqc program starts with two backslashes (//):

```
// ZBB.nqc - A simple program for the Zip-Bam-Bot chassis
```

These two backslashes create a *comment*. You can see many comments in ZBB.nqc; these are purely for the reader's aid and do not affect the code in any way. They inform the person reading the program about how the program is structured, how individual sections and commands work, and anything else the program writer wants to bring to the reader's attention. All the text after // is considered a comment. Anything that might be before // on the same line is not considered a comment, and the next line is also not a part of the comment. The two backslashes create a comment for only one line—the line on which they appear. They also don't add to the real size of the program which is downloaded to the RCX.

> **TIP** *Don't hesitate to add comments to your programs. Adding comments helps others to understand your programs and is also considered good practice.*

One of the first things we did in this program was to define resources using the #define keyword, which is known as a *directive*.

```
// motors
#define Left OUT_A
#define Right OUT_C

// constants
#define TURN 35
#define FORWARD 200
```

By doing this, we can actually change the name of a resource to something we would like to use, which can be useful for a number of reasons. Changing the name with this method is called creating a *macro*. Let's examine one of our definitions to see why defining is useful:

```
#define Left OUT_A
```

This line of code renames OUT_A to Left. Left is the macro. Now that we have created a macro, we can call the motor Left, rather than OUT_A, in the rest of the program. Not only is this name easier to write (and often remember), it is more efficient. We'll be taking a closer look at the efficiency of defining in Chapter 4.

> **NOTE** *Defining objects in a program does not permanently change the name; it is only for use in that program. Also, #define directives do not add to the size of a program downloaded to the RCX. Definitions are dealt with in what is called a preprocessor. A preprocessor looks at and deals with directives (directives start with a pound sign, #) before the program is downloaded. Because of the preprocessor, you can define as many resources or constants as you like with the #define directive, and it will not add to the real size of the program.*

We next start off the program with the mandatory main task, and then use a *control structure*.

```
task main()         // main task
{
  while(true)       // infinite loop
  {
    OnFwd(Left+Right);  // turn on both motors forward
    Wait(FORWARD);      // wait two seconds
    Rev(Right);         // reverse right motor
    Wait(TURN);         // wait 0.35 seconds
    Fwd(Right);         // forward right motor
  }
}
```

The control structure here is the while statement. By adding the *constant condition* true, we get while(true) to create what is often called an *infinite loop*—a loop that repeats itself forever.

Immediately following the infinite loop line is the actual code that will move Zip-Bam-Bot around. The first line of code here turns both motors on in the forward direction:

```
OnFwd(Left+Right);    // turn on both motors forward
```

To turn on the motors in the forward direction, we use the OnFwd(*motor*) command (where *motor* is a motor name). The motors we picked are Left and Right, which are macros representing OUT_A and OUT_C.

The rest of the code within the infinite loop has the motors running in different directions for different periods of time using the Wait(*time*) command. In NQC, all time periods are in hundredths of a second (with the exception of a fast timer clocking in tenths of a second). The code in the infinite loop starts off by running both motors forward for two seconds (designated by the macro FORWARD defined as 200 hundredths of a second), and then reverses one of them for 35 hundredths of a second.

In the program, we change the direction of one of the motors to reverse by using the Rev(*motor*) command. After reversing one of the motors, the program puts it back in forward using the Fwd(*motor*) command, and then this bit of code ends. However, because of the infinite loop, it will repeat all the code perpetually, resulting in the Zip-Bam-Bot chassis running around forever (or actually until the batteries run out).

Running Around Randomly

Seeing the Zip-Bam-Bot chassis do the same thing over and over again can quickly get boring. Wouldn't it be nice if you could add some random actions? The revised program shown in Listing 3-2 shows how that can be accomplished.

Listing 3-2. ZBB2.nqc

```
/* ZBB2.nqc - A simple program for the Zip-Bam-Bot chassis
 with some random movements */

// motors
#define Left OUT_A
#define Right OUT_C

// constants
#define TURN 10
#define FORWARD 50

task main()             // main task
{
  while(true)           // infinite loop
  {
    OnFwd(Left+Right);
    Wait(FORWARD+Random(200));  // wait .5 seconds + random
```

```
    PlaySound (SOUND_CLICK);      // play sound "click"
    Rev(Right);
    Wait(TURN+Random(50));        // wait .1 seconds + random
    PlaySound (SOUND_CLICK);      // play sound "click"
    Fwd(Right);
  }
}
```

A Quick Test of ZBB2.nqc

Download ZBB2.nqc to Zip-Bam-Bot, and place it in an open area, as before. Press the Run button on the RCX and watch carefully. You'll see that Zip-Bam-Bot doesn't always move forward for the same amount of time. With a bit of randomness added into the program, it has the ability to change the time spent going forward every time. And notice that when it turns, the amount of time spent turning changes, too. Another difference is that Zip-Bam-Bot is playing a noise every once in a while, instead of being quiet. The program (which continually repeats itself) has it play a sound at about the end of the program.

Now that Zip-Bam-Bot has random movements, let's find out how that was done.

Understanding ZBB2.nqc

This time, we took the instances where the motor is powered for a certain period of time and went a bit further by adding onto the mandatory waiting period a random amount of time. When the robot is going forward, it waits 0.5 second before doing anything else, but it must also wait an *additional* amount of time, *anywhere* between 0 and 200 hundredths of a second. Look at the line of code responsible for this:

```
Wait(FORWARD+Random(200));
```

The Random(*n*) *expression* (where *n* is a number between 0 and *n*) is what adds the unpredictability.

The amount of time the robot waits while turning also has an additional waiting time, amounting to anywhere between 0 and 50 hundredths of a second—this means the robot could turn a little or a lot.

```
    Wait(TURN+Random(50));
```

You probably noticed that the comment at the top of the program looked a bit different. This is because that comment is in the other style NQC offers. This type of comment starts with /*; anything beyond those characters is a comment. The characters */ end the comment. I used this type of comment here because what I wanted to say required two lines. I could also have used the // style by just placing // on two different lines, like this:

```
// ZBB2.nqc - A simple program for the Zip-Bam-Bot chassis
// with some random movements
```

Also included in the midst of this action are some sounds known as *clicks*. After the robot has finished either going forward or turning, it is programmed to play a click by using the PlaySound() command. This tells you when that snippet of code has finished running. Although this procedure is not too important right now, playing sounds in code can be helpful when you need to debug your sumo-bot programs. It is often good programming practice to put sounds in various places in a program to indicate if sections of code have executed properly.

Running Around with Organization

Since the program is so small right now, it is easy (and okay) to just put the code right into the main task and have it executed immediately. However, when you get into more complicated programs, you need to take a more organized approach.

For good programming practice (and quite possibly to save some time later on), you can organize your code easily and efficiently by using *functions*. Take a look at this example:

```
void Practice()
{
   OnFwd(OUT_A+OUT_C);
   Wait(200);
   Off(OUT_A+OUT_C);
}
```

This is a function called Practice(). As you can see here, the void keyword is used to create a function. Now all you need to do is call the Practice() function in the main task, and it will execute the function immediately.

Let's create a new, organized version of the program for the Zip-Bam-Bot chassis, as shown in Listing 3-3.

Listing 3-3: ZBB3.nqc

```
/* ZBB3.nqc - A simple program for the Zip-Bam-Bot chassis
   with some random that is in a function */

// motors
#define Left OUT_A
#define Right OUT_C

// constants
#define TURN 10
#define FORWARD 50

task main()
{
  while(true)
  {
    Running();    // execute Running() function
```

```
    }
}

void Running()                  // here is the function
{
    OnFwd(Left+Right);          // all this is the same code
    Wait(FORWARD+Random(200));
    PlaySound (SOUND_CLICK);
    Rev(Right);
    Wait(TURN+Random(50));
    PlaySound (SOUND_CLICK);
    Fwd(Right);
}
```

All the previous code that makes the chassis move is now in a function named Running(). The program declares the function with the void keyword, and then requests that it be executed in the main task by calling Running(). Like the rest of the examples, the program runs indefinitely. This is because the call to execute Running() was placed inside the braces of a while(true) statement, just as in the previous program. If you ran ZBB3.nqc, you would see that it makes the chassis do the same things as it did with the ZBB2.nqc program. It is just the code structuring that makes this program different.

This is all great, but it is not very practical for a real sumo-bot. For a more realistic program, less running around like crazy would be better. Let's cut back on the action a bit and come up with something more efficient.

Improving the Program for Running Around with Organization

To reduce the amount of running around, the program will run the motors only straight, *until* a timer runs out. Listing 3-4 shows the new program.

Listing 3-4: ZBB4.nqc

```
/* ZBB4.nqc - A simple program for the Zip-Bam-Bot chassis.
   It has some random in a function and is suitable
   for being the "running around" code in a sumo-bot */

// motors
#define Left OUT_A
#define Right OUT_C

// constants
#define TURN 10
#define LIMIT 35

// The main task
task main()
{
```

```
    // Clear the timer we are going to use
    ClearTimer(0);

    // Start the motors
    OnFwd(Left+Right);

    while(true)      // here is the infinite loop
    {
      Running();     // this command executes the Running() function
    }
}

// This is the function
void Running()
{
    until(Timer(0)>=LIMIT);    // here we are checking the timer
    Rev(Left);                 // reverse the left motor
    Wait(TURN+Random(40));     // wait 0.1 seconds and random amount
    Fwd(Left);                 // this makes the robot go forward
    ClearTimer(0);             // don't forget to clear the timer
}
```

A Quick Test of ZBB4.nqc

Download ZBB4.nqc to Zip-Bam-Bot, place it in the open area once again, and press the Run button on the RCX. It should be obvious that the erratic turning has been greatly reduced. In this program, Zip-Bam-Bot spends a lot of time going forward, and then executes a simple turn. That simple turn, however, isn't really all that simple. It, too, has random movements in it, making the action more fun to watch.

Understanding ZBB4.nqc

In the beginning of the main task, the following line clears a timer that will tell the robot to change its direction after a specified amount of time (with the random timing).

```
    ClearTimer(0);
```

We need to clear the timer, because the previous timer amount (from when the RCX was last on) is remembered.

In real robotic sumo, if the robot doesn't find the opposition after a certain amount of time going in one direction, it's a good idea to change that direction. The following line of code is responsible for watching the timer:

```
until(Timer(0)>=LIMIT);
```

The code here is based around a specified amount of time, LIMIT, whose value is 3.5 seconds. When Timer(0) is more than or equal to (designated by >=) LIMIT, the program knows it's time to change the direction of the robot; then the process starts all over again. Also notice the use of the until statement. Used this way, until creates a *condition*. The program waits until the timer is more than or equal to 3.5 seconds—a condition that must be met. The program also clears the timer once it has reached 3.5 seconds, using the ClearTimer(0) command again—otherwise, the timer would continue counting upwards past 3.5 seconds.

For the sumo-bots in later chapters, you'll probably need to modify this program. With functions doing line detecting, touch sensor sensing, and who knows what else, the Running() function will need to be integrated smoothly within the program. But, of course, getting your code to work and execute smoothly is half the fun isn't it?

Testing the Zip-Bam-Bot Chassis

You have seen various programs for this little bot and done some quick tests with them, but you still might have a yearning to see some robotic sumo action. Great! That's a sure sign of a robotic sumo fan. Let's set up a project that resembles what would happen in a robotic sumo arena. You don't need to use the RIS Test Pad or a sumo-bot arena for this project, because the chassis can't tell if it has passed over a line or hit something (later versions of Zip-Bam-Bot *will* be able to detect their surroundings).

First, place the Zip-Bam-Bot chassis on the outskirts of an open space, facing towards the center. To make the test run robotic-sumo-oriented, place various objects around that open space. These can be little blocks of wood, some of the extra-large LEGO bricks for kids, and anything else that is fairly small and easily pushed. Their sole purpose is to be shoved and moved around—whether 1 foot or 1 inch. Remember that pushing is what a sumo-bot is supposed to do!

Using the download procedure outlined in the "Downloading Programs to the RCX" section earlier in this chapter, load the ZBB.nqc program into the RCX slot 1, ZBB3.nqc into slot 2, and ZBB4.nqc into slot 3. Test each program, one at a time (staying nearby, in case Zip-Bam-Bot goes somewhere it shouldn't), and observe Zip-Bam-Bot's performance at pushing objects around using each program. Then experiment with objects of varying weights to test Zip-Bam-Bot's pushing abilities. If you would like to see some heavier objects being pushed, try canned food, books, and even the lid to the RIS.

Time the chassis; for example, give it a minute for each program. See how many objects it can find (run into) and move during that time period. Determine which program you think is best for this situation. When picking sumo-bot strategies, you'll need to decide which type of program would work well in a particular situation. For this situation, the "Running Around with Organization" program (ZBB3.nqc) might be the best pick. Because it keeps Zip-Bam-Bot moving quickly, it increases the chances of hitting something; however, this depends on how you've positioned the objects around Zip-Bam-Bot. If the objects are close together and near Zip-Bam-Bot, ZBB3.nqc probably would be the best choice. But if you placed the objects in a different setup—say they are widely spaced and the area you are using for Zip-Bam-Bot is very large—one of the other programs might work better.

Conclusion

This chapter gave you an introduction to the basis of the next two chapters: the Zip-Bam-Bot chassis. You built it, programmed it, and (I hope) understood how it worked. More about Zip-Bam-Bot should make sense when you see the purposes behind its design and layout in the next chapters. In Chapter 4, you'll see a fully developed sumo-bot made with the Zip-Bam-Bot design: Zip-Bam-Bot version XK1.

CHAPTER 4

Zip-Bam-Bot Version XK1

ZIP-BAM-BOT VERSION XK1 makes for a unique yet efficient sumo-bot. XK1 takes the features its chassis provides (speed, agility, and so on) and puts them to good use. More specifically, it relies on speed, momentum, and some programming smarts to win the round and become top sumo-bot. As shown in Figure 4-1, XK1 is designed with a slope, two touch sensors, and two large claws—features that will frustrate the opponent and gain superiority in the arena. All the pieces that make up XK1 are found in just one RIS.

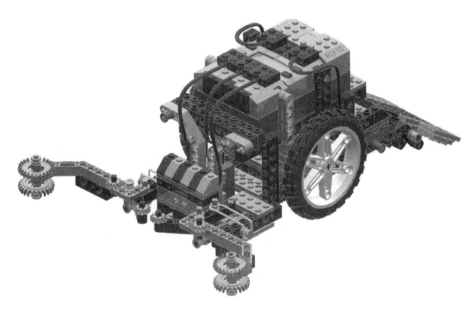

Figure 4-1. Completed Zip-Bam-Bot Version XK1

You will first construct a number of subassemblies, and then attach them and several other pieces in the final assembly to the Zip-Bam-Bot chassis to make the complete sumo-bot. However, before you start building, you should understand the strategy XK1 will use—which forms the basis for its design—and take a look at the parts you'll use as well.

Understanding XK1's Strategy

As mentioned in Chapter 3, there are two approaches your small-and-fast sumo-bots can take: the hit-and-hit-again approach, also known as the *repeated ramming method*, and the hit-and-run approach. XK1 uses the first approach. Here is the basic idea of how the repeated ramming method works: On contact at high speed, the sumo-bot that gets hit has its wheels taken off the ground for just a split second, and this enables your sumo-bot to push the opponent back a little distance. Your sumo-bot then repeatedly rams the opponent until it is pushed off the arena.

There is also a second way you can approach the repeated ramming method—here is how this second approach works: Your sumo-bot, upon contact at high speed, completely demobilizes (flips over) the opponent by using mechanisms or subassemblies. Since the opponent may not have been demobilized at the first hit, repeated ramming is also used. You'll see this small-and-fast approach in action in the next chapter.

XK1's substrategy is based on feedback from two touch sensors, which are depressed by liftarms. Here is the basic idea of the substrategy: The front of the robot holds two large claws, which, on impact, place XK1 facing directly at the opponent. Moments later, or even at the same time, its bumper(s) is triggered. Once this has happened, XK1 will crash into its opponent again and again, until it pushes its competitor completely out of bounds, correcting its position as necessary with the claws at each hit.

Constructing Subassemblies for XK1

As noted at the beginning of the chapter, XK1 requires only one RIS. The bill of materials for XK1, minus the chassis, is shown in Figure 4-2.

Now you're ready to start building XK1. You'll build the following subassemblies:

- Light sensor subassembly

- Back slope subassembly

- Touch sensors subassembly

- Left claw subassembly

- Right claw subassembly

First, you'll build the essential light sensor subassembly.

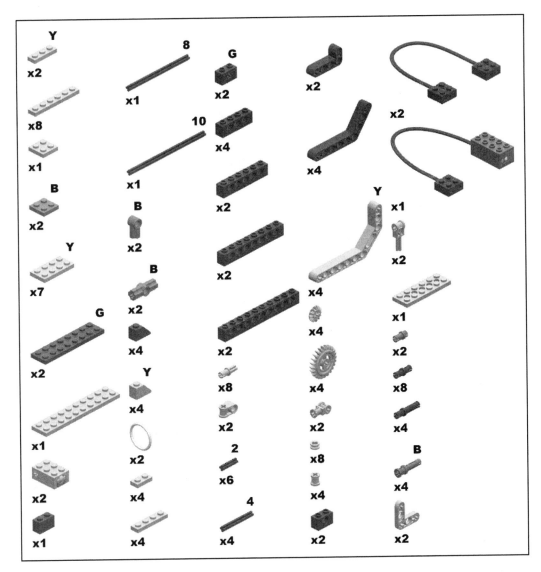

Figure 4-2. XK1's bill of materials

Light Sensor Subassembly

Despite the fact that the light sensor subassembly is made from only a handful of pieces, it has a unique design. It also gives XK1 personality: it looks like a face with two eyes. Figure 4-3 shows the completed light sensor subassembly.

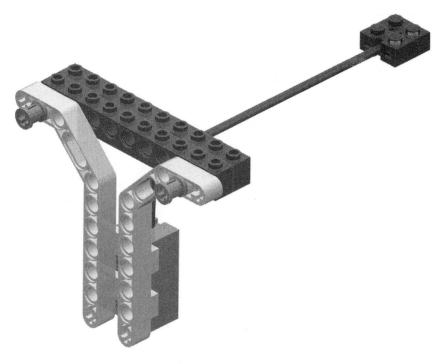

Figure 4-3. The completed light sensor subassembly

The exact placement and positioning of the light sensor are very important. Take a look at the completed sumo-bot shown in Figure 4-1, at the beginning of this chapter, to see where the light sensor is placed. The reason for this placement is a simple one: you don't want the opponent to ram the light sensor and break it off midway through a competition! The light sensor in a sumo-bot must always be placed in a protected area and/or with an extremely strong attachment. If you have the light sensor in an exposed area or with a weak connection—or even worse, both—it will probably get taken off pretty quickly. In this model, opposing sumo-bots never even touch the light sensor!

By placing the light sensor a little bit farther back, as opposed to right up front, you gain two advantages:

- The shock of a crash is not directly on the light sensor, or even on the light sensor subassembly, but on the chassis in general.

- XK1 can push the other sumo-bot off the arena without detecting the line and turning around before the job is finished.

In steps 1 and 2, you connect the beams and friction pins. The two beams, firmly snapped together with friction pins, are what connect to the chassis. The attachment point on the chassis is the 2x8 space in front of the RCX.

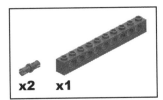

 Light Sensor Subassembly Step 1: *Snap two friction pins into a 1x10 beam.*

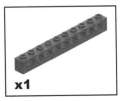

 Light Sensor Subassembly Step 2: *Snap another 1x10 beam onto friction pins.*

Next, in step 3, add two yellow *11.5 angular liftarms* and connect them to the beams by means of two blue pins, sometimes called *long pins with stop bush*. The liftarms and stop pins give the subassembly the appearance of a face, but they also make it clean and easy to use, which is, in reality, more important.

> **TIP** *Adding some character to your sumo-bots is important. The blue stop bushes and yellow liftarms, which outline a face in this assembly, make XK1 look like some sort of creature. Giving your sumo-bot characteristics makes it easier to name and also helps it to keep a unique profile at a competition. Also, when you're participating in an event, an amusing, ingeniously designed, or unique characteristic can impress the audience (and even other participants) and draw a lot of attention. After all, you want people to like your creation! Who's going to be interested in a "plain" sumo-bot?*

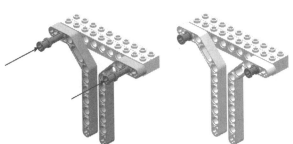
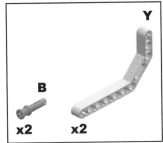

 Light Sensor Subassembly Step 3: *Add two yellow liftarms and two blue pins.*

In step 4, turn the model around to the back and connect the two "free" liftarms together with 1x3 yellow plates. But wait! In step 4, you have these plates *pushed stud-first into a liftarm!* For those of you new to the TECHNIC line of pieces, this attachment might seem odd. While unusual, it is a very strong connection and quite acceptable. You'll see this type of attachment again in the claw subassemblies you'll build later.

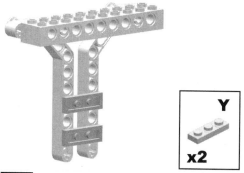

 Light Sensor Subassembly Step 4: *Push two yellow 1x3 plates into liftarms.*

To complete the light sensor subassembly, place the light sensor directly in the middle (on the back side) of the newly added yellow plates, as shown in step 5. Placing a brick—in this case a light sensor—in the middle like this is possible, although it may not be how it is usually done. This method just makes it unique and puts the light sensor in a better position: the middle.

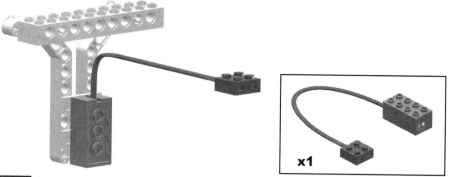

 Light Sensor Subassembly Step 5: *Push a light sensor into 1x3 plates.*

You have now completed the light sensor subassembly. It should look like the one shown in Figure 4-3, at the beginning of this section.

Back Slope Subassembly

The back slope subassembly, shown in Figure 4-4, is designed for cases when XK1 is backing up directly into the opposing sumo-bot. Instead of XK1 simply getting rammed by the other sumo-bot, the opponent can actually go *up* the smooth incline, and if you're lucky, end up less mobile than it was before. In addition, XK1 is designed to prevent the opposing sumo-bot from getting stuck on its chassis in the event it does go upwards and onto it. On some sumo-bots, this could be a plus, but for XK1, it is not, as it does not have much pulling power. Instead, two sloped pieces stationed on the chassis, which you will add in the final assembly, serve as a stopping point.

> **NOTE** *The back slope subassembly uses two blue pins with a stop bush and two long friction pins to attach to the chassis. The only reason the steps call for long friction pins instead of blue pins is that the RIS has only four blue pins. Since two of them are used in the light sensor subassembly, you have only two left for the back slope subassembly. However, if you have more blue pins, feel free to use them.*

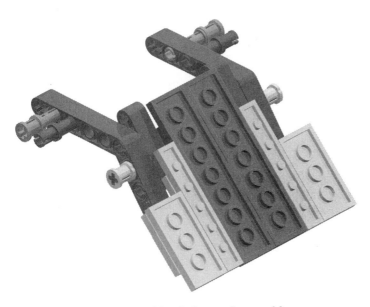

Figure 4-4. The completed back slope subassembly

Begin construction by taking two of the longer, black angular liftarms in the RIS set and pushing in friction pins, as shown in step 1.

 Back Slope Subassembly Step 1: *Push four friction pins into black liftarms.*

Step 2 snaps *2x4 L-shaped liftarms* onto the friction pins.

 Back Slope Subassembly Step 2: *Snap 2x4 L-shaped liftarms onto friction pins.*

Step 3, on the other hand, doesn't snap—it *slides*. To be more specific, you slide a #10 axle through the liftarms, and as the axle is going from one side to the other, you slide 1x2 and 1x4 beams and two *bushings* onto the axle. Don't forget to add the plates to the beams in step 3 as well.

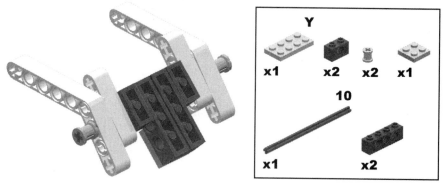

 Back Slope Subassembly Step 3: *Slide axle through liftarms and position bushings and beams with plates on axle.*

Step 4 uses more plates! The plates in this step form the actual slope. Attach two 2x8 green plates to the beams, and attach all the other plates onto the 2x8 plates.

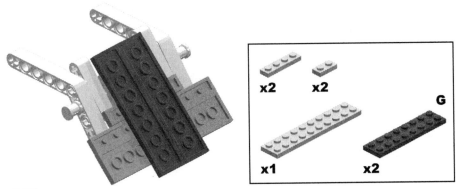

 Back Slope Subassembly Step 4: *Add 2x10, 2x8, 1x4, and 1x2 plates.*

Step 5 adds *more* plates to finish the slope and also the pins that allow the back slope subassembly to attach to the chassis. Once you've completed this step, you're finished with the back slope subassembly, which should look like the one shown in Figure 4-4, at the beginning of this section. You're ready to move on to the touch sensors subassembly.

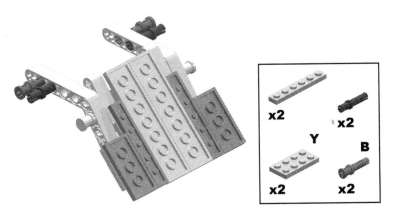

 Back Slope Subassembly Step 5: *Add two 2x4 yellow plates, two 1x6 plates, and push long friction and blue pins into liftarms.*

Touch Sensors Subassembly

The two touch sensors are used together with the two claw subassemblies you'll be building next. As you'll soon see, the bumper system uses a very interesting bumping technique. Figure 4-5 shows the completed touch sensors subassembly.

Figure 4-5. The completed touch sensor subassembly

To begin, take two touch sensors and place an electrical wire on each of them facing backwards, and then add two 2x2 blue plates and two 1x6 plates as shown in step 1.

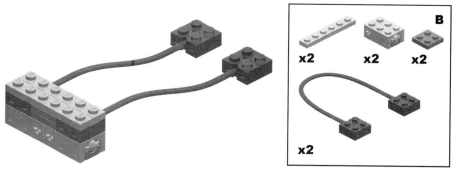

 Touch Sensors Subassembly Step 1: *Place electrical wires on two touch sensors and add two 2x2 plates and two 1x6 plates.*

Then, take both black and yellow *1x2 sloped bricks*, and place them on top of everything, as shown in step 2.

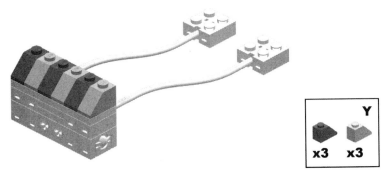

 Touch Sensors Subassembly Step 2: *Add three black and yellow 1x2 sloped bricks.*

Left Claw Subassembly

The claws have a special purpose: on impact, they direct XK1 in the direction of the opposing sumo-bot. The ends of the claws are tipped with 24t (24 tooth) crown gears, which allow the adversary to run smoothly along them (as opposed to getting stuck or worse). The claws are specially designed and attached so they won't fall off at the first crash. Because of the role the claws play, a lot of force will be exerted on them, and a strong design is very important. Figure 4-6 shows the completed left claw subassembly.

Figure 4-6. The left claw subassembly

By placing itself in the proper direction with its claws, XK1 can better use its momentum to give the competition the hardest hit. This design also sets XK1 up in a straight line for the next hit. The touch sensors and the black liftarms pointing out toward the front of XK1 (which I call *feelers*) detect the other sumo-bot after the large, yellow claws have done their job. All the different pieces you see on the black feelers are specially designed to register a hit in as many situations as possible.

Steps 1 and 2 build up the core center of this assembly, which is "core" because almost everything connects to it. The core center is constructed out of *axles*, various pins, a *crossblock*, and *angle connectors*. Notice this part is made without any beams. The types of pieces used here are sometimes called *axle accessories*.

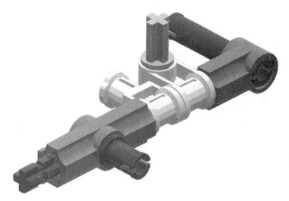

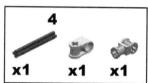

 Left Claw Subassembly Step 1: *Slide crossblock and connector with axle hole onto #4 axle.*

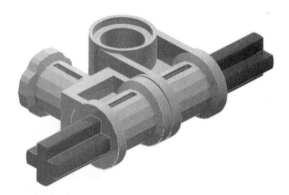

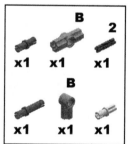

Left Claw Subassembly Step 2: *Add angle connectors, notched #2 axle, and pins.*

Step 3 introduces a beam, the black feeler I mentioned earlier, and a piece called a *pole reverser handle,* or a *catch.*

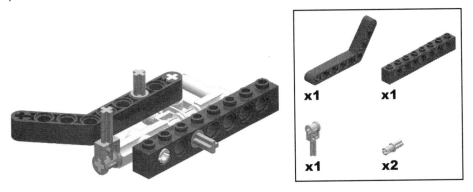

 Left Claw Subassembly Step 3: *Add 1x8 beam, black liftarm, two axle pins, and catch.*

In step 4, you add a rubber band and some bushings. Do you see those axle pins you added in step 3? Put a half-bushing on the upper one, and a bushing on the lower one. Take one of the white rubber bands included in the RIS and stretch it across both of them.

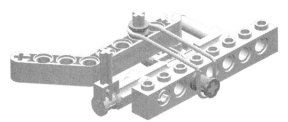

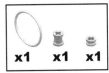

 Left Claw Subassembly Step 4: *Position bushing and half-bushing, then add rubber band.*

Now you're going to work on the "arm" in steps 5 and 6. The first step consists of a large, yellow liftarm (one of my favorite pieces in the RIS), an axle, and a beam that goes stud-first into the liftarm. This connection is just like the one you used in the light sensor subassembly. Although this beam is not entirely necessary, it can be useful for helping to contain the opponent and preventing a slope from going underneath the arm.

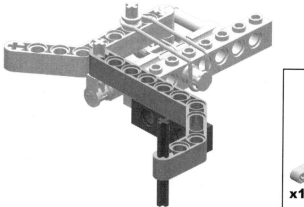

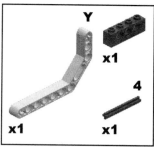

 Left Claw Subassembly Step 5: *Place liftarm, #4 axle, and 1x4 beam onto catch.*

In step 6, you add the 24t crown gears. Not only do these allow the opposing sumo-bot to "slide" along them, but they also help the arm by giving it more bulk at the tip, which, overall, helps the performance.

 Left Claw Subassembly Step 6: *Add two 24t crown gears and three half-bushings.*

In steps 7 and 8, you add some parts that help to register hits on the feeler. After pushing in a *3/4 pin*, axle pin, and a notched #2 axle as shown, add a *12t bevel gear* (mainly for decoration) and an *L-shaped liftarm* with its own bevel gear. Once you've done some testing, it will be easier to see how this L-shaped liftarm improves the bumper system's performance.

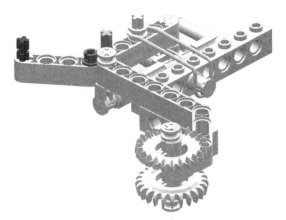

 Left Claw Subassembly Step 7: *Push 3/4 pin, axle pin, and notched #2 axle into liftarm.*

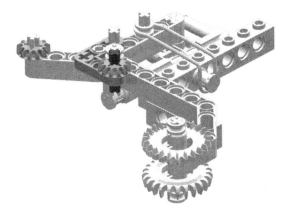

 Left Claw Subassembly Step 8: *Add L-shaped liftarm, notched #2 axle, and two bevel gears.*

You're now finished with the left claw subassembly, which should look like the one shown in Figure 4-6, at the beginning of this section.

Right Claw Subassembly

The right claw subassembly, the last subassembly for XK1, is a mirror image of the left claw subassembly, as shown in Figure 4-7. In other words, everything is built the same, except that the orientation of the pieces is switched. To build the right claw subassembly, follow the instruction steps given for the left claw subassembly, but change the orientation of the pieces so that the completed assembly looks like Figure 4-7. Remember, you can always download the actual building instructions for the mirror subassemblies from the Downloads section of the Apress website (www.apress.com) if you would rather follow those. Once you're finished with the right claw subassembly, all the assemblies have been built and you are ready to move onto the next phase: the final assembly of XK1.

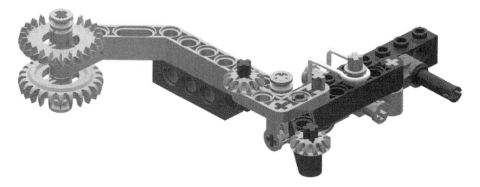

Figure 4-7. The right claw subassembly

Putting XK1 Together

The first step is to modify the chassis you built in Chapter 3—there are actually several things you need to do in this step. First, on the front end, remove (temporarily) the 2x6 TECHNIC plate on the top, pull out the 2x4 black brick occupying the space underneath, and add a 1x2 black brick, two *1x2 green bricks with axle holes*, and a #8 axle, which goes through the green bricks.

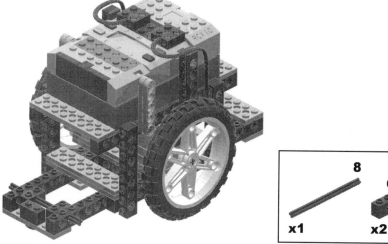

XK1 Final Assembly Step 1: Modify front end of the Zip-Bam-Bot chassis.

Once you've done this, replace the 2x6 TECHNIC plate, and then turn the model around to the back and add plates to the very back end of the chassis, as shown in step 2.

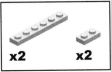

XK1 Final Assembly Step 2: *Replace 2x6 plate on front end of chassis and add two 1x2 and 1x6 plates to back of chassis.*

In step 3, you finish off the back end with beams and sloped bricks.

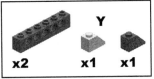

XK1 Final Assembly Step 3: *Place two 1x6 beams and two sloped bricks onto chassis.*

Now connect the **back slope subassembly**, as illustrated in step 4, by pushing its blue and long friction pins into the chassis.

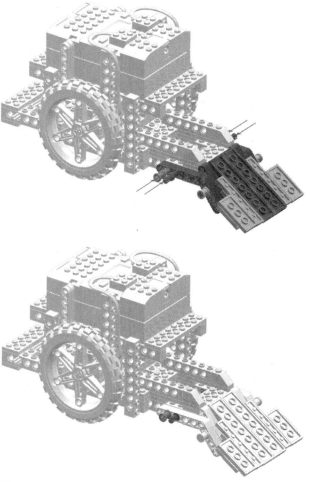

 XK1 Final Assembly Step 4: *Attach back slope subassembly to chassis.*

TIP *Did you notice how easily the back slope subassembly connected to the chassis? This ability—the ability to connect to the chassis or base quickly and easily—is known as* modularity. *Modularity is an important concept to understand, and implement, in robotic sumo. Some rule sets allow participants to change assemblies on their sumo-bot after the game has started! If you have a few assembled and easily connected assemblies on hand, and decide one of them would work better for the current match, you're allowed to switch them out. This is why it is important to try to have a design that allows different parts to be easily removed and added.*

After this, turn the model back around to the front. Add the **light sensor subassembly** in step 5, and add the **touch sensors subassembly** in step 6. Here is the scheme for attaching the electrical wires to the RCX:

- The **touch sensor** on the right side goes on **input port 3.**

- The **touch sensor** on the left side goes on **input port 1.**

- The **light sensor** goes on **input port 2.**

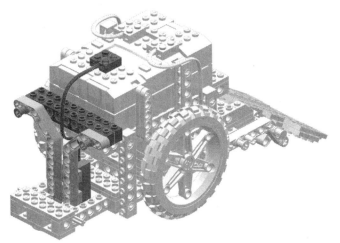

 XK1 Final Assembly Step 5: *Attach light sensor subassembly to chassis.*

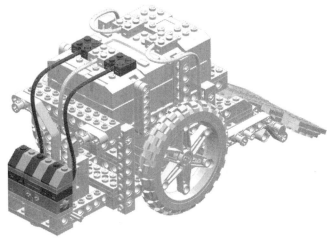

 XK1 Final Assembly Step 6: *Attach touch sensors subassembly to chassis.*

Now take the **left** and **right claw subassemblies** and connect them as shown in step 7. The long friction pins on the claw subassemblies should go one stud's space into the structure's beams, and the catches should go into the #8 axle you added in step 1.

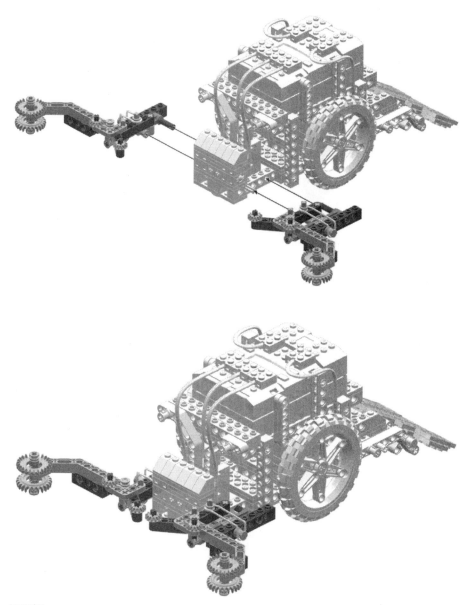

 XK1 *Final Assembly Step 7:* *Attach the left and right claw subassemblies to chassis.*

You are (obviously!) not finished attaching the claws, however. To continue, add two yellow 2x4 plates, which go from the claw assemblies to the chassis, in step 8.

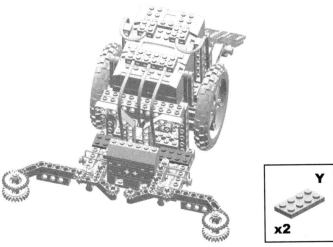

 XK1 Final Assembly Step 8: *Add two 2x4 plates for strengthening.*

Lastly, flip XK1 on its top and add the six various plates, as shown in step 9. These plates help to—once again—strengthen the claw subassemblies.

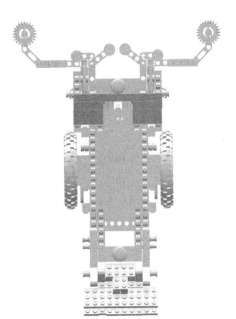

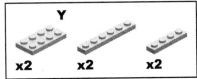

 XK1 Final Assembly Step 9: *Add two 2x4, 1x4, and 1x6 plates to bottom of chassis.*

The model is now finished and should look like the sumo-bot shown in Figure 4-1, at the beginning of this chapter. Zip-Bam-Bot Version XK1 is in your hands!

Before we move on, let's take a closer look at some of the aspects of XK1's design:

No gears: You most likely noticed that there are no gears involved in the drivetrain of XK1. Consider that the ultimate goal of Zip-Bam-Bot is to go *fast*. Introducing gears results in friction, which results in less power and speed. By connecting the wheels directly to the motor, friction is at an absolute minimum. Making the gears go faster to make XK1 go faster wouldn't work very well, since there would be a reduction in torque. XK1 would then go slower, since there wouldn't be enough power to properly push it along.

> **NOTE** *There is nothing wrong with using gears in a small-and-fast sumo-bot. For this model, I simply chose not to. Also, if there are gears in a model, that doesn't necessarily mean they are used to change the speed. Often, gears are necessary to transmit power from one place to another.*

Big wheels: If you used a smaller wheel, Zip-Bam-Bot wouldn't go as fast. Using a bigger wheel basically makes XK1 go faster. More specifically, the larger the diameter of the wheel, the more speed.

Ground clearance: You must always (or as in many cases as possible) try to keep your sumo-bot low to the ground, or else a sneaky opponent will take the incentive to run itself under it. XK1 has most of its subassemblies attached to the front end, which results in the robot tipping forwards and onto its skid plate. Although this doesn't immunize XK1 against slopes, it's much better than leaving a nice-sized gap for the opponent to run under. (However, dragging on the ground isn't always the best method, as you'll learn in the "Considering the Pros and Cons of XK1's Design" section later in this chapter). A back-end hit would result in the opposition going up XK1's slippery slope, and a side hit on the wheels would result in nothing more than a little jolt, because of the traction the wheels provide.

Now that you're finished with building this sumo-bot, you're ready to move on to the programming.

Formulating a Solid Programming Solution for XK1

The first task is to consider how you want XK1 to accomplish its job—the job of being a sumo-bot! It has three sensors, which offer you a variety of possibilities. For the sub-strategy you're using for XK1, you have at least two separate tasks that need to be accomplished, with the possibility of a third task as well:

Watching for the line: This task is responsible for watching out for that thick, black line encircling the arena. You need to set up a system where XK1 can use its light sensor to detect the difference between the line and playing ground, and then react to that difference. This is the most important task in terms of priority. If XK1—or any sumo-bot for that matter—fails to give the "watching for the line" task ultimate authority, it could accidentally drive itself out of bounds.

Responding to the other sumo-bot: Second in importance, XK1 must carefully monitor if the other sumo-bot has made contact via its two touch sensors in the front. If the sensors are pressed (or just one of them is pressed), XK1 should respond by ramming the opposition repeatedly (attacking).

Running around on the playing ground: Last in priority, and ironically what your sumo-bot will spend the most time doing, is maneuvering on the playing ground. In a possible stratagem, XK1 will not just move straight all the time, but will perform some random turns in its navigation to increase its chances of finding the other sumo-bot.

Actually, you need to create only two different tasks for XK1. The first task will watch for the line and use an auto-calibration process (internally storing the values of the line, playing ground, and so on) for the light sensor. The second task will check on the touch sensors to see if they have been pressed. Once a touch sensor is pressed, XK1 will back up for a specified amount of time, and then go forward again. You won't create the third task—running around with random turns—for XK1, for the following two reasons:

- XK1 is so fast that it can easily cover any robotic sumo arena in a flash. With speed like that, the random turns are almost unnecessary.

- You can have the wheels going forward (to travel) in both of the other tasks. With that capability, the need for a third task diminishes.

On the other hand, having a random maneuvering task can be helpful in certain situations. In the next chapter, you'll implement this type of task in another sumo-bot.

Programming XK1 with the Solution

Now that you have decided on a programming solution, you're faced with a predicament: How do you get two different tasks to properly work with each other? Or how do you give the light sensor task top priority? If you have two tasks running, and the RCX is busy with a touch sensor hit, and suddenly the robot goes over the line...well, it wouldn't be pretty. The RCX is so preoccupied that it misses the light sensor reading completely!

You need to think of some other way to attack this problem rather than simply running task 1 and task 2. You don't need to use multitasking (more than one task running at the same time), but you do need to have the right task doing the right thing at the right time. How can you do this? You can use either of two NQC features added in the 2.0 release:

- *Access control* allows you to actually set priority ranks for different tasks using the SetPriority() command. In this way, you can give the line-detecting code highest priority, the touch sensors next highest, and so on.

- *Event monitoring* is an elegant feature of NQC that makes sure *nothing* (like an important light-sensor reading) goes unnoticed by accident.

We're going to try out both of these NQC features, but first, we need to make the vital functions that we'll use often and that both approaches can share.

> **NOTE** *Remember that you don't need to retype the programs in this book into BricxCC. All of the programs for this book are available from the Downloads section of the Apress web site (*www.apress.com*).*

Creating the Functions

The first function we'll create is a calibration process for the light sensor. Then we'll create an attacking function, and finally, the function for avoiding the line that encircles the arena, which XK1 uses after it has detected the line.

The Calibration Function

First, you need to understand the method by which you are calibrating and "starting up" the robot (after calibration, the robot must be started up by telling it to get the main part of the program underway). In a robotic sumo event, the sumo-bots are either started with a remote control or by the creator. Not all events use remote-control activation, so we'll be going with the more user-oriented activation approach.

The calibration and startup approach is based around a touch sensor. By pressing and releasing a specified touch sensor, you can tell the robot when to take the reading of the line and when to start. Okay, let's get into the actual code!

> **TIP** *You should always introduce some method of auto-calibration in your program for the light sensor. When you go to a robotic sumo event, you probably won't know what kind of value your light sensor will read on the arena, and that's why you need the auto-calibration. Failure to do so could cause some obvious problems.*

The code that does the calibration is really not that complex (two lines of code), as it simply takes a reading with the light sensor and tweaks it a bit. The function as a whole might seem complex, but after a little explanation, it should be easy to understand, and you'll see that the code actually makes the calibration process easier for you. Take a look at the `Calibrate()` function:

```
// sensor and constants
#define See SENSOR_2
#define AMOUNT 3
#define LIMIT 35

int line=0,threshold=0;    // variables
```

```
// this is the calibrating function
void Calibrate()
{
    until(RBump==1);
    line=See;
    threshold=line+AMOUNT;
    until(RBump==0);
    PlaySound(SOUND_CLICK);
    until(RBump==1);
    until(RBump==0);
    PlaySound(SOUND_CLICK);
    Wait(LIMIT);
}
```

As you can see at the top, a few resources were defined for the calibrating function's use.

```
#define See SENSOR_2
#define AMOUNT 3
#define LIMIT 35
```

Then, to begin the process, two variables are declared and initialized at zero for later use.

```
int line=0,threshold=0;      // variables
```

Variables are used in all types of programming. Simply put, a variable is something the programmer names and then stores information in. This line uses the variable declaration keyword int, which stands for *integer*. After declaring int, the name of each variable with its initialization (=0) is written. Also, a comma is placed in between the two variables (line and threshold) to separate them. To start with, we store the values 0 in both of our variables. Later on in the function, the variable line equals the same amount the light sensor does, which could be anywhere from 100 to 0.

> **NOTE** *Variables are very powerful but can be a little confusing at times. This is partly due to the fact that there is more than one type of variable in NQC, and some of these variables are specific to NQC. For more information about variables and how they work, look in the* NQC Programmer's Guide *that comes with BricxCC, or check out* Definitive Guide to LEGO MINDSTORMS *by Dave Baum (Apress, 2002).*

All those until statements can be confusing, so let's talk about those before we get into the rest of the function. The main purpose of these statements is to assist you with calibration. With them, you can easily and quickly tell the robot when to take the readings and start the main part of the program. All the until statements are based around XK1's bumpers; that is, they are used with XK1's bumpers to form the statement. For example, the first line of code within the calibration function is:

```
until(RBump==1);
```

This makes XK1 wait until its right bumper is pressed, which is the first step in the calibration process. Then it takes the readings for the light sensor and waits until the right bumper is released.

For the actual calibration process, after the right bumper has been pressed, the light sensor (named See) puts a reading into the variable named line.

```
line=See;
```

The threshold variable is then made the same amount as the line variable plus AMOUNT (which equals 3).

```
threshold=line+AMOUNT;
```

Adding 3 to the threshold ensures that XK1 will not miss the line. When we call the <= (less than or equal to) *operator* later in the program (shown in Listing 4-1, later in this chapter) to look for the line, the addition of 3 will keep the threshold variable slightly higher than the value of the actual line. Therefore, when the light sensor detects the line, it will be darker than the threshold variable, and XK1 will not miss it.

> **NOTE** *Adding a small amount to the* threshold *variable works for a black line and white surface, but for a white line and a black surface, you need to take a slightly different approach. For this situation, subtract a small amount from* threshold *and call* >=.

Now that the calibration has been done, the sumo-bot needs to be started up in orderly fashion. This is done in the same way as the calibration: wait until the right bumper is pressed then released. But that isn't all; as is the practice with this approach for starting up at a robotic sumo event, we introduce a small amount of waiting time in the program after the bumper has been pressed and released.

```
until(RBump==1);
until(RBump==0);
PlaySound(SOUND_CLICK);
Wait(LIMIT);
```

The Wait() time amount is named LIMIT, which is 0.35 second. Using LIMIT, you can step back from XK1 before it starts up.

As explained in Chapter 3, placing some sounds (in this case, SOUND_CLICK) strategically in the function help to confirm that the robot is properly responding. Look through the function again, and you'll see that there are two clicks programmed into this function, and both are played after the right bumper has been pressed and released:

- After the reading for the light sensor has been taken, the RCX will emit a click.

- After you press and release the right bumper to start up the main part of the program, the RCX will emit another click.

The Attacking Function

Now you need to think of how you want XK1 to react to a touch sensor hit. You *could* tell it to run back a little bit and then go forward *until* it hits the other robot again. However, that introduces some complicated programming issues. Instead, we'll tell XK1 to run back a little bit and then go simply *forward*. Here is the function for reacting to a sensor hit, appropriately named Win():

```
// constant
#define BACK_TIME 70

// attacking function
void Win()
{
    Rev(OUT_A+OUT_C);      // reverse both motors
    Wait(BACK_TIME);       // wait 0.7 seconds
    OnFwd(OUT_A+OUT_C);    // turn on both motors in forward direction
}
```

This function is pretty simple. We first define a constant called BACK_TIME that is 70 hundredths (0.7) of a second for use in the Win() function. The first line of code in the function makes XK1 reverse both motors, and the second line causes the program to wait for those 70 hundredths of a second. Lastly, the function turns both motors back on in the forward direction. In the end, all this little function does is make XK1 back up a little and go forward again. It's great for the repeated ramming method, but can cause problems when XK1 is near the line. We'll talk more about this later in the "Understanding the Pros and Cons of XK1's Design" section.

The Line-Avoiding Function

The third function we'll create is one that XK1 uses to avoid the line after it has detected the line. When the light sensor detects the line, XK1 should back up just a little bit, spin around, and then go forward. Here is what this approach looks like:

```
// motors
#define Left OUT_A
#define Right OUT_C

  //constants
#define LIGHT_BACK 20
#define TURN 45

void Avoid()
{
    OnRev(Left+Right);    // reverse both motors
    Wait(LIGHT_BACK);     // wait a small amount of time
    Fwd(Left);            // left motor go forward, which makes XK1 turn in place
    Wait(TURN);           // wait .45 seconds
    OnFwd(Left+Right);    // both motors go forward again
}
```

As you can see, the function basically turns the robot in a different direction. The time amounts determine how much the sumo-bot runs backwards and spins. Through testing, I've found that the time amounts used here are, generally speaking, good timing; however, feel free to modify them.

Programming XK1 with Access Control

Now that we have these functions completed, we're going to create a full-blown sumo-bot program that uses them and NQC's access control feature (among other things). Listing 4-1 shows the completed access control program.

Listing 4-1. XK1_Access_Control.nqc

```
// XK1_Access_Control.nqc
// A sumo-bot program for Zip-Bam-Bot Version XK1

// motors
#define Left OUT_A
#define Right OUT_C

// sensors
#define LBump SENSOR_1
#define RBump SENSOR_3
#define See SENSOR_2

// constants
#define BACK_TIME 70
#define TURN 45
#define AMOUNT 3
#define LIMIT 35
#define LIGHT_BACK 20

// variables for calibration
int line=0,threshold=0;

task main()
{
    // initialize sensors
    SetSensor(LBump,SENSOR_TOUCH);
    SetSensor(RBump,SENSOR_TOUCH);
    SetSensor(See,SENSOR_LIGHT);

    // calibrate light sensor
    Calibrate();

    // start motors and tasks
    OnFwd(Left+Right);

    // start tasks
```

```
   start LWatch;
   start Crash;
}

// this task watches for the line
task LWatch()
{
   SetPriority(0);    // highest priority

   while(true)
   {
      until(See<=threshold);  // if we see the line...

         acquire(ACQUIRE_USER_1)
         {
           Avoid();          // ...take control and avoid it
         }
   }
}

// this task watches the touch sensors
task Crash()
{
   SetPriority(1);       // second highest priority

   while(true)
   {
      until(LBump|RBump==1);  // if touch sensors are pressed...

         acquire(ACQUIRE_USER_1)
         {
             Win();      // ...take control and crash repeatedly
         }
   }

}

// this function sets the robot up for another crash
void Win()
{
  Rev(Left+Right);
  Wait(BACK_TIME);
  OnFwd(Left+Right);
}

// this function avoids the line
 void Avoid()
{
   OnRev(Left+Right);
   Wait(BACK_TIME);
   Fwd(Left);
```

```
    Wait(TURN);
    OnFwd(Left+Right);
}

// this is the calibrating function
void Calibrate()
{
    until(RBump==1);
    line=See;
    threshold=line+AMOUNT;
    until(RBump==0);
    PlaySound(SOUND_CLICK);
    until(RBump==1);
    until(RBump==0);
    PlaySound(SOUND_CLICK);
    Wait(LIMIT);
}
```

For those of you new to NQC, this program probably looks a little intimidating, but don't worry. All of those #defines and comments (// lines) make the program look more complicated that it actually is.

Near the top of the program are a number of predefined constants and definitions for motors and sensors.

```
// motors
#define Left OUT_A
#define Right OUT_C

// sensors
#define LBump SENSOR_1
#define RBump SENSOR_3
#define See SENSOR_2

// constants
#define BACK_TIME 70
#define TURN 45
#define AMOUNT 3
#define LIMIT 35
#define LIGHT_BACK 20
```

The values for the constants were determined through testing, but you can easily change them to your liking. With a full-scale program, it's easy to see why defining is efficient and should be used. Let's look at one of the definitions from the top of the program again, which we also used in the previous chapter:

```
#define Left OUT_A
```

Let's say you have a large program in which you used the Left resource many times. Suddenly, you decide you don't want to use OUT_A anymore; now you want to use OUT_C (remember that Left stands for OUT_A). To fix this, you could simply go to the #define

Left OUT_A line of code and change the letter A to C. This is *very* easy. The alternative (if you didn't use the defining method) would be to change every occurrence in the code, one by one, from OUT_A to OUT_C. By defining resources in your programs, you make your programs more flexible, because they are easier to modify.

Now let's turn our attention to the rest of the program. It has some new features that I have not introduced or fully explained yet, including tasks, sensor initializations, and more. Let's start by discussing how to initialize sensors. The program includes three sensor initializations:

```
// initialize sensors
SetSensor(LBump,SENSOR_TOUCH);
SetSensor(RBump,SENSOR_TOUCH);
SetSensor(See,SENSOR_LIGHT);
```

The SetSensor(sensor, configuration) function initializes sensors and sets how they read information. In other words, it's used to set the type and mode of a sensor you would like to use. You can set both the type and mode by using special constants. For the touch sensors, we use the constant SENSOR_TOUCH, which sets the most common type and mode for touch sensors. For the light sensor, we used the constant SENSOR_LIGHT.

Another new feature is *tasks* (although you saw the main task in the previous chapter). Tasks are declared with the task keyword and can be started using the start task_name; command. As discussed earlier, there are two distinct tasks (disregarding the main task) in this program: one for detecting the line and one for watching the touch sensors. They are started with these two commands (after the sensor initializations, calibration, and other little chores):

```
start LWatch;
start Crash;
```

Calling start on the light (LWatch) and touch (Crash) sensor tasks in the main task starts the "real" part of the program.

Let's take a closer look at the light task:

```
// this task watches for the line
task LWatch()
{
    SetPriority(0);

    while(true)
    {
        until(See<=threshold);

            acquire(ACQUIRE_USER_1)
            {
                Avoid();
            }
    }
}
```

This task is named LWatch() and can be executed with start LWatch(). We gave it the highest priority, with the SetPriority() command, because of the important role it plays. Accordingly, we assigned the touch sensor task the second highest priority. Once something happens that the task is interested in (and this applies to both tasks), it requests control of the ACQUIRE_USER_1 resource. In the light sensor task's case, it is interested in a reading from the light sensor that is darker than the predefined threshold:

```
until(See<=threshold);
```

Once all this has taken place, the task is in complete control until it lets go of that resource or another task with a higher priority (if there is one) requests control.

> **NOTE** *In access control, the highest priority is 0. The next highest is 1, then 2, and so on, up to 255. This is a bit counterintuitive, so when using access control, double-check your work to make sure you have your numbers right.*

The two sensor tasks are in infinite loops, so once you press the Run button on the RCX, XK1 will keep on running until you stop it by pressing the On/Off button or by pressing the Run button a second time.

This is the essence of an organized, working, NQC access control program. You have your functions that will be executed at various times to do little jobs, your tasks that watch for certain things happening, and—nicely blended in between—the access control part.

Now that you've seen how access control works, let's move on to event monitoring.

Programming XK1 with Event Monitoring

The previous program is great, but it's not the only way to program a robot that needs to monitor several things. So for variety's sake, let's experiment with event monitoring. First, we'll look at a complete event monitoring program, and then I'll do some explaining. The NQC syntax for event monitoring and access control are nearly identical, and a quick glance at the two programs shows their similarities. Speaking of similarities, this program makes XK1 act the same as it did using the previous program— and yet it is shorter and cleaner! Event monitoring is responsible for this, and you'll see how in Listing 4-2, which shows the XK1_Event_Monitoring.nqc program.

Listing 4-2. XK1_Event_Monitoring.nqc

```
// XK1_Event_Monitoring.nqc
// A sumo-bot program for Zip-Bam-Bot Version XK1

// motors
#define Left OUT_A
#define Right OUT_C
```

```
// sensors
#define LBump SENSOR_1
#define RBump SENSOR_3
#define See SENSOR_2

// constants
#define BACK_TIME 70
#define TURN 45
#define AMOUNT 3
#define LIMIT 35
#define LIGHT_BACK 20

// variables for calibration
int line,threshold;

task main()
{
   // initialize sensors
   SetSensor(LBump,SENSOR_TOUCH);
   SetSensor(RBump,SENSOR_TOUCH);
   SetSensor(See,SENSOR_LIGHT);

   // initializing events
   SetEvent(0,LBump,EVENT_TYPE_PRESSED);
   SetEvent(1,RBump,EVENT_TYPE_PRESSED);

   // calibrate light sensor
   Calibrate();

   // turn on both motors
   OnFwd(Left+Right);

   while(true)    // infinite loop
   {
      monitor(EVENT_MASK(0) + EVENT_MASK(1))
      {
         while(true)   // another infinite loop
         {
            until(See<=threshold);  // if we see the line avoid it
            Avoid();
         }
      }
      catch   // if the touch sensors are pressed, do this function
      {
         Win();
      }
   }
}

// this function sets the robot up for another crash
void Win()
```

```
{
    Rev(Left+Right);
    Wait(BACK_TIME);
    OnFwd(Left+Right);
}

// this function avoids the line
void Avoid()
{
    OnRev(Left+Right);
    Wait(LIGHT_BACK);
    Fwd(Left);
    Wait(TURN);
    OnFwd(Left+Right);
}

// this is the calibrating function
void Calibrate()
{
    until(RBump==1);
    line=See;
    threshold=line+AMOUNT;
    until(RBump==0);
    PlaySound(SOUND_CLICK);
    until(RBump==1);
    until(RBump==0);
    PlaySound(SOUND_CLICK);
    Wait(LIMIT);
}
```

In event monitoring, different events you would like to use must be initialized. This time, we initialized events 0 and 1 (the numbers for event monitoring are irrelevant), gave them SENSOR_1 and SENSOR_3 as their sensors, and specified EVENT_TYPE_PRESSED as the event type they are interested in. The event type is self-explanatory. Once the sensor is pressed, the code under catch is activated. In this case, the individual sensor's reading is irrelevant (we are not concerned with whether the hit came from the left or right touch sensor), so the program monitors both touch sensor events and activates the catch code when either is pressed.

> **NOTE** *There are 11 different types of events and a variety of resources you can use for event monitoring (timers, message buffer, and so on). For more information about programming event monitoring, see the* NQC *Programmer's Guide,* which comes with BricxCC. For additional examples of event monitoring, see the book Extreme MINDSTORMS: An Advanced Guide to LEGO MINDSTORMS, *by Dave Baum et al (Apress, 2000).*

Take a look again at one of the first lines of real code under the main task:

```
monitor(EVENT_MASK(0) + EVENT_MASK(1))
```

This tells the program to monitor those events (events 0 and 1). The code within the braces of monitor is what's normally running in the program. Note that putting the line-detecting code in here does have some disadvantages. If a touch sensor is pressed, the touch sensors are given more weight than the light sensor. A different way would have been to make a light sensor event and have the touch sensor code within the braces of the monitor keyword. For XK1's purposes however, the approach taken here will suffice.

Testing XK1

Now that you have a working program in a working sumo-bot, how do you test it? Where should you test it? Against what sumo-bot should you stage it? Your first inclinations might be to test XK1 on the RIS Test Pad, and to stage it against another sumo-bot. But these solutions might present problems.

First, XK1 can, in some instances, get snagged on the RIS Test Pad. To avoid this, it would be in your best interest to make a robotic sumo arena (see Chapter 11). Not only does having your own arena get rid of the snagging problem, but it also gives you the advantage of being able to thoroughly test your sumo-bots. If you haven't built an arena yet but want to try XK1 out *now*, feel free to temporarily substitute the RIS Test Pad—but do make an arena for yourself in the near future.

Regarding what to stage XK1 (and any of your other sumo-bots) against, the main problem is that not everyone has enough parts (mainly a second RCX) to make two sumo-bots. Instead of constructing another sumo-bot, you can place different objects with different weights in your arena (similar to how you tested the chassis in the previous chapter) for your test.

> **TIP** *If you do have the extra materials to build a second sumo-bot, or have another working sumo-bot on hand, do use this to your advantage for testing purposes. However, you should not only use this approach; a balanced testing method is important. Part of balanced testing is to use stationary objects to test your sumo-bots. Create different situations with stationary objects to test your sumo-bot's response—you might be surprised at what you can find out by using this method!*

After you've set up your testing area, follow these steps:

1. Upload the programs to the RCX as outlined in Chapter 3. Put XK1_Access_Control.nqc into program slot 1 and XK1_Event_Monitoring.nqc into program slot 2.

2. Place XK1's light sensor directly on the line encircling the arena.

3. Select the desired program, activate it by pressing the Run button on the RCX, and, with the light sensor still over the line, press and then release the right bumper. XK1 should perform the calibration and confirm the action by emitting a little click.

4. With the calibration done, pick up XK1 and place it in the middle of your arena.

5. Press and release the right bumper again, and after a small wait and another little click, XK1 should shoot forward.

> **NOTE** *Both programs presented in this chapter will cause essentially the same set of actions in XK1, but why not try out both? The best way to do this is, after using one program for a while, stop it and run the other program. The calibration for both of the programs is the same, so there is no difference in setting them up.*

On contact with an object, XK1 should back up and go forward again. If it does not, the touch sensor is not reading a hit. Check to see if the wires are connected firmly enough. When it sees the line, XK1 should back up just a bit and make a turn amounting to about 180 degrees. For most purposes, this turn suffices; however, feel free to change the timing for this and any of XK1's actions. Also, remember that the battery power level in the RCX affects the performance of XK1.

See how much weight XK1 can shove around. Indeed, in some robotic sumo events, participants take a test in which their sumo-bots shove a wooden block out of the arena. The entry sometimes must pass this test before it is admitted! With this in mind, set up a variety of objects on your arena and watch XK1 push them out, one by one.

Besides letting XK1 beat up stationary objects, you should move objects around on your arena with your hands to create specific situations. While XK1 is happily running around, pick up an object—whether a large LEGO block, small book, or a block of wood—and position it in front of XK1. Wait until XK1 hits the object, and watch as it repeatedly rams that object (whether the object is pushed backwards or not is up to you!). Now suddenly remove the object—what does XK1 do? It should run straight ahead but stop on the line. This is one of the nice features of these types of programs: XK1 is as ready to ram something as it is to stop at the line. Create other interesting situations like this one and see what happens.

Considering the Pros and Cons of XK1's Design

XK1 may have strengths, but it also has weaknesses. As I said in Chapter 2, there is no perfect sumo-bot. However, part of the challenge of making a sumo-bot is to find those weaknesses and see if it's possible to fix them. But let's begin by taking a look at the good side: the pros.

The Pros

Here are the advantages of XK1's design:

- XK1 easily positions itself in the direction of the opponent with its two large claws.

- XK1's slope can neutralize the effects of back-ramming sumo-bots.

- XK1's light sensor is highly protected.

- XK1's drivetrain system provides a maximum in speed and minimum in friction.

- XK1 can easily outmaneuver larger and slower sumo-bots.

The Cons

The following are some disadvantages of XK1's design:

- XK1 can accidentally *back over* the line encircling the arena.

- There are a few rare instances where XK1's claws can get stuck on the other sumo-bot or the feelers will not register a reading.

- XK1's wheels are unprotected from a direct hit.

- XK1's front end runs along the ground (on the black skid), which creates some friction.

Don't be discouraged by the cons list; every sumo-bot out there has its own list of pros *and* cons.

The truth is XK1 *could* back over the line; this problem is caused by its attacking function. For instance, if XK1 were right next to the line, hit the other sumo-bot, and backed up, it would back over the line. Since the task for detecting the line tells it to back up, and since XK1 was already backing up when it detected the line, it will gladly oblige and continue on its way. You could fix this problem by adding another light sensor, but that would require more parts than are available within a single RIS.

XK1's wheels are unprotected, but because they are added directly to the motor, they are in a largely inaccessible geometry (inaccessible to other pieces, that is). You could just build bricks in front of the wheels, but this would add to the overall weight of the robot, which is not desirable. In reality, XK1's unprotected wheels are not a big problem and not worth the extra bricks to make them protected.

How would you solve the friction problem? You could change the mobility design and add a swivel wheel. However, this can't really be done to XK1 without changing it into another sumo-bot.

To solve some problems, you simply need to build a different type of robot—which then, of course, introduces other problems! So, in the end, you just need to deal with your problems the best you can and make your sumo-bot in the best possible way. You can't have everything absolutely perfect; you'll need to make some compromises.

Conclusion

Congratulations! You have just built and programmed a real LEGO MINDSTORMS sumo-bot! By now, you should see the essence of the small-and-fast strategy. It's all about speed, momentum, and a few smooth getaways. Sometimes, the need to just zip away (*Zip*-Bam-Bot?) comes up, and any member of the small-and-fast strategy should be able to accomplish that task just fine.

In the next chapter, you'll meet another sumo-bot: XK2. Your first foray into the small-and-fast strategy with XK1 was—in all probability—interesting and instructive, but with XK2, you'll take the small-and-fast strategy a bit further. You'll learn new things, see a new substrategy, and encounter some interesting building methodology. With all that you're learning, you're well on your way to becoming a sumo-bot expert!

CHAPTER 5

Zip-Bam-Bot
Version XK2

EVEN IF **XK2** had feelings, it wouldn't mind being called flat-face; in fact, that would be a compliment! Take a look at Figure 5-1, which shows the sumo-bot we're going to build in this chapter, to see what I mean.

Figure 5-1. Completed Zip-Bam-Bot Version XK2

Still retaining the trademark speed of the Zip-Bam-Bot design, XK2 uses this to assist a super-smooth, large slope covering its whole front—indeed, the slope is its "head!" However, this large slope, predominately made out of liftarms, is not the most important one in the robot. The more vital slope is smaller, but more lethal, and is positioned on the very front. This slope complements the bigger slope; it does the initial "running underneath," while the larger one furthers the process. Together, their sole purpose is to allow XK2 to run underneath opposing sumo-bots in an attempt to push back or actually flip the opponent—a timeless trick in the robotic sumo world.

> **NOTE** *What I refer to as a slope can also be called by several other names, including inclined plane, wedge, and more. However, to stay consistent, I have chosen one name—slope—and will be referring to it as such throughout the book.*

Among its other features, XK2 possesses a special subassembly that prevents other robots from flipping *it*. This subassembly is located in the back of the sumo-bot and comes in the form of specially positioned tires.

XK2's substrategy is based on the second approach to the repeated ramming method discussed in the previous chapter: using a mechanism or subassembly to demobilize the opponent on contact. For XK2, the slope is the subassembly responsible for demobilizing the opponent. This is all very incredible, but the structural changes aren't the only changes. There are new programming techniques to try out as well!

Constructing Subassemblies for XK2

Like the previous version of Zip-Bam-Bot, XK2 can be built with a single RIS. The bill of materials is shown in Figure 5-2.

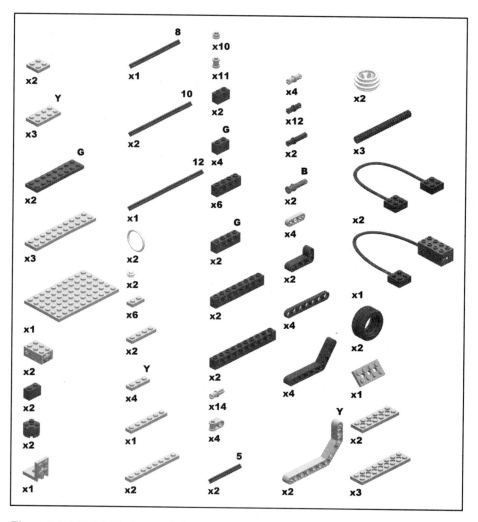

Figure 5-2. XK2's bill of materials

You'll build the following subassemblies:

- Head subassembly

- Back skid subassembly

- Light sensor subassembly

Since there are only three subassemblies for XK2, you might think this sumo-bot is smaller than XK1. However, this isn't true; their weight and size are quite similar. You have fewer subassemblies because XK2's head subassembly is somewhat large (for a small robot). Also, because some modularity must often be sacrificed in smaller robots, the touch-sensing mechanism and other structures, parts, and modifications are built and added in the "Putting XK2 Together" section, after you construct the subassemblies. In reality, XK2 has almost the same number of subassemblies that XK1 does; they're just "hidden" in the final assembly.

Let's begin with the largest subassembly: the head subassembly.

Head Subassembly

Figure 5-3 shows the head subassembly. This assembly possesses the smaller slope, which is made out of plates and is positioned on the very front, and also the much larger liftarm slope. Besides acting as a slope, the head also gives XK2 its characteristic look—whatever that might be!

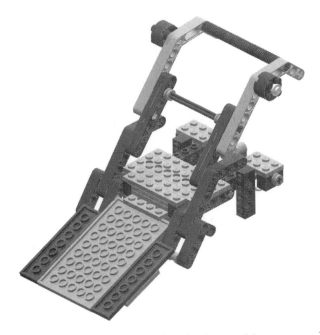

Figure 5-3. The completed head subassembly

NOTE *Using plates is a common way to run under other sumo-bots, and in the non-LEGO robotic sumo world, using material similar to LEGO plates for slopes is common as well.*

The head subassembly is not rigidly attached to the chassis, but instead pivots on two points. This flexibility allows the entire head to move on impact, acting as a sort of bumper (which it is). After XK2 has been completely assembled, you'll be able to observe much more clearly how the bumper system works. But let's quickly go over the bumper system's operation.

Once the head has moved backwards (by getting hit), two special pieces called *perpendicular axle joiners*, or *crossblocks*, activate touch sensors, which are facing completely upside down, by running across their yellow "clickers." (You'll build and attach the touch sensors later in the chapter.) When the bumper—the head—is no longer being pressed inwards, two rubber bands will draw it back out.

In step 1, locate two 1x10 beams, two axle pins, four friction pins, and then position them as shown. As you might imagine, these parts lay the framework for the assembly.

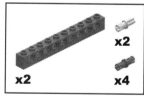

 Head Subassembly Step 1: *Snap four friction and two axle pins into 1x10 beams.*

Next in line—and shown in step 2—is the addition of two black liftarms, which are snapped onto the pins closest to the front of the beams, more pins, a 2x6 TECHNIC plate, and two 1x2 black bricks.

NOTE *The RIS contains four 2x6 TECHNIC plates. All four of these are currently on the Zip-Bam-Bot chassis, but step 2 adds another one. However, you don't need the 2x6 TECHNIC plates positioned on the front of the chassis for XK2, so you can take one of them off to use for this subassembly (the front of the chassis will be reconstructed a little later).*

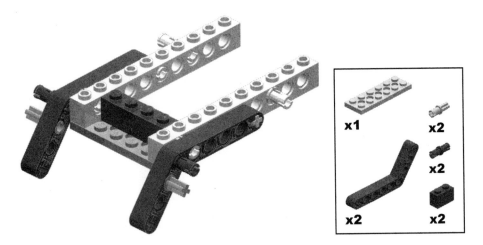

 Head Subassembly Step 2: *Add four pins, two liftarms, and a 2x6 plate with two 1x2 bricks.*

In step 3, you add a few plates, which connect the two sides together, and two 1x4 beams onto the back friction pins. These beams will serve as the connection point later on, when you do the final assembly (in the "Putting XK2 Together" section).

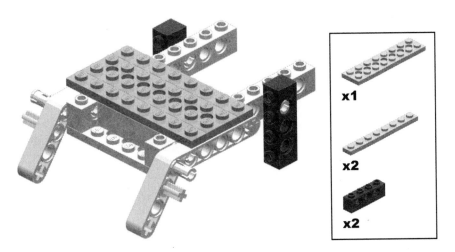

 Head Subassembly Step 3: *Attach two 1x8 plates, one 2x8 plate, and two 1x4 beams.*

Now for an interesting part! In this assembly, there are two rubber bands; both of them are the small, white ones included in the RIS, and both of them go in the back. You'll add these (and other pieces) in a creative way in steps 4 through 6.

First, slide #5 axles into the beams as shown in step 4. Then position the various bushings and crossblocks on those axles.

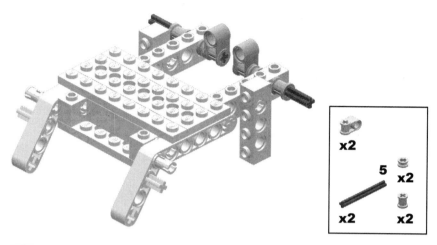

 Head Subassembly Step 4: *Slide #5 axles through beams, and bushings and crossblocks onto the axles.*

Once this is finished, put a white rubber band on the end of each axle. After adding the white rubber bands, place 1x2 green bricks with an axle hole and half-bushings on the last remaining spaces of the axles, thus blocking the rubber band's only exit. You are *not* connecting the rubber bands to anything in particular right now; they are for later use.

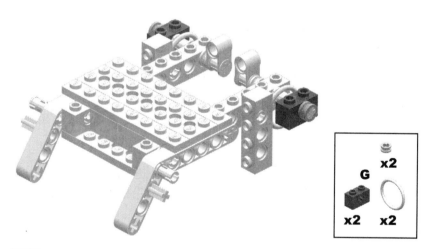

 Head Subassembly Step 5: *Add 1x2 axle bricks, half-bushings, and two rubber bands.*

Step 6 has two parts. First, place 1x3 yellow plates going from the green bricks to the beams. These plates "lock" the green bricks in place and prevent them from swinging around. Second, you'll start working on the very front—the protruding slope part. There is not too much to this, except the pieces will be at an odd slant; well, an odd slant for most cases, but not for a sumo-bot's slope! This slant is intentional and a good thing.

Begin by pushing a #12 axle through the black liftarms. While you're going along, slide bushings and 1x4 beams onto the axle. The slope, which is made out of plates, will connect directly into these beams.

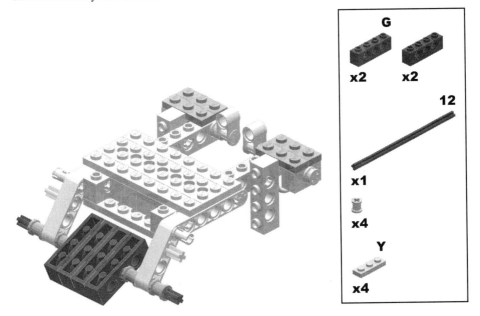

 Head Subassembly Step 6: *Add four 1x3 yellow plates and begin construction on the slope.*

NOTE *There are four 1x3 yellow plates used in this assembly, and the RIS has only two of them. If you do not have extra 1x3 plates, use 1x4 plates. They will project out a stud's space on the sides, but that's okay.*

After this, snap a 6x10 plate onto the inverted 1x4 beams; this is the first piece of the slope. Also connect some 2x10 plates to the 6x10 plate—these will provide an attachment point for additional plates for the slope.

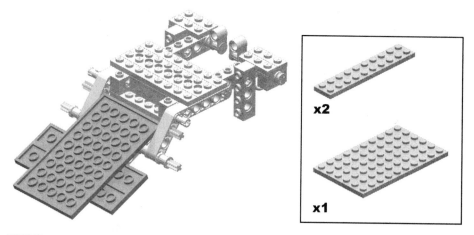

 Head Subassembly Step 7: *Snap a 6x10 plate with two 2x10 plates onto 1x4 beams.*

Using more plates, widen the slope. Also position several plates directly above the slope, as shown in step 8. The slightly odd array of plates positioned above the slope has an important purpose: these plates, along with the 2x6 TECHNIC plate beneath them, reduce the amount of free room for the slope to a negligible amount. That means you now have a fully operable slope!

> **TIP** *Inverted (upside-down) plates provide a smooth surface, and, when combined with other plates, can form very large slopes. In other words, they're efficient and have the potential to cover large areas with relatively few pieces.*

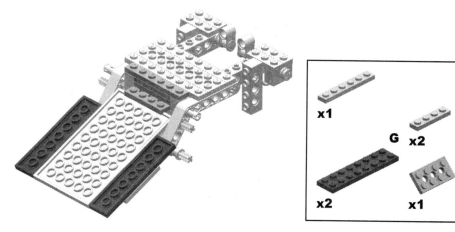

 Head Subassembly Step 8: *Add two 2x8 plates, one 2x4 plate, one 1x6 plate, and two 1x4 plates.*

With the slope built, the final stage of construction, for the "face," commences. Steps 9 and 10 build up the face with liftarms, axles, pins of this and that type, and well... I think you probably get the idea.

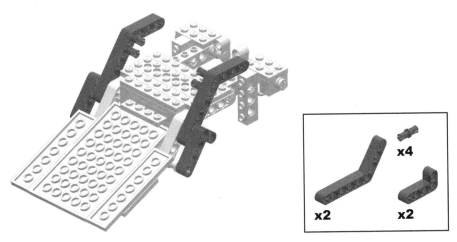

 Head Subassembly Step 9: *Add four liftarms and four friction pins.*

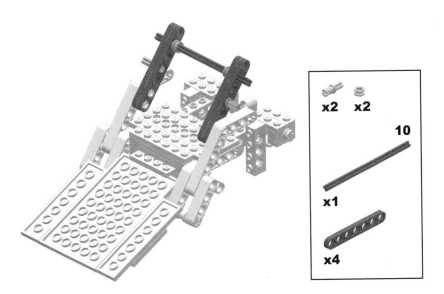

 Head Subassembly Step 10: *Build up liftarm slope with four 1x7 half-liftarms and add two axle pins, a #10 axle and two half-bushings.*

In step 11, you begin working with the final section of the head. This step uses a large, yellow liftarm (the liftarm's curve at the end is perfect for the head-like appearance!) and two pins. One pin is the connection point for an eye (the outer pin), and the other pin is for *ribbed hosing* (the inner pin).

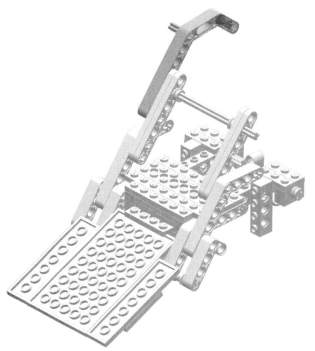

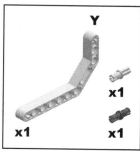

 Head Subassembly Step 11: *Add large, yellow liftarm, friction pin, and axle pin.*

Step 12 adds the ribbed hosing, which is the green, medium-sized type included in the RIS. When completed, the head appears as if the ribbed hosing fits perfectly, but this is actually not true. The single piece of green, ribbed hosing you add in step 12 is just a little bit wider than the head, and it pushes the yellow liftarms out to the side a little. This is okay—it will not harm or hinder XK2.

In step 13, add a yellow liftarm and a pin to the left side of the face, just as you did for the right side, and add the eyes as well—these give the sumo-bot that characteristic appearance!

> **TIP** *When adding the eyes, put the 1x1 white round plates onto the "black eye piece" first, and then attach the whole eye onto the assembly. If you do it the other way around, it will be very difficult to add the white plates.*

You're now finished with the head subassembly. It should look like Figure 5-3, shown at the beginning of this section.

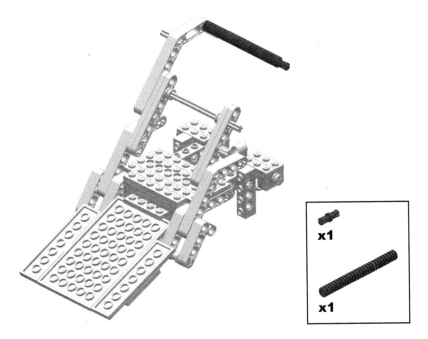

 Head Subassembly Step 12: *Push green, ribbed hosing with friction pin into friction pin.*

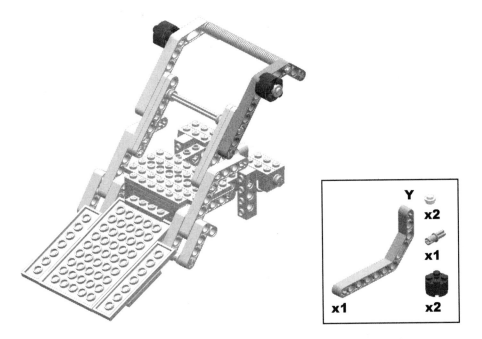

 Head Subassembly Step 13: *Add yellow liftarm and axle pin and push 2x2 round bricks with 1x1 round plates into axle pins.*

Back Skid Subassembly

The back skid subassembly, shown in Figure 5-4, is responsible for counteracting any slope that is trying to run itself under XK2 in the front. If the enemy's slope has lifted XK2's nose into the air and then tries to push XK2 forward, the rubber wheels hit the ground and generate friction, making it harder (impossible?) for the opposition to push XK2 backwards.

Figure 5-4. The back skid subassembly

Because this assembly is prone to high amounts of pressure, it needs to be firmly attached to the chassis; the long friction pins are responsible for this. However, almost more important is that the section of the chassis to which this assembly is attached should not be able to break off. With a little modification of the chassis, this is easily accomplished. You'll use bracing—an extremely powerful strengthening technique, as you saw in Chapter 3—to secure the attachment. As you'll see later, two *1x3 half-liftarms* play an important role in this particular bracing setup.

The construction is very easy and consists of only two steps. Step 1 slides bushings, half-bushings, and two crossblocks on a #8 axle.

Step 2 adds two wheels and the long friction pins. This particular type of wheel is probably one of the lesser-known pieces of the RIS, especially since there are only two of them, but they can certainly be helpful. What are these wheels called? One name, although in no way official, is *30.4 x 14 tire*, which corresponds to the dimensions of the tire.

 Back Skid Subassembly Step 1: *Slide crossblocks, bushings, and half-bushings onto #8 axle.*

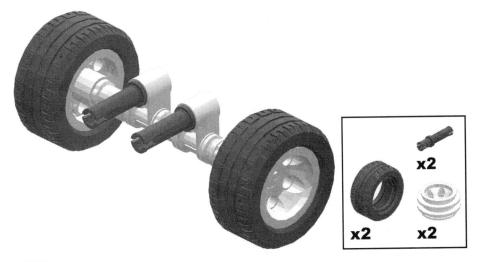

 Back Skid Subassembly Step 2: *Add two long friction pins and two wheels.*

TIP *The specific type of wheel chosen for this subassembly works well, but it is not the only choice, and, for a stopper, this is not the only way to orient the wheels. Try using different wheels and see how and if they work, and come up with new ways to position the wheels. Also be sure to implement these tricks in your own sumo-bots!*

The back skid subassembly is now complete, and it should look like the one shown in Figure 5-4, at the beginning of this section.

Light Sensor Subassembly

The light sensor subassembly, shown in Figure 5-5, consists of just a few pieces and takes just two steps to assemble, like the previous subassembly. It's made out of several plates, including an angle plate for the light sensor, and the light sensor itself.

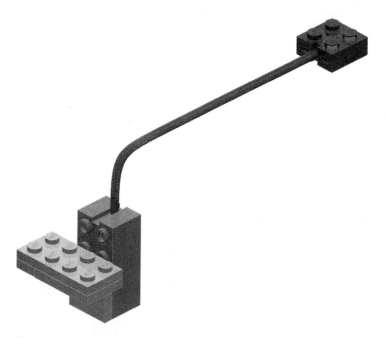

Figure 5-5. The completed light sensor subassembly

In step 1, three plates, including 1x2 plates and an angle plate, are positioned side by side—and in midair! However, a 2x4 yellow plate brings them all together.

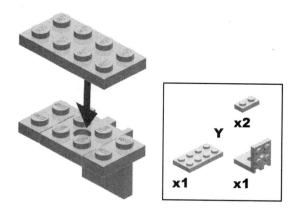

 Light Sensor Subassembly Step 1: *Lay down two 1x2 plates and an angle plate then bring them together with a 2x4 yellow plate.*

Add the light sensor to the angle plate in step 2, and then you are ready to move on to the final assembly!

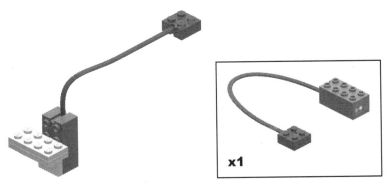

 Light Sensor Subassembly Step 2: *Connect a light sensor to angle plate.*

Putting XK2 Together

Before you begin adding subassemblies to XK2, you need to modify the chassis you built in Chapter 3, as was necessary for XK1 in Chapter 4.

At the very front, take away the 2x6 TECHNIC plates and expand the area to an eight studs' width. To do this, replace the bottom plate with a 2x8 TECHNIC plate and put a 2x4 brick (you can use the same one that was there before) and two 1x2 beams onto the new plate, as shown in step 1. Don't forget the skid plate! Simply remove it from the previously used 2x6 TECHNIC plate and place it onto the bottom 2x8 TECHNIC plate. Last, you should remove the top 2x6 TECHNIC plate on the very back end of Zip-Bam-Bot and the 2x8 TECHNIC plate in front of the RCX.

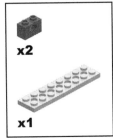

 XK2 Final Assembly Step 1: *Modify front end of chassis to eight studs' width, and remove top 2x6 plate on back end of chassis and 2x8 plate in front of RCX.*

In step 2, place a 2x8 TECHNIC plate on top of the little space, and put two axle pins with half-bushings into the 1x2 beams you just added.

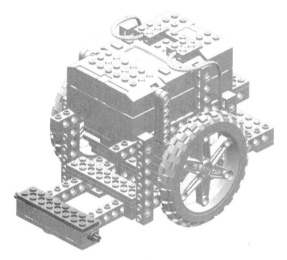

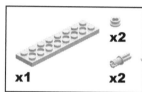

 XK2 Final Assembly Step 2: *Add 2x8 plate, two half-bushings, and two axle pins.*

Add the **light sensor subassembly** as shown in step 3. You're not connecting the electrical wire to the RCX right now; you'll do that in the next step.

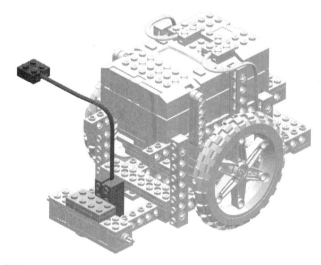

 XK2 Final Assembly Step 3: *Attach the light sensor subassembly to chassis.*

Add the **head subassembly** in step 4 by pushing two blue stop bushes into the head's 1x4 beams and into the chassis. *Now* connect the light sensor's wire, attaching it to **sensor input port 2** on the RCX.

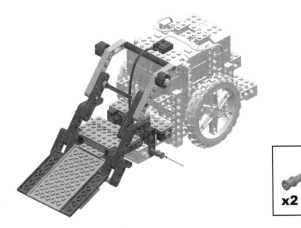

 XK2 Final Assembly Step 4: *Attach head subassembly to chassis and light sensor's wire to RCX.*

Do you remember the small, white rubber bands you added earlier to the head subassembly? Take the rubber bands *on both sides* and stretch them across and onto the half-bushings at the front of the chassis, as illustrated in step 5 (the rubber band on the right side is not visible). Something interesting to note is how the light sensor prevents the head from going too far out. The crossblocks on the head subassembly are pressing on the light sensor, which acts as a sort of stopper. Even though there is a noticeable amount of pressure being exerted on the light sensor subassembly, the special design and setup keeps it from breaking.

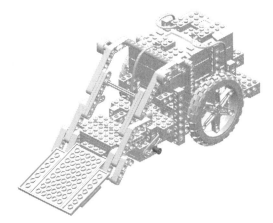

 XK2 Final Assembly Step 5: *Stretch rubber bands onto half-bushings at front of chassis.*

In steps 6 through 8, you'll build the touch sensors into the chassis. Take a #10 axle and push it through the two protruding beams in the front, sliding two touch sensors on them and two bushings on the axle as it goes from one beam to the other. After this, attach electrical wires to the touch sensors and then onto the RCX. Connect the electrical wires as specified in the following:

- The **right touch sensor** connects to **sensor input port 3.**

- The **left touch sensor** connects to **sensor input port 1.**

Once the touch sensors are in place, position 1x2 green axle bricks onto the ends of the #10 axle. Add some plates as directed, and the touch sensor system is complete.

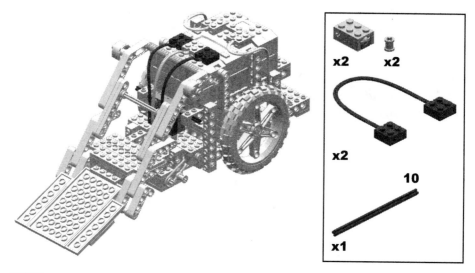

 XK2 Final Assembly Step 6: *Add a #10 axle, two bushings, two touch sensors and their electrical wires to front of chassis.*

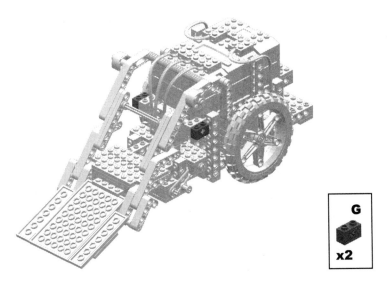

 XK2 Final Assembly Step 7: *Add 1x2 green bricks with an axle hole onto end of #10 axle.*

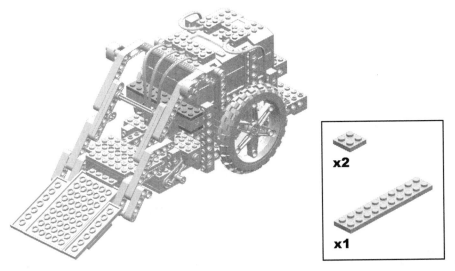

 XK2 Final Assembly Step 8: *Attach a 2x10 plate and two 2x2 plates.*

Turn the model around to the back. You are now going to construct the section that will hold the back skid subassembly, and then add the back skid subassembly itself. In steps 9 and 10, you add plates and beams to the back end of XK2. As you can see, you are adding "bulk" to the back of the chassis.

 XK2 Final Assembly Step 9: *Connect two 1x4 beams and four 1x2 plates to back of chassis.*

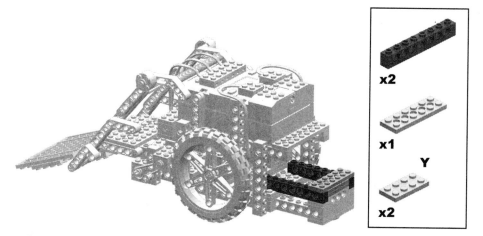

 XK2 Final Assembly Step 10: *Add two 1x8 beams, two 2x4 yellow plates and a 2x6 plate.*

In step 11, add the various pins as shown.

 XK2 Final Assembly Step 11: *Snap four axle pins and four regular pins into back end of chassis.*

In step 12, add the green, ribbed hoses and four 1x3 half-liftarms to the back of the chassis, as directed.

Contrary to how it might look, the hosing is not merely for decoration. Instead, the hoses prevent opposing sumo-bots from running into the general area that they surround. If a sumo-bot runs into these, it will just push XK2 around and not get caught on that section of the chassis. The position the hoses are in keeps them extremely rigid; they are almost impossible to bend.

What you just did with the 1x3 half-liftarms is bracing; this will prevent any of the recently added parts from breaking off. And that is pretty important, considering the possible amounts of force that can be exerted on this section of XK2!

 XK2 Final Assembly Step 12: *Attach two pieces of green, ribbed hosing and brace back end of chassis with four 1x3 half-liftarms.*

In step 13, pull out the **back skid subassembly** and push its long friction pins into the chassis about one stud's space.

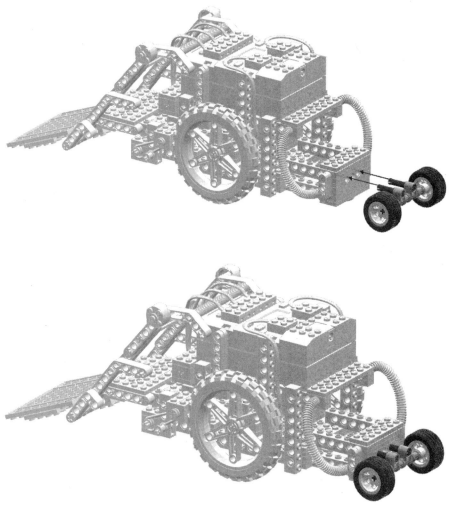

![hammer icon] *XK2 Final Assembly Step 13: Attach back skid subassembly to chassis.*

You are finished! Your sumo-bot should look like the one shown in Figure 5-1, at the beginning of the chapter. It's now ready for some action and programming.

> **NOTE** *You might consider removing the two 2x8 TECHNIC plates positioned on the chassis directly behind XK2's head. After several hard hits, these plates can become loosened and eventually knocked out of place. Removing these two plates does not weaken XK2 in any way.*

Formulating a Solid Programming Solution for XK2

As I stated at the beginning of the chapter, XK2 takes the second approach of the repeated ramming method. So what does this mean in the way of tasks for its program? Well, we know for sure that XK2 will possess a line-detecting task and a touch-sensing task. Having these behaviors and tasks is essential, but it would be nice if we could add something else to go along with the program. So, let's introduce a new task to the program: a "maneuvering task."

The maneuvering task will do what we left out in XK1's programming: random turns. We didn't use this for XK1 because any of the Zip-Bam-Bots can cover an arena, regardless of size, in just a few seconds. However, it's still a good idea to add a maneuvering task. If XK2 gets rammed in the front, doesn't detect it, and somehow ends up with its nose in the air, both sumo-bots might become stuck, and neither would make any progress. This would happen because XK2's wheels would be trying to go forward and its back skid subassembly would be generating friction. This stalemate might burn out XK2's motors! With this new task, after a few seconds of inactivity, the program will tell XK2 to change its position and direction. A task like this one could be a lifesaver.

Now consider another scenario: What would happen if XK2 were running up against a big sumo-bot—big enough that even a nicely placed hit hardly budges it. Instead of concentrating on attacking and ramming, XK2 could do the opposite; that is, rather than going *towards* the enemy sumo-bot, XK2 could go *away* from it. However, XK2 would go away only after it has given the opposition a nice hit (it has to hit something before it knows it's time to run away!). To implement this behavior, which I like to call *ram-and-run*, we'll create a second version of XK2's program.

> **NOTE** *In reality, no one would stage a small sumo-bot like this one against a monstrously large sumo-bot—at least not with the goal of winning in mind. However, the second program demonstrating the ram-and-run approach is still a good example, because it can be used against other small-and-fast sumo-bots (and sumo-bots using other strategies as well). So, remember that even though the second program in this chapter portrays small versus large, it doesn't necessarily mean that this approach is used only against large sumo-bots.*

Take a look at the different tasks or behaviors we now have:

Line-detecting task: Just as in Chapter 4, this task is responsible for watching for the line. Most everything about this task remains the same as the previous line-detecting task.

Touch-sensing task: This, too, is nearly identical to the touch-sensing task described in Chapter 4. Once it registers a hit, it calls another function to execute the proper maneuver. We'll also create another version of this function for the second program, whose primary purpose is to combat bigger robots.

Maneuvering task: This task, after a specified amount of time, makes XK2 execute a turn for a random amount of time. You saw this when you did some programming to test Zip-Bam-Bot's chassis in Chapter 3. The radius of the turn amount will not be huge, since we don't want XK2 to continually run into the line.

> **NOTE** *There are other approaches to the maneuvering task, as you'll see in later chapters.*

Now that we have our tasks outlined, we're ready to create the programs.

Programming XK2 with the Solution

To program XK2, we'll use the access control feature of NQC and the same basic structure that we used for XK1 in Chapter 4. And, as noted in the previous section, we'll also create a second version of the program with ram-and-run behavior.

Adding the Maneuvering Task

Do you remember how the Running() function we created back in Chapter 3 worked? That function was introduced in the ZBB4.nqc program (Listing 3-4). It used a timer to tell when to execute a turn. Let's look at it again:

```
void Running()
{
    until(Timer(0)>=LIMIT);
    Rev(Left);
    Wait(TURN+Random(40));
    Fwd(Left);
    ClearTimer(0);
}
```

In Chapter 3, I noted that this function would probably need some modification before it could be integrated within a complete sumo-bot program. Right now we're going to mentally modify the name of this function to Change() since it changes XK2's direction, but before we go any further, we need to work on the task that will use the function—the maneuvering task. The new maneuvering task will be given lowest priority (2), since line-detecting and sumo-detecting (the touch sensor's task) are more important. The finished task looks like this:

```
// this task introduces some random turns
task Maneuver()
{
    // third highest priority
    SetPriority(2);

    // infinite loop
    while(true)
    {
    // until timer is >= 2.5 seconds which is determined by LIMIT
        until(Timer(0)>=LIMIT);

        acquire(ACQUIRE_USER_1)
```

```
        {
            Change();    // execute our new function
        }
    }
}
```

Now we can turn our attention to the modification of the Running() function. Besides changing its name to Change(), there is one other modification we need to make. This modification is to delete the line of code which refers to the timer, as the maneuvering task holds that code. So the completed function, now the Change() function, looks like this:

```
// this function changes the direction of the robot
void Change()
{
    Rev(Left);
    Wait(TURN+Random(40));
    Fwd(Left);
    ClearTimer(0);
}
```

We will use this code, along with much of the code from the previous program (XK1_Access_Control.nqc) to make the new program for XK2. The entire program, with line-detecting and touch-sensing support, the maneuvering task, and other vital functions and code, is shown in Listing 5-1.

Listing 5-1. XK2_Access_Control.nqc

```
// XK2_Access_Control.nqc
// A sumo-bot program for Zip-Bam-Bot Version XK2

// motors
#define Left OUT_A
#define Right OUT_C

// sensors
#define LBump SENSOR_1
#define RBump SENSOR_3
#define See SENSOR_2

// constants
#define BACK_TIME 50
#define TURN 40
#define AMOUNT 3
#define LIMIT 25
#define LIGHT_BACK 40

// variables for calibration
int line=0,threshold=0;
```

```
task main()
{
   // initialize sensors
   SetSensor(LBump,SENSOR_TOUCH);
   SetSensor(RBump,SENSOR_TOUCH);
   SetSensor(See,SENSOR_LIGHT);

   // calibrate light sensor
   Calibrate();

   // start motors
   OnFwd(Left+Right);

   // let's clear the timer we are going to use
   ClearTimer(0);

   // start tasks
   start LWatch;
   start Crash;
   start Maneuver;
}

// this task watches for the line
task LWatch()
{
   // highest priority
   SetPriority(0);

   // infinite loop
   while(true)
   {
      until(See<=threshold);    // until we see the line

         acquire(ACQUIRE_USER_1)
         {
           Avoid();       // avoid the line
         }
   }
}

// this task watches the touch sensors
task Crash()
{
   // second highest priority
   SetPriority(1);

   // infinite loop
   while(true)
   {
      // until left or right touch sensors are pressed
      until(LBump|RBump==1);
```

```
      acquire(ACQUIRE_USER_1)
      {
         Win();    // take control and crash repeatedly
      }
   }
}


// this task introduces some random turns
task Maneuver()
{
   // third highest priority
   SetPriority(2);

   // infinite loop
   while(true)
   {
      // until timer is >= 2.5 seconds which is determined by LIMIT
      until(Timer(0)>=LIMIT);

         acquire(ACQUIRE_USER_1)
         {
            Change();   // execute our new function
         }
   }
}


// this function sets the robot up for another crash
void Win()
{
   Rev(Left+Right);
   Wait(BACK_TIME);
   OnFwd(Left+Right);
   ClearTimer(0);
}


// this function avoids the line
void Avoid()
{
   OnRev(Left+Right);
   Wait(LIGHT_BACK);
   Fwd(Left);
   Wait(TURN);
   OnFwd(Left+Right);
   ClearTimer(0);
}


// this function changes the direction of the robot
void Change()
{
   Rev(Left);
   Wait(TURN+Random(40));
```

```
        Fwd(Left);
        ClearTimer(0);
    }

    // this is the calibrating function
    void Calibrate()
    {
        until(RBump==1);
        line=See;
        threshold=line+AMOUNT;
        until(RBump==0);
        PlaySound(SOUND_CLICK);
        until(RBump==1);
        until(RBump==0);
        PlaySound(SOUND_CLICK);
        Wait(TURN);
    }
```

Wow! That's a lot of code for a little bot! But it gets the job done, and that's what is important.

This program makes XK2 act much like XK1, but this is good since the repeated ramming method is very effective (especially when the sumo-bot has a slope on the front). However, the repeated ramming method is not effective when staged against *every* sumo-bot. Let's look into the particulars of a different approach: the ram-and-run approach.

Creating a Program for the Ram-and-Run Approach

Whether you call it ram-and-run or hit-and-run, this approach resembles a sort of guerrilla warfare. Once the touch sensor has registered a hit, the program backs up the sumo-bot, and then turns it around. The effectiveness of this approach (in terms of *winning* the round) is debatable, but it sure beats getting beat!

To start off, let's modify our attacking function. Remember that once the touch sensors have registered a hit, XK2 needs to run in the *opposite* direction. With the addition of a slight amount of waiting time to allow the momentum of XK2 to do its work, the new Win() function looks like this:

```
// constants
#define BACK_TIME 50
#define TURN 40

// this function avoids the other sumo-bot
void Win()
{
    Wait(20);
    Rev(Left+Right);
    Wait(BACK_TIME);
    Fwd(Right);    // this turns XK2 in the other direction
    Wait(TURN);
    OnFwd(Left+Right);
    ClearTimer(0);
}
```

With this function, XK2 will not continually ram, but instead will ram and run. Now how about that line-avoiding function? Modifying it, too, would not be such a bad idea. Instead of turning right, let's turn left, just to do something different. With this change, here's the new line-avoiding function:

```
// constants
#define LIGHT_BACK 40
#define TURN 40

// this function avoids the line
void Avoid()
{
   OnRev(Left+Right);
   Wait(LIGHT_BACK);
   Fwd(Right);
   Wait(TURN);
   OnFwd(Left+Right);
   ClearTimer(0);
}
```

That's interesting, but for good measure, let's also modify the maneuvering function. A little change of the motor direction, a little change of the random timing, and we have ourselves a new version of the Change() function:

```
// constant
#define TURN 40

void Change()
{
   Rev(Right);
   Wait(TURN+Random(30));
   Fwd(Right);
   ClearTimer(0);
}
```

Now that we have made these changes, the new functions are combined into the program XK2_Access_Control_Two.nqc, which gives us a completed ram-and-run NQC program. Listing 5-2 shows the new program.

Listing 5-2. XK2_Access_Control_Two.nqc

```
// XK2_Access_Control_Two.nqc
// A sumo-bot program for Zip-Bam-Bot Version XK2

// motors
#define Left OUT_A
#define Right OUT_C
```

```
// sensors
#define LBump SENSOR_1
#define RBump SENSOR_3
#define See SENSOR_2

// constants
#define BACK_TIME 50
#define TURN 40
#define AMOUNT 3
#define LIMIT 25
#define LIGHT_BACK 40

// variables for calibration
int line=0,threshold=0;

task main()
{
   // initialize sensors
   SetSensor(LBump,SENSOR_TOUCH);
   SetSensor(RBump,SENSOR_TOUCH);
   SetSensor(See,SENSOR_LIGHT);

   // calibrate light sensor
   Calibrate();

   // start motors
   OnFwd(Left+Right);

   // let's clear the timer we are going to use
   ClearTimer(0);

   // start tasks
   start LWatch;
   start Crash;
   start Maneuver;
}

// this task watches for the line
task LWatch()
{
   // highest priority
   SetPriority(0);

   // infinite loop
   while(true)
   {
      until(See<=threshold);   // until we see the line

         acquire(ACQUIRE_USER_1)
         {
           Avoid();       // avoid the line
         }
```

```
    }
}

// this task watches the touch sensors
task Crash()
{
    // second highest priority
    SetPriority(1);

    // infinite loop
    while(true)
    {
        // until left or right touch sensors are pressed
        until(LBump|RBump==1);

            acquire(ACQUIRE_USER_1)
            {
                Win();    // take control and crash repeatedly
            }
    }
}

// this task introduces some random turns
task Maneuver()
{
    // third highest priority
    SetPriority(2);

    // infinite loop
    while(true)
    {
        // until timer is >= 2.5 seconds which is determined by LIMIT
        until(Timer(0)>=LIMIT);

            acquire(ACQUIRE_USER_1)
            {
                Change();  // execute our new function
            }
    }
}

// this function avoids the other sumo-bot
void Win()
{
    Wait(20);
    Rev(Left+Right);
    Wait(BACK_TIME);
    Fwd(Right);    // this turns XK2 in the other direction
    Wait(TURN);
    OnFwd(Left+Right);
    ClearTimer(0);
}
```

```
// this function avoids the line
void Avoid()
{
    OnRev(Left+Right);
    Wait(LIGHT_BACK);
    Fwd(Right);
    Wait(TURN);
    OnFwd(Left+Right);
    ClearTimer(0);
}


// this function changes the direction of the robot
void Change()
{
    Rev(Right);
    Wait(TURN+Random(30));
    Fwd(Right);
    ClearTimer(0);
}


// this is the calibrating function
void Calibrate()
{
    until(RBump==1);
    line=See;
    threshold=line+AMOUNT;
    until(RBump==0);
    PlaySound(SOUND_CLICK);
    until(RBump==1);
    until(RBump==0);
    PlaySound(SOUND_CLICK);
    Wait(TURN);
}
```

There you have it: the essence of the ram-and-run approach. As you can see, the ram-and-run behavior itself is actually fairly simple. And watching it in action is quite interesting—so why don't we do some testing?

Testing XK2

First, download XK2_Access_Control.nqc to program slot 1 on your RCX, and then download XK2_Access_Control_Two.nqc to program slot 2. Use the procedure outlined in Chapter 3, in the "Downloading Programs to the RCX" section, to download the programs to your RCX using BricxCC.

> **NOTE** *Remember that you can download all the programs presented in this book from the Downloads section of the Apress web site (www.apress.com).*

To test the first program—the one portraying the classic repeated ramming method—make sure the RCX is on program slot 1, and position the light sensor over the line encircling the perimeter of your arena with the aid of the LED. Press the "head bumper" back until it touches the touch sensors, then let go ("letting go" releases the touch sensors as the rubber bands pull the head forwards). XK2 should emit a click to indicate that it has successfully calibrated the light sensor. Now place XK2 in the center of your arena and, once more, press and release the touch sensors by pushing the head in and then letting go. After about half a second, XK2 will start moving. Notice the degree of the turn it executes when it sees the line. Use your hand to activate the touch sensors and see how it responds.

> **NOTE** *Having a second line-detecting light sensor in the back of small-and-fast sumo-bots is highly advantageous and will greatly improve your sumo-bot's survivability. In fact, you should always do this if you own a second light sensor and if the rule set for the competition you're participating in allows it. In Chapter 7, you'll see one possible way to use and program two line-detecting light sensors in a sumo-bot. You can also download a bonus chapter, which covers how to build Zip-Bam-Bot version XK3, from the Downloads section of the Apress web site (www.apress.com). The bonus chapter has coverage on using two line-detecting light sensors, and, of course, shows you how to do it in a small-and-fast sumo-bot.*

Now let's experiment with that maneuvering task. Right after XK2 has completed a task (detected line, touch-sensor hit), pick it up so its wheels are not touching the ground, count to two seconds, and then set it back down. In about a half second, XK2 should execute a random turn, and then resume normal behavior. This little action is the maneuvering task kicking in.

Place something in the arena, and see how long it takes XK2 to find it and get rid of it. Try increasingly larger objects to test XK2's overall pushing ability. Also, try to manipulate different situations by moving objects with your hands.

When you're ready, experiment with the ram-and-run program. Turn the program slot on the RCX to slot 2 and do the calibrating process as before. Test all the situations as previously mentioned, but this time, notice XK2's "runaway" behavior. Place a large object in the arena and "chase" XK2. See if it can successfully elude the object that you're holding (but don't be too hard on your bot, now!).

Considering the Pros and Cons of XK2's Design

Some of the same problems pestering XK1 are still here, but (on the brighter side), we now have some new features and goodies.

The Pros

The following are the advantages of XK2's design:

- XK2 can run its slope under a variety of opponents.

- XK2 can easily outmaneuver larger and slower sumo-bots.

- XK2 can use its stopping mechanism to prevent other sumo-bots from flipping it.

- XK2's slope keeps its front low to the ground.

- XK2's drivetrain system provides maximum speed and minimum friction.

- XK2's light sensor is highly protected.

The Cons

The following are some disadvantages of XK2's design:

- XK2 can accidentally back over the line encircling the arena.

- If cornered, XK2 could get pushed out of the ring.

- XK2 is vulnerable to a side hit of its head.

- XK2 is vulnerable to back ramming.

As you can see, some of the same problems we had with XK1 are still here. However, these are not critical, and the pros of the design should even things out.

Something you might have noticed absent from the cons list is the friction problem. Why is the friction problem not much of a disadvantage? The answer is simple: XK2's front end *skips* across the ground! This skipping is primarily a combination of its fast speed and the distribution of its weight. This means that XK2 isn't in contact with the ground as much as XK1, and the end results are higher speed and efficiency.

Conclusion

XK2 takes the concept of repeated ramming and gives it a twist by using the second approach to the repeated ramming method. Now, instead of just using momentum to defeat the opponent, a slope aids the process. You were also introduced to a few new mechanisms. Subassemblies like the back skid subassembly can come in quite handy, and the head subassembly shows the advantage of having the whole head act as a bumper—it's harder to miss detecting a hit when done this way.

You also saw new programming procedures. We introduced an extra task into our ram-and-ram-again strategy that makes XK2 turn after a predefined amount of inactivity. We also tried a second strategy: the "ram-and-run" approach. Instead of continually ramming, this strategy makes XK2 run away after detecting a hit.

Well, you have done it—you have built, programmed, and tested all the small-and-fast sumo-bots presented in this part of the book. (And remember, a bonus chapter you can download from the Downloads section of www.apress.com shows how to build a third version of Zip-Bam-Bot.) Through this interactive journey into the small-and-fast strategy, you have learned several important concepts and principles. Some of these pertain to robotic sumo in general, but many of these tips and tricks are specific to this strategy. Each strategy has its own perks and secrets, and it's largely your job to find them—with the help of this book, of course!

Here are the important points to remember when creating sumo-bots for the small-and-fast strategy:

- Keep the weight and size to a minimum.

- Use the ram-and-ram-again or ram-and-run approaches only.

- Although important for all sumo-bots, building a highly durable structure is especially important for small-and-fast sumo-bots.

- Things happen fast in this strategy. The program should keep the sumo-bot moving and well informed at all times.

- Use fewer gears (this doesn't necessarily mean no gears) and bigger wheels for less friction and more speed.

- If possible, use a second light sensor in the back of your sumo-bot for enhanced line-detecting capabilities.

Keep in mind that there is far more that you can do with the small-and-fast strategy than you've seen in these examples. I've seen some pretty amazing mechanisms and techniques used on small sumo-bots including transmissions (which we'll discuss in the next chapter), position-changing light sensors, and more—all implemented within a small sumo-bot *and* under restrictive rules. So keep experimenting and trying new things, and don't let anyone ever tell you that small sumo-bots aren't any fun!

Part Three

The Second Approach: The M-Class Strategy

CHAPTER 6

The Brain-Bot Chassis

BE PREPARED TO throw off every last remnant of RIS-only restrictions and delve into a large and fascinating section of robotic sumo: the M-class strategy. No longer will we build simple and small chassis and sumo-bots; no longer do rule sets tie us down to single-set restrictions; no longer is robotic sumo a "little game" of tiny bots and little pushes. In this strategy, just about every definable factor and variable are quite different from those contained in the small-and-fast strategy; you could almost say it's a different game. In the midst of all these changes, one of them is extremely important: the plan of attack. Speed is still important, but having a powerful gear train for pushing is essential, too.

In the M-class strategy, many different kinds of gear trains become viable options, and methods that help to find the opposing sumo-bot abound. Complex and ingeniously designed sumo-bots are commonplace. However, more simple sumo-bots—which can be just as effective—use this strategy as well. The bottom line is that the diversity in the M-class strategy is simply amazing.

Why does the M-class strategy have these characteristics? The answer is simple: it is *in between* the small-and-fast and big sumo strategies. Small sumo-bots rely on speed and almost no push; big sumo-bots rely on push and almost no speed. Medium sumo-bots can cover a wide spectrum of designs and configurations, and they even have the potential to possess more than one aspect or ability. For example, how about a sumo-bot that can go both fast *and* slow?

In this chapter, you'll meet the Brain-Bot chassis, discover the meaning behind its name, and learn how to make a sumo-bot that can change its speed. Figure 6-1 shows the completed model.

Figure 6-1. The finished Brain-Bot chassis

Building the Brain-Bot Chassis

Brain-Bot may seem kind of large (which it is), but this doesn't mean you'll need
to build two dozen subassemblies to construct it. Instead, the majority of the construction happens in the drive subassemblies. These hold the motors that power
the wheels, additional motors (as you will see in the final assembly), and, of course,
the wheels. Fortunately, the designs for the left and right sides are identical; this
means that you can build two drive subassemblies, and they will make up the core
base of the robot. As for the rest of the robot, there is an RCX subassembly, two middle
bulk subassemblies, bottom bracer subassembly, and two gear-switch subassemblies.
In the final assembly, described in the "Putting the Brain-Bot Chassis Together" section,
you will also add some additional pieces to the sumo-bot.

Brain-Bot is constructed mainly out of pieces from the RIS 2.0 and the Ultimate
Builders Expansion Pack (UBEP). In addition to these sets, you will need one more
motor, some extra #4 and #6 axles, and extra gears. Fortunately, the model doesn't
have any rare or hard-to-find gears. However, you'll need quite a few common gears to
complete Brain-Bot. Among these are more than a dozen 8t gears and eight 40t gears.
Figure 6-2 shows Brain-Bot's bill of materials.

At this point, you might be wondering how Brain-Bot can use four motors, since
there are only three output ports on the RCX. Four (or more) motors *can* be added to
the RCX; you'll see how this works when you put the chassis together later in this
chapter.

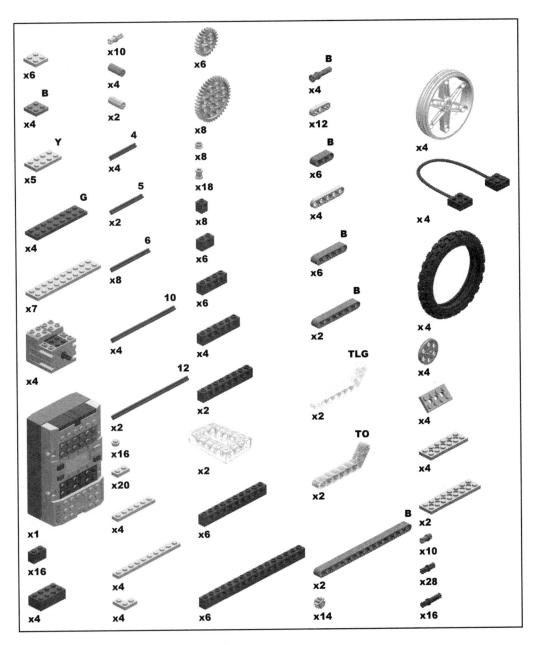

Figure 6-2. Brain-Bot's bill of materials

The Drive Subassembly

The drive subassembly is shown in Figure 6-3. The gearing in this assembly might leave you scratching your head, but once you have actually built it and seen it in action, it will make a lot more sense than it does at first glance.

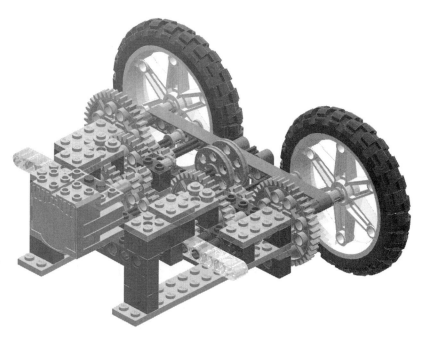

Figure 6-3. The completed drive subassembly

The primary purpose of this drive subassembly is mobility: it makes the robot go (a pretty simple concept). It can also switch to two different speeds—when another assembly is added later—but *that* isn't such a simple concept. The speed-control system as a whole is known as a *transmission*, and the system that actually changes the speed is known as a *gear switch*. And the gear switch does just that: switch gears.

Brain-Bot is designed to go a relatively fast speed in one mode, but slow (meaning a lot of torque, or pushing power) in another mode. This is so the sumo-bot can go fast while searching for the opponent and go slow while pushing the opponent. However, I encountered a difficulty in designing this. The problem is that gear switches don't work that way, or so it seems. Most gear switches give only a small change in speeds as they use 8t, 24t, or 16t gears to do the switching (giving only 1:3 or 3:1 ratio boosts, for instance). I wanted something quite different: a *slow* speed and a *relatively faster* speed. Tiny changes in the speed and torque just wouldn't do.

Ratios and Gears

What's the deal with ratios and how do they work? A ratio—for example, 1:3—will ultimately represent the rotation of the gears. I say *ultimately* because there are two ways to do your ratios, which we will examine in a moment. What's important to realize when making ratios and observing ratios is *which gear is turning which*. The ratio will always depend on which is the *powered gear* and which gear is being turned by the powered gear, or, in a setup involving multiple gears, which gear is the final output gear.

Here are the two ways to do your ratios, or, better put, the two views on ratios:

- **Rotation view:** This view has the ratios corresponding exactly to the rotations of the gears, which means an 8t gear turning a 24t gear would result in a 3:1 ratio; that is, the 8t turns three times for every one turn of the 24t. Likewise, a 24t turning an 8t would result in a 1:3 ratio, as the 24t turns once for every three turns of the 8t.

- **Gear teeth view:** This view goes by the number of teeth on the gears, which means an 8t gear turning a 24t gear would result in a 1:3 ratio. This ratio is achieved by counting the gear's teeth, putting them together as a ratio—8:24—and then simplifying them: 1:3. Likewise, a 24t gear turning an 8t gear would result in a 3:1 ratio, as the ratio would be 24:8, which would then simplify to 3:1.

To truly explain gears and ratios, and to comprehend the actual physical forces a ratio represents, you must consider the rotations of the gears. However, the gear teeth view can also effectively explain ratios and is easier to understand and use. Although gear ratios have plenty to do with LEGO MINDSTORMS robotic sumo, they aren't what it's all about. We'll be concentrating more on robotic sumo itself in this book, so we'll take the easier-to-understand gear teeth view.

Which ratio view should you use in your MINDSTORMS career? Really, it's nothing more than a matter of personal opinion. If you choose the rotation view, you'll be using true ratios that refer to the actual rotation of the gears. If you choose the gear teeth view, the numbers in the ratios can be easier to comprehend and use.

After a great amount of experimentation and work, the end result is what you see: the drive subassembly. This assembly uses 40t gears to attain greater ratio boosts instead of using only 24t and 8t gears. However, it also uses other gears, which combine to make up a complex gear train that gives the final (and desired) result. That result is a 1:15 ratio in fast speed, obtained by multiplying these ratios: 1:3 × 1:5 = 1:15. This would be considered slow by the small-and-fast strategy's standard, but for the M-class strategy, it's a quite acceptable ratio, since the sumo-bots are bigger and heavier. Figure 6-4 highlights the gears responsible for the fast speed in the drive subassembly.

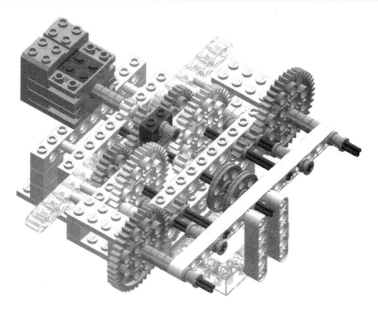

Figure 6-4. The drive subassembly's fast speed

For the slow speed, Brain-Bot has only one additional set of gears that the power is transferred through, but this makes all the difference. Figure 6-5 highlights the gears responsible for the slow speed. Now let's do the math: 1:3 × 1:5 × 1:5 = 1:75! That's a lot of torque! And these are just the kinds of numbers I wanted to see.

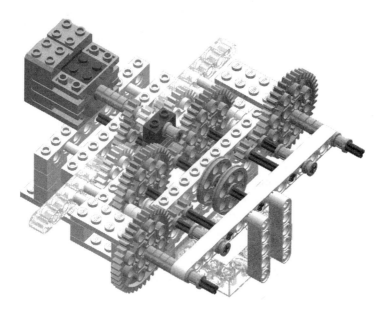

Figure 6-5. The drive subassembly's slow speed

Now that you know what it does, let's build the drive subassembly—the first (and the most important) assembly. Note that you will build *two* drive subassemblies. In the final assembly, one goes on the right side and one goes on the left side; together, they make up the majority of the sumo-bot and the core chassis itself.

Steps 1 and 2 do some simple and basic work with beams and plates.

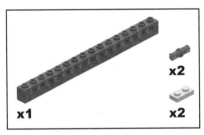

Drive Subassembly Step 1

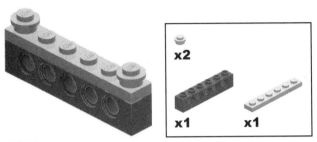

Drive Subassembly Step 2

Step 3 braces the beams with a piece from the UBEP—the 1x3 blue liftarm—and adds more plates.

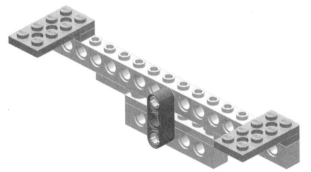

Drive Subassembly Step 3

Steps 4 and 5 build the assembly up another layer, and then brace that as well; this time with axle pins and the 1x3 gray half-liftarms that are easily found in the RIS.

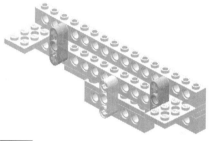
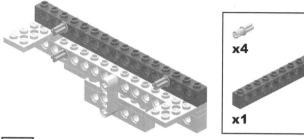

Drive Subassembly Step 4

Drive Subassembly Step 5

Now things begin to get a little more interesting. The assembly needs to be widened—no problem! Steps 6 through 9 stretch out the structure a good amount. This is accomplished with a special method: connect long friction pins into a beam or liftarm, attach another beam/liftarm, put more long pins in that, and keep going! This climaxes in step 9 with one last beam—you also add four 1x2 black bricks and two 2x10 plates to the bottom of this beam.

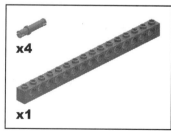

Drive Subassembly Step 6

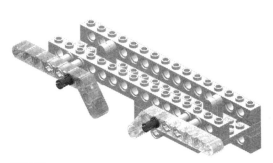

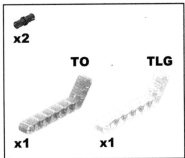

x2

TO   TLG

x1   x1

 Drive Subassembly Step 7

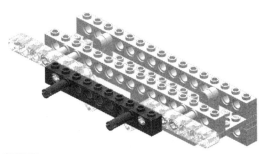

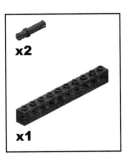

x2

x1

 Drive Subassembly Step 8

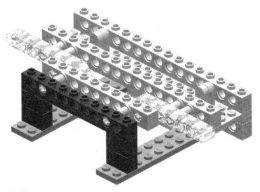

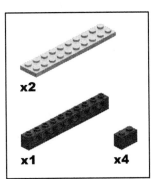

x2

x1   x4

 Drive Subassembly Step 9

With the main bulk of the assembly done, you are now ready to work on the gearing. Turn the model so the other side is facing you. In step 10, add 40t gears along with bushings and #6 axles.

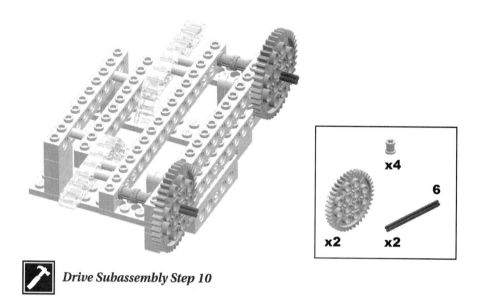

Drive Subassembly Step 10

Step 11 adds plates, axle extenders, and more gears—this time, 8t gears.

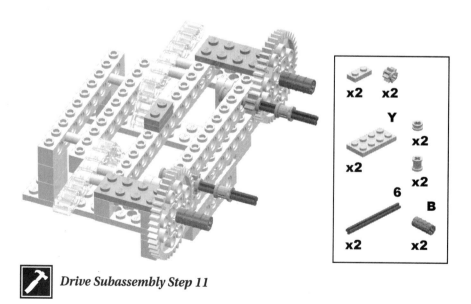

Drive Subassembly Step 11

In step 12, build and add the main switching axle as shown. Notice the "breathing space" of one stud for the 24t and 8t gears added in this step. When you move the switching axle (to switch the speed), the gears on that axle can easily be moved as well.

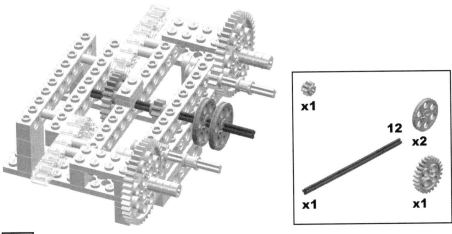

 Drive Subassembly Step 12

Now, in step 13, add the final gears, which include two more 40t gears, 24t gears, and 8t gears.

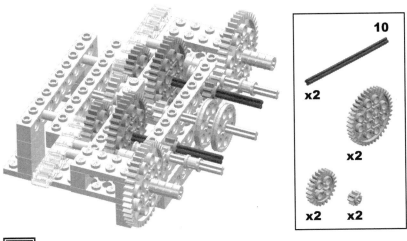

Drive Subassembly Step 13

As you have probably noticed, all those gears have their accompanying axles protruding out into space. You are now going to take care of this. As shown in step 14, take one of the *1x15 straight liftarms* from the UBEP, slide it onto the axles, and top off two of them with half-bushings.

There is one other part to this step. Underneath all this building activity is a single 1x6 beam—the one you added back in step 1. It is now time for this beam to do something! There will be a number of pieces attached either directly or indirectly to this beam, and you start off by snapping two friction pins into it.

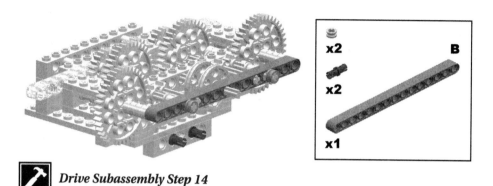

Drive Subassembly Step 14

In step 15, connect one of the transparent TECHNIC 4x6 bricks with an open center onto the friction pins from the previous step, and add four *more* friction pins to the assembly.

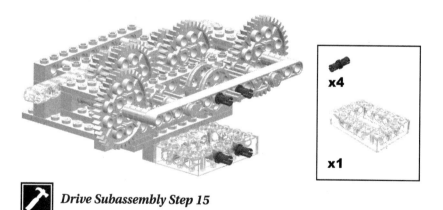

Drive Subassembly Step 15

Step 16 makes it easy to see the purpose behind all this: bracing! This step uses two of the 1x5 blue, straight liftarms from the UBEP for the bracing, and also adds some axles for the wheels.

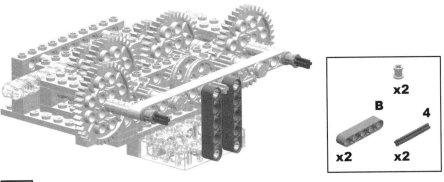

Drive Subassembly Step 16

Step 17 adds the wheels for this sumo-bot.

> **NOTE** *You might be wondering, "Why these wheels again? Why not different wheels?" We're using these wheels again because they provide good traction and speed. Also, they are readily available; every version of the RIS includes four of them. Smaller wheels don't give as good of a performance, and, actually, using smaller wheels won't work in this model. Try putting some on and see what happens.*

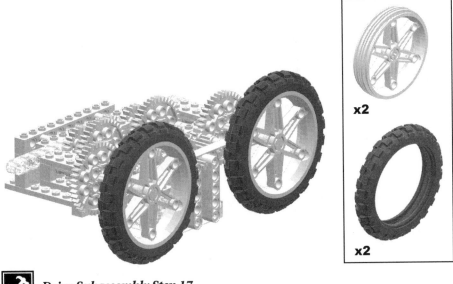

Drive Subassembly Step 17

Step 18 builds up some bricks and plates for later use.

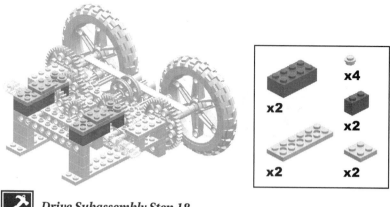

![icon] *Drive Subassembly Step 18*

In step 19, pull out a motor and attach the various pieces to it as shown.

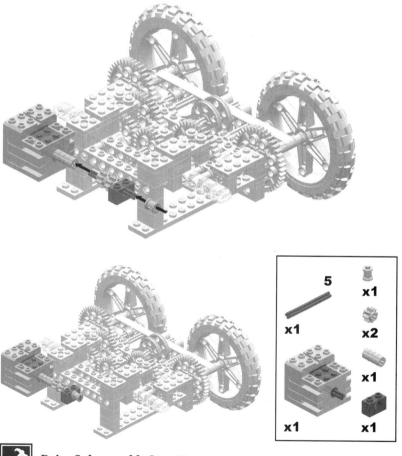

![icon] *Drive Subassembly Step 19*

Lastly, in step 20, after you've added the pieces to the motor, add the motor itself to the assembly.

 Drive Subassembly Step 20

You've completed the last building step for the drive subassembly, but right now there's a potential problem in the assembly. Do you see the axle on the motor's shaft, which holds two 8t gears and goes into a 1x2 beam at the end? Well, on that axle is a bit of "extra breathing space", and this will cause a gap—the gap could appear in between the two 8t gears, in front of the 8t gears, or in other places along the axle. Although this gap is very small, it will eventually cause problems when trying to switch speeds by snagging the moving gears. You need to eliminate this little gap, but how? You can't add anything else to the axle—is there any solution?

MindStormers (like you and me) sometimes come up against a problem like this one. Often, the answer to the problem is to redesign the problem spot; but redesigning really wouldn't work here because of the nature of the problem. A major redesign might solve the problem, but then the sumo-bot wouldn't be Brain-Bot anymore. Instead, here are the two simple steps you can perform to remove the little gap:

1. Take the axle extender on the motor and push it forward against the gap until it disappears. Once you do this, the gap is transferred to the other side of the 1x2 beam.

2. While firmly holding the axle extender so that it can't move backwards, push the bushing at the end of the axle all the way towards the 1x2 beam.

This solves the problem and properly seals the axle on that end. There is a bit of extra axle coming out of the bushing, but it can be safely disregarded. This little fix works excellently; sometimes the best solutions are the simplest ones.

CAUTION *Fixing the gap is a small but crucial task. If you don't do it, the whole sumo-bot might not work properly.*

After fixing the gap on your drive subassembly, you are finished with your first subassembly. Your drive subassembly should look like Figure 6-3, shown at the beginning of this section.

Now, follow the same steps to build another drive subassembly (remember that you need *two* drive subassemblies). Don't forget to fix the gap problem on both of them!

The Left Switch Subassembly

The left switch subassembly, shown in Figure 6-6, is responsible for switching the gears that will change the output speed of the robot. How does it work? First, the RCX sends a short burst of power—at a certain power level—to the motor. Then 1x3 liftarms connected directly to the motor move thin *wedge wheels* (located on the drive subassembly); these wedge wheels are on the main switching axle, so the switching axle is moved. This also means the gears on the switching axle are moved, and that is how you change the speeds.

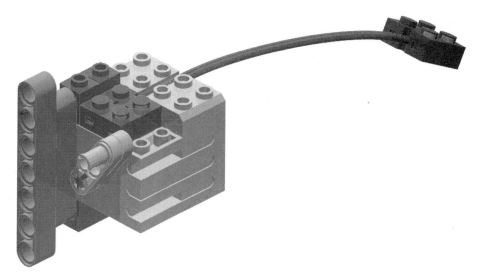

Figure 6-6. The completed left switch subassembly

In step 1, you add an electrical wire, facing towards the back, on a motor, and some pieces you haven't used yet in this book: *1x1 bricks with a hole*. Put four of these on, as shown, with a long friction pin running through them.

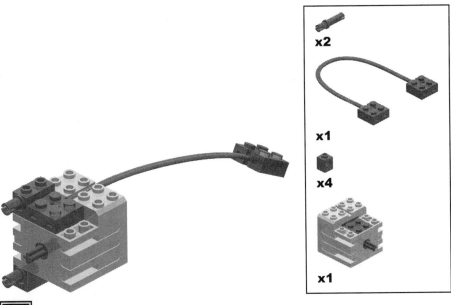

 Left Switch Subassembly Step 1

Steps 2 and 3 add the actual switching mechanism to the motor and construct the section that will connect to the chassis (you'll see exactly how it connects in the final assembly).

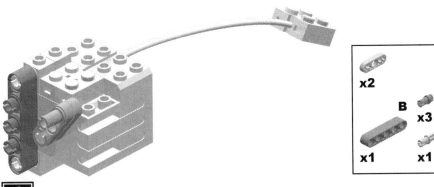

 Left Switch Subassembly Step 2

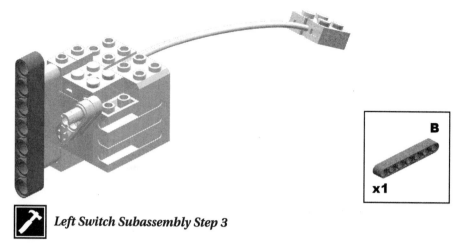

Left Switch Subassembly Step 3

Your left switch subassembly is now complete. It should look like Figure 6-6, shown at the beginning of this section.

The Right Switch Subassembly

The construction for the right switch subassembly, shown in Figure 6-7, is exactly the same as for the left switch subassembly, except that everything is mirrored. And as you would expect, this assembly will be going on the right side of the sumo-bot. To build a right switch subassembly, follow the instructions given for the left switch subassembly, but change the orientation of the pieces while you're building so that the completed subassembly looks like Figure 6-7.

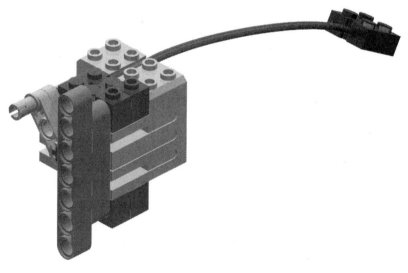

Figure 6-7. The completed right switch subassembly

The Middle Bulk Subassembly

With a name like "middle bulk subassembly," you can't help but wonder, "What exactly is this?" It is just what its name implies: bulk that goes in the middle. Once the basic layout of Brain-Bot is put together, there seems to be an "unfinished" spot in the middle—a spot that needs something to be there to make the sumo-bot complete. This is where the middle bulk subassembly, shown in Figure 6-8, comes in. Not only does it make the robot complete, the middle bulk subassembly is a great place to attach other pieces. In fact, the spot in this model where the RCX will rest is on top of the middle bulk subassemblies. This brings up another point: you will need to build *two* of these subassemblies. The left and right sides of Brain-Bot are identical, so two middle bulk subassemblies are necessary.

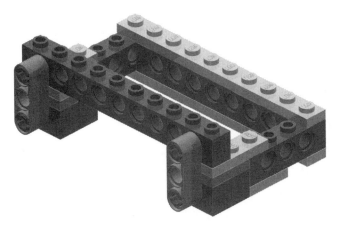

Figure 6-8. The completed middle bulk subassembly

In steps 1 and 2, you add a series of plates and beams, which are stacked up, to form the base.

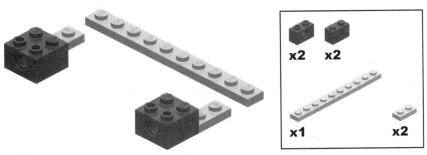

Middle Bulk Subassembly Step 1

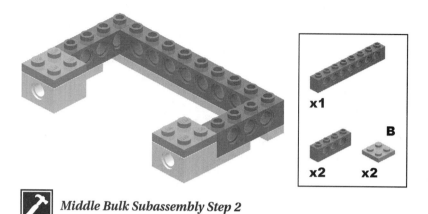

![hammer icon] *Middle Bulk Subassembly Step 2*

Step 3 adds more plates; these are mostly for reinforcement.

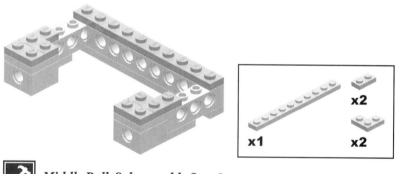

![hammer icon] *Middle Bulk Subassembly Step 3*

Step 4 places another beam on top of the plates closest to the front and four friction pins in the beams.

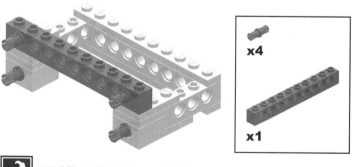

![hammer icon] *Middle Bulk Subassembly Step 4*

Bracing time again! In step 5, take two 1x3 blue liftarms, found in the UBEP, and snap them directly onto the friction pins.

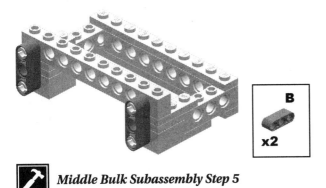

Middle Bulk Subassembly Step 5

That completes the middle bulk subassembly construction, and it should look like Figure 6-8, shown at the beginning of this section. Remember to build *two* of these.

The RCX Subassembly

The RCX subassembly, shown in Figure 6-9, will make your life easier when you do the final assembly. Instead of needing to build this directly onto the chassis in the final assembly, you can build it here and then easily slip it onto the chassis. Once again, in the final assembly, the RCX will not be directly attached or pushed onto bricks. Just as in the Zip-Bam-Bot chassis, only the edges of the RCX, which cannot attach to anything, are placed on studs. Therefore, this assembly—or should I say the RCX—is attached to the chassis by means of four of those ever-useful blue pins.

Figure 6-9. The completed RCX subassembly

NOTE *A bit of LEGO MINDSTORMS history: If you have only owned the RIS 2.0, you might not know that the blue pins used in this RCX subassembly did not make their appearance until the RIS 1.5. The RIS 1.0 didn't have quite as many axle accessories, and instead was more "brick-oriented." When the RIS 1.5 came out, some of the bricks were removed and several more "axle-oriented" pieces were introduced, including the blue pins with stop bushings.*

Construction is quite simple. In step 1, push four 3/4 pins into the RCX. In step 2, attach 1x6 beams and double layers of 1x5 half-liftarms onto the pins, and then push four blue, long pins with stop bushings into the liftarms and beams.

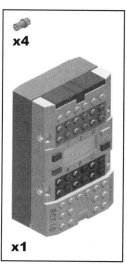
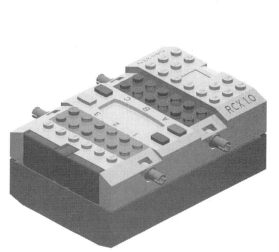

 RCX Subassembly Step 1

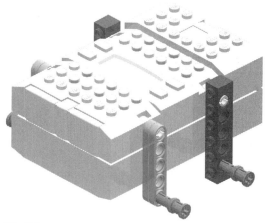
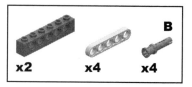

 RCX Subassembly Step 2

The Bottom Bracer Subassembly

The bottom bracer subassembly, shown in Figure 6-10, is nothing more than plates connected together in a certain pattern—a pattern that will conform perfectly to the bottom of the robot and strengthen the chassis. Without this subassembly, Brain-Bot would be much weaker. In a sense, the bottom bracer subassembly welds the robot together by attaching to both of the drive subassemblies.

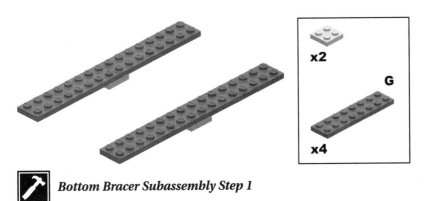

Figure 6-10. The completed bottom bracer subassembly

The construction involves only two steps.

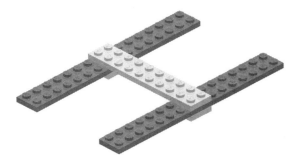

 Bottom Bracer Subassembly Step 1

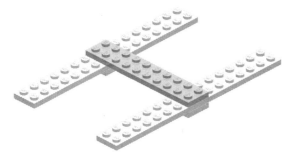

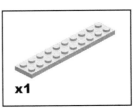

Bottom Bracer Subassembly Step 2

Putting the Brain-Bot Chassis Together

With all the subassemblies finally completed, the long-awaited moment has come: the final assembly of the Brain-Bot chassis.

To begin, get both **drive subassemblies** you constructed at the start of this chapter. Place them with their wheels facing away from each other and their motors touching together. Attach a 2x4 yellow plate to the two motors, and two 2x10 plates to the two assemblies, as shown in step 1.

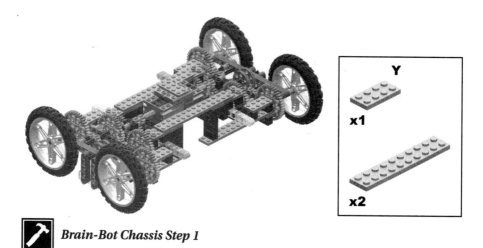

 Brain-Bot Chassis Step 1

Before you start putting on vital pieces such as the motors or the RCX, you need to strengthen the chassis quite a bit more. You will do this by firmly bringing the two drive subassemblies together in steps 2 through 4. In step 2, turn the model on its top (carefully!) and put two 1x4 beams onto the bottom of the motors. These beams further connect the two motors together.

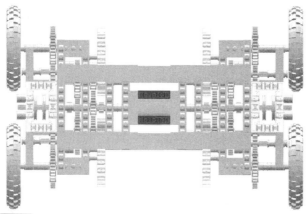

Brain-Bot Chassis Step 2

Now attach two 2x8 TECHNIC plates, as shown in step 3. These plates further strengthen the motors and also the whole chassis.

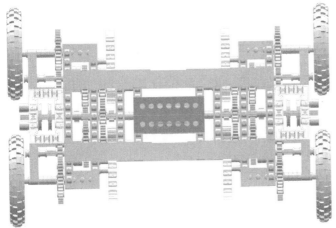

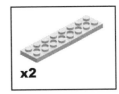

 Brain-Bot Chassis Step 3

However, the chassis is still not strong enough. One more series of plates is necessary. How can you do this? It's easy: pull out the **bottom bracer subassembly** and attach that! While you're at it, also add two 1x6 plates to the front and back of the sumo-bot. These plates attach to the bottom bracer subassembly and both sides of the robot, as shown in step 4 (one of the 1x6 plates is not visible in the image).

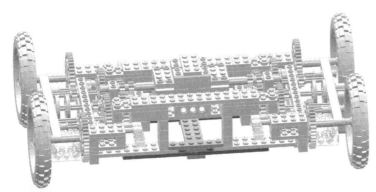

 Brain-Bot Chassis Step 4

Now you can whip out your two **middle bulk subassemblies**, and attach them as shown in step 5. Actually, first you attach an electrical wire to each motor, then two 1x1 round plates to each electrical wire's 2x2x2/3 plates which are connected to the motors, and then you place the middle bulk subassemblies on top.

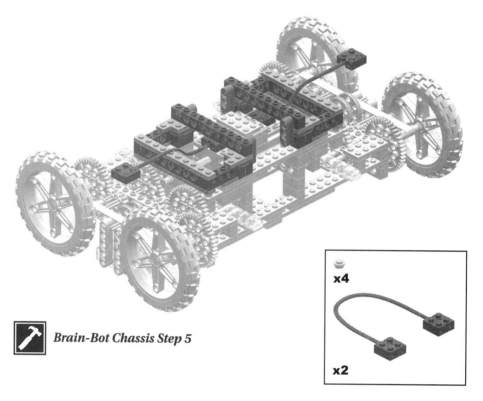

Brain-Bot Chassis Step 5

Step 6 adds the **RCX subassembly**, uses the four blue stop pins to firmly attach it to the chassis, and connects the "free" electrical wires to the RCX. Remember that all you need to do to remove the RCX is pull out those blue pins. There are a number of reasons why this is a great feature to possess, but here is one of them: changing the batteries is painless! Connect the motor's electrical wires to the RCX like this:

- The **right drive subassembly's motor** goes on **output port C.**

- The **left drive subassembly's motor** goes on **output port A.**

> **TIP** *Among MINDSTORMS fans (and LEGO fans as a whole) there are no rules, but there are a few guidelines that are recognized and generally followed. Among these guidelines is the RCX rule: make access to the RCX easy, prevent the infrared port from being obstructed, and allow easy detachment and attachment of the RCX. As you can see, Brain-Bot abides by these guidelines. However, these guidelines are only suggestions, and not all models have the capability to use them. So, if you use them, that's great! If you don't, that's just fine, too.*

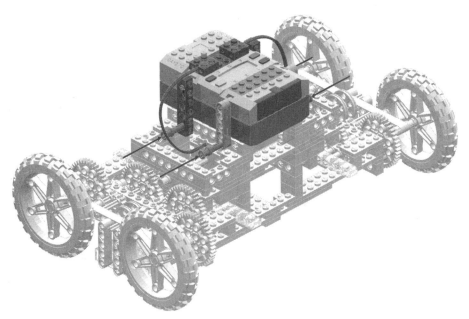

 Brain-Bot Chassis Step 6

Only one step left! In step 7, add the **left** and **right switch subassemblies**. As you can see, they are pushed down onto the drive subassemblies. The blue liftarms on the switch assemblies actually go down onto the beam's studs and make a connection. Do you remember this type of connection from Chapter 4? It's a slightly unusual connection, but it's a useful one!

> **CAUTION** *When pushing the switch subassembly's 1x7 blue liftarms onto the chassis, make sure you push them all the way onto the beam's studs. If the connection isn't solid, the switch subassemblies might work themselves off the chassis. One way to ensure you have a firm connection is to take the 1x7 blue liftarms off the switch subassemblies, attach those to the chassis first, and then snap on the rest of the assemblies.*

As mentioned at the beginning of this chapter, having more motors than there are motor outputs isn't a problem—there is an easy way to work with more than three motors. And you can see how to do it in step 7: both of the switch subassembly's wires connect to *one* port (**output port B**) on the RCX! This is completely "legal" and will not harm the RCX or motors in any way. The important thing to remember is the orientation of the wires. The motor on the right should have its wire on the bottom and going out the back; the motor on the left should have its wire on top and going out the front towards the LCD.

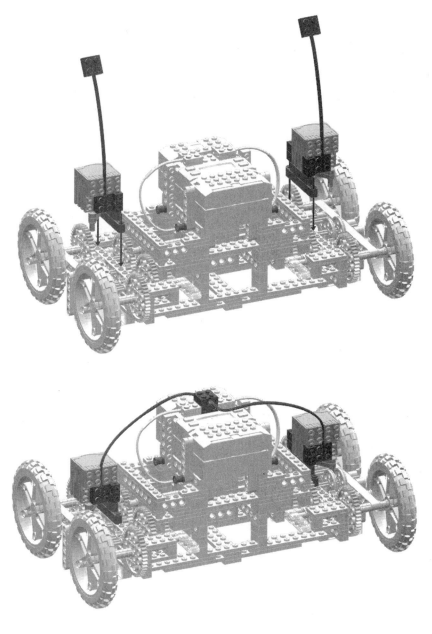

Brain-Bot Chassis Step 7

Once you've completed step 7, you are finished building the Brain-Bot chassis. Your model should look like the completed chassis shown in Figure 6-1, at the beginning of the chapter.

Programming the Brain-Bot Chassis

After seeing cool gear switches and impressive gear trains, you are probably ready to see Brain-Bot really work. Besides that though, it's a good idea to test the basics of a chassis before doing some serious sumo-bot programming on it (although, in this case, the chassis has been rigorously tested).

But how did Brain-Bot get its name? *Brain* signifies, as you probably guessed, thinking power or being smart. Not only does this allude to the fact that Brain-Bot is smart, it also means Brain-Bot has the *capabilities* to be smart; the M-class strategy allows this to happen. With all the amazing features it has to offer, the M-class strategy holds endless "smart" possibilities. Most of this smartness goes on in the programming; in other words, the program that runs the sumo-bot is what will make it truly smart.

In the programs for Brain-Bot, we will add something new: a *header*. A header is a separate, different file from your .nqc program and has the filename extension .nqh.

Programming Brain-Bot with a Header

Before we go any further, we need to take a closer look at headers and why they are useful.

In the C or C++ language, which NQC is based on, most programs have code at the very top that serves the purpose of including certain files for that program, so it can access specific functionality. As an example, let's say we are writing a program to create textures for a racecar game in C or C++ (however out of place that example may be). To get the textures for the cars, we need to include a file in the program with a line of code that says:

```
#include <cartexture.h>
```

Notice that it is of a file type .h instead of the typical .c in the C language. NQC has a file type of .nqc, which mimics .c, and it also has a file type of .nqh, which mimics the .h files of the C language. To include files in your NQC programs, you use the following line of code (the filename is robot.nqh in this example):

```
#include "robot.nqh"
```

Along with the different filename extension, an important difference you should note between the C and NQC code is that NQC uses *double quotes* (") around the filename. C uses *angle brackets* (< and >). Official NQC documentation states that enclosing a filename in angle brackets is forbidden.

So, why use these files called headers? If you are using a chassis and making several robots out of it, those robots are likely to have something in common. Instead of needing to add the same basic functions in each of the programs for those robots, we can put all those functions in one .nqh file, and then include them in whatever program we want with just one line of code! To execute those functions, all we need to do is call their name within the program as is ordinarily done. This whole process makes our life easier and our programs much cleaner.

> **NOTE** *Including more than one header in a NQC program is legal, but it isn't always practical. If you were making a header for a specific type of robot, it would be a good idea to put all the code in one header instead of multiple ones. However, if the set of commands you're using are distinct and separate, including more than one header in a NQC program is fine.*

Now let's look at the NQC header we'll use for our Brain-Bot chassis, shown in Listing 6-1. As you can see, it has some basic actions and also some constants, which can be included and used in an NQC program.

Listing 6-1. Brain-Bot.nqh

```
/* Brain-Bot.nqh - A file holding important instructions
 * for the Brain-Bot chassis. To be included in any Brain-Bot
 * programs */

// motors
#define Left OUT_A
#define Right OUT_C
#define Switch OUT_B

// constants
#define Change 25
#define Position 200
#define Straight 300

// go forward
void Forward()
{
   OnFwd(Left+Right);
}

// go in reverse
void Reverse()
{
   OnRev(Left+Right);
}

// switch gears to fast speed
void SwitchF()
{
   On(Left+Right);
   OnRev(Switch);
   Wait(Change);
   Off(Switch);
}
```

```
// Switch gears to slow speed
void SwitchS()
{
    On(Left+Right);
    OnFwd(Switch);
    Wait(Change);
    Off(Switch);
}

// turn right
void TurnR()
{
    Fwd(Left);
    Rev(Right);
    Wait(Position);
    Fwd(Left+Right);
}

// turn left
void TurnL()
{
    Fwd(Right);
    Rev(Left);
    Wait(Position);
    Fwd(Left+Right);
}

// stop
void Stop()
{
    Off(Left+Right);
}
```

> **NOTE** *You will notice that there is no main task in this program (or actually header). That is correct. In headers, there are no main tasks. If you try to compile this header, you will get, "Error: task 'main' not defined." This is okay. BricxCC can't quite tell the difference between an .nqh file and an .nqc file, which does need a main task. Just ignore this error message, or even better, don't compile the header at all.*

Now that the header is set up, the next logical step is to create a full-blown NQC program and include this header in that program. As with the Zip-Bam-Bot chassis program in Chapter 3, we are not going to create a "real" sumo-bot program—just think of this as a test drive. We want to try out Brain-Bot's different features and get a feel for how it works. For this test drive, I wrote a relatively simple program that moves the robot around for a while and then stops. The program is called Brain-Bot-One.nqc and is shown in Listing 6-2.

> **NOTE** *Make sure that your headers are always in the same directory as the program that includes them. For instance, if you have an NQC program in C:\Robot that includes a header, the header must also be in C:\Robot. Otherwise, the compiling or downloading procedure will produce an error message.*

Listing 6-2. Brain-Bot-One.nqc

```
// Brain-Bot-One.nqc - a program for the Brain-Bot chassis.

// let's include the header for this program
#include "Brain-Bot.nqh"

task main()
{
  SetPower(Switch,3);    // set power for switch motors to 3

  // let's do this twice
  repeat(2)
  {
  Forward();
  Wait(Straight);
  TurnR();
  PlaySound(SOUND_CLICK);
  }

  // and this twice
  repeat(2)
  {
  Reverse();
  Wait(Straight);
  TurnL();
  PlaySound(SOUND_CLICK);
  }

  SwitchS();      // let's try out the switching mechanisms

  // we'll do this twice in slow mode
  repeat(2)
  {
  Wait(Straight);
  TurnR();
  PlaySound(SOUND_UP);
  }

  SwitchF();      // switch back to fast

  // then do this twice
  repeat(2)
```

```
{
Wait(Straight);
TurnL();
PlaySound(SOUND_UP);
}

Stop();        // we're done, turn off motors
PlaySound(SOUND_DOWN);   // play a sound so we know we're done
}
```

A Quick Test of Brain-Bot-One.nqc

Just as in Chapter 3, we are going to do some quick tests of each of the programs, and then do more thorough testing later. Download Brain-Bot-One.nqc to program slot 1 on the RCX using BricxCC, following the procedure outlined in Chapter 3, in the "Downloading Programs to the RCX" section. Then press the Run button on the RCX. Brain-Bot should begin the program by moving forward. After waiting a specified amount of time, Brain-Bot should turn right, play a sound, and then repeat that set of actions one more time.

> **CAUTION** *Brain-Bot should* always *be on fast speed when starting a program. The fast speed is the basic, or usual, driving speed, and the slow speed is the secondary driving speed. When you start the program, it assumes that the fast speed is the current one, and Brain-Bot's program will eventually turn it to slow speed. But if it's already on slow speed, its switching motors won't be able to move! This won't burn out your motors, but it is most assuredly not desirable.*

Now Brain-Bot should do something else: instead of going forwards, it should go backwards for a certain amount of time, and then turn left. This set of actions should be repeated twice as well.

At this point, Brain-Bot should switch gears to slow speed. Then the program should make Brain-Bot do another set of actions in slow speed, switch back to fast speed, do another set of actions, and finally stop, sounding the end of the program with SOUND_DOWN.

Understanding Brain-Bot-One.nqc

Brain-Bot-One.nqc doesn't contain anything outstanding or earth-shattering, but it does have two things you haven't seen in previous programs. One is the #include command, which as discussed earlier, includes header files:

```
#include "Brain-Bot.nqh"
```

The other new code is the repeat() statement. As you can guess, it's used to repeat something. It takes one argument, an *expression*, and repeats anything within its braces that number of times.

```
repeat(2)
{
Wait(Straight);
TurnL();
PlaySound(SOUND_UP);
}
```

The number 2 is the expression, and the repeat() statement will execute anything within its braces two times. It's pretty easy to use repeat()!

The rest of the program doesn't require much explanation. The individual commands included from Brain-Bot.nqh are put to good use (like calling SwitchS();), there are a few sounds played here and there to confirm when something is finished, and several Wait(); commands are used to have the robot move or do an action for a certain period of time.

Creating a More Complex Header-Based Program for Brain-Bot

The previous example just executed little chunks of code a repeated number of times. Couldn't we do something a bit more interesting? Of course! Because Brain-Bot doesn't have any sensors right now, our programming is somewhat limited, but there is still a lot more we can do. Although this next example doesn't boast of being super-complex, it executes commands based on the values of a timer. Therefore, the sumo-bot depends on an external source—time. This should definitely be more interesting, especially since you can change the waiting time periods, resulting in infinite possibilities.

Listing 6-3 shows Brain-Bot-Two.nqc. This program makes use of timers, until, and a special command—introduced with the RCX 2.0 firmware and parallel NQC 2.0 release—that controls the LCD: SetUserDisplay().

Listing 6-3. Brain-Bot-Two.nqc

```
// Brain-Bot-Two.nqc - a program for the Brain-Bot chassis

#include "Brain-Bot.nqh"

task main()
{
  SetUserDisplay(Timer(0),0);   // let's set the RCX's LCD to Timer 0

  SetPower(Switch,3);      // set power for switch motors to 3

  ClearTimer(0);   // clear the timer
```

```
    Forward();          // go forward

    until(Timer(0) >= 25);  // until timer is >= 2.5 seconds
    PlaySound(SOUND_CLICK);
    ClearTimer(0);             // clear the timer

    SwitchS();       // switch to slow mode
    Reverse();       // then reverse

    until(Timer(0) >= 35);   // until timer is >= 3.5 seconds
    PlaySound(SOUND_CLICK);

    TurnR();                 // turn right
    Forward();               // go forward
    SwitchF();               // switch back to fast
    TurnL();                 // now turn left

    ClearTimer(0);           // then and only then clear the timer

    Reverse();               // now put in reverse

    until(Timer(0) >= 45);   // until timer is >= 4.5 seconds

    Stop();   // stop!!!

    PlaySound(SOUND_DOUBLE_BEEP); // we're done
}
```

A Quick Test of Brain-Bot-Two.nqc

Once again, download the program to the RCX. You can place it in slot 1 (which erases any previous program in slot 1), slot 2, or any other slot. Position Brain-Bot somewhere with a little moving space, make sure it is on fast mode, and press the Run button on the RCX.

The first thing you should notice is that the display on the RCX changes from its normal state (system clock) to something different: a timer. This is not just any old timer, but the timer *we are using*; that is, Timer(0). We set this up at the beginning of the program to be able to visually observe when the robot makes its decisions (the program clears the timer about the time a set of different commands executes).

After 2.5 seconds, Brain-Bot should play a sound, clear the timer, change to slow speed, and go in reverse. After reversing for 3.5 seconds, it should play another sound, turn right, put the motors in the forward direction, switch back to fast, and *then* turn left. Once that burst of activity is finished, Brain-Bot will once again clear the timer in use, go in reverse for 4.5 seconds, and finally stop, playing DOUBLE_BEEP to let you know it's finished.

Understanding Brain-Bot-Two.nqc

As noted before Listing 6-3, this program uses the `SetUserDisplay()` command to control the LCD:

```
SetUserDisplay(Timer(0),0);
```

The format for using this command is `SetUserDisplay(value, precision)`. *Value* is the source to be displayed. This could be a constant (for example, 54), a variable, a timer, a sensor, and even the message buffer. *Precision* deals with a decimal point. The number entered here determines the position of the decimal point. If we have 1 for precision, the decimal point would move one space to the left (starting from the right). A precision of 0, as in our example, means that there won't be a decimal point displayed.

What's the purpose of using this in our case? There isn't any particular reason really, but it does show the potential usefulness of `SetUserDisplay()`. When you are using something frequently in a program, like a timer, it can be extremely helpful to actually monitor its progress. With `SetUserDisplay()`, you can determine where bugs are in your programs and do many other useful and interesting things. The program here shows just one example of controlling the LCD.

> **TIP** *To find out more about setting the LCD, look in the* NQC Programmer's Guide, *which comes with BricxCC. For more thorough coverage, check out* Extreme MIND-STORMS: An Advanced Guide to LEGO MINDSTORMS, *by Dave Baum et al (Apress, 2000). This book also covers other features of the RCX 2.0 firmware.*

In the rest of the program, the sumo-bot executes an action or series of actions until the allotted amount of time has run out. It is done with a line of code like this:

```
until(Timer(0) >= 45);
```

The program then clears the timer and executes another set of actions until another predefined period of time runs out. There is one exception in this program where it runs some actions without worrying about time, but the main part of the structure operates this way.

> **TIP** *Make your own program for Brain-Bot and see what you can come up with. String together a few commands from the header file and add some statements such as* repeat *and* until *(or both) to control the structure of the program. Also see if you can figure out how to use* Random() *to give Brain-Bot some unpredictability.*

Testing the Brain-Bot Chassis

Now that you have seen these programs, let's retest them, but in some "sumo-like" situations. First, make sure that Brain-Bot-One.nqc is in program slot 1 on the RCX and Brain-Bot-Two.nqc is in program slot 2. Place Brain-Bot in your arena and put some relatively small and heavy objects—as you did in Chapter 3—in the general area where Brain-Bot will be going.

NOTE *Remember that you don't need to retype the programs in this book into BricxCC. All of the programs for this book are available from the Downloads section of the Apress web site (www.apress.com).*

Press the Run button on the RCX, for Brain-Bot-One.nqc, and watch carefully. How does Brain-Bot manage hitting an object on fast speed? How about on slow speed? What about the same object on different speeds? Set up different situations to see the different reactions.

Now change the program to Brain-Bot-Two.nqc. Run the program and, once again, watch the reactions with the objects. This time, however, let's make things a little more interesting. Grab an object and position it in front of Brain-Bot, without letting go. Use your hands to increase or decrease the resistance of the object once Brain-Bot has run into it. Try holding an object somewhat firmly in front of Brain-Bot when it is on slow speed—the reaction you see is similar to Brain-Bot shoving another sumo-bot.

Now try this: while Brain-Bot is running along—whether in slow or fast mode—place your finger, or even hand, in front of one of the tires. What happens? Brain-Bot will go right over it! But it's not the fact that Brain-Bot can go over your finger or hand that is interesting; it is *why* Brain-Bot can go over it that is interesting. It's because of the type of wheels—believe me, big wheels are a good thing!

CAUTION *The switch subassemblies can slightly separate the wedge wheels on the drive subassemblies over time; this could possibly lead to problems when attempting to change the speed. Therefore, you'll need to properly reposition the wedge wheels if they get out place. To do this, put the switching axle in fast speed with the outer wedge wheel touching the 1x15 blue, straight liftarm (as it should always be on fast speed), and push the other wedge wheel towards it until there are no more gaps between the switching motor's axle pin and the wedge wheels. You don't need to check to see if the wedge wheels have come apart every time you start up Brain-Bot, but be sure to check this occasionally.*

Conclusion

Brain-Bot shows you just how different things can be when switching from one strategy to another. Right from the start in the M-class strategy we are getting into some complex sumo-bots—and this is just the chassis! However, this chassis is so full-featured it could almost be called a sumo-bot in itself; almost, but not quite. It's missing something quite vital: sensors. In the next chapter, you will meet ZR2. This M-class sumo-bot adds more fun and interesting subassemblies, quite a few sensors, and utilizes the features of this chassis and some nice programming to become a formidable foe.

However, before continuing, keep in mind that the examples in this book are not intended to be a comprehensive representation of the M-class strategy, because there are just too many possibilities (it would be like trying to make a book conclusive on all the things you can make with LEGO). The purpose of the examples in Part Three of this book is to generalize the M-class strategy, and to help you to understand and appreciate this strategy. Because of the way Brain-Bot is designed, it is limited in one way or another. In other words, Brain-Bot can't be everything!

But Brain-Bot *can* show you many M-class tricks, substrategies, mechanisms, and more. Learn from these examples; adapt the mechanisms into your own designs; take the information, tips, and tricks presented and store them in your brain; and most of all, remember to have fun while you're doing it!

CHAPTER 7

Brain-Bot Version ZR2

BRAIN-BOT VERSION ZR2 is huge, fearsome-looking, and a competitor's biggest nightmare: a tough, pushy, and aggressive opponent with brains. And with two sets of "eyes" on the ends of "tentacles," it looks like some kind of alien creature. But what does this sumo-bot do? ZR2 is summed up in just a few words: two-sided, double trouble. Observe Figure 7-1, which shows ZR2, and you'll understand why.

Figure 7-1. Completed Brain-Bot Version ZR2

Two-Sided, Double Trouble?

Two-sided, double trouble may be somewhat redundant, but it accurately describes who ZR2 is and what it can do. You know how some sumo-bots have a strong front side but a weak back side? Well, ZR2 solves this problem in an unconventional way: why not make the back the front and the front the back—at any time! In other words, the back and the front are going to be the same. This ability can be mainly attributed to Brain-Bot's nearly perfect symmetry. Its left side is equal to its right side, and its front is nearly equal to its back.

With this approach in mind, ZR2 has the potential to "attack" from either end. "Wait a second—how can ZR2 detect the opponent? I don't see any bumpers!" It's quite true that ZR2 lacks bumpers, but ZR2 isn't lacking a means of detecting sumo-bots. Right at the front and back of the sumo-bot, directly connected to the chassis, are touch sensors, which allow ZR2 to detect the opponent. These sensors do not detect by impact with the opponent—at least not directly—but instead impact with *gears*. Each of these touch sensors keeps track of the speed of a 40t gear on the Brain-Bot chassis, and when these gears have slowed down, ZR2 can tell it has run into the opponent. It takes some special programming to accomplish this, and you'll see what it is and how it works when we program ZR2. We'll also discuss the mechanical aspects of this setup in more detail in the final assembly, when we add the touch sensors.

ZR2 holds even more surprises: when it detects the line, it can simply go in reverse without turning. After all, the front is the back and the back is the front. You might be thinking, "To use this 'two-sided, double-trouble approach,' aren't we going to need to rig the robot in a special way? For example, won't we need *two* light sensors?" You're absolutely right. We'll need two line-detecting light sensors *and* more programming genius. You can set up a sumo-bot to use two line-detecting light sensors in several ways; in this chapter, you'll see one way to do this.

In this chapter, we're going to discuss two subjects that we will implement into ZR2's program: *speed theory* and *direction theory*. Speed theory has to do with keeping track of the robot's speed with a variable. Direction theory has to do with keeping track of the robot's direction of travel with variables. We'll go into detail on these subjects when we do the programming.

There are yet two more features of ZR2 to mention: its counter-rotating wheels (CRWs) and a slope that covers the entire back (except that there isn't a back or front now!). CRWs come in a variety of sizes and configurations. In ZR2, they are four medium-sized wheels positioned on the front that are always rotating at the same speed as ZR2's main wheels. And since ZR2's main wheels can change speed with a transmission, the CRWs can change speed, too! But what exactly is the purpose of the CRWs? You'll find out as you build ZR2, but I'll tell you this much: in ZR2, the CRWs are an offensive mechanism.

ZR2's slope is unique and built predominately with parts from the RoboSports Expansion Pack (RSEP). What makes this slope unique is its method of attachment to the chassis. Slopes can be a little difficult to attach and orient, and we'll get into how we attach this one in the sections about the light sensor mount subassembly and final assembly.

So, what's ZR2's substrategy? ZR2's first goal is to find the opponent (which should be any sumo-bot's first goal). After detecting the opponent, using its special touch sensor setup, it switches to slow speed and attacks the opponent with the end holding the slope or the end with the CRWs, depending on whether ZR2 is in forward or reverse. ZR2, as previously mentioned, will go in the opposite direction upon detecting the line and also employs an efficient maneuvering strategy. Now that you know the basics of ZR2, let's construct this sumo-bot!

Constructing Subassemblies for ZR2

To construct ZR2, you will need pieces from the RIS and two expansion packs: RoboSports Expansion Pack (RSEP) and Ultimate Builders Expansion Pack (UBEP). To get an idea of the types and number of parts that are necessary, take a look at the bill of materials in Figure 7-2.

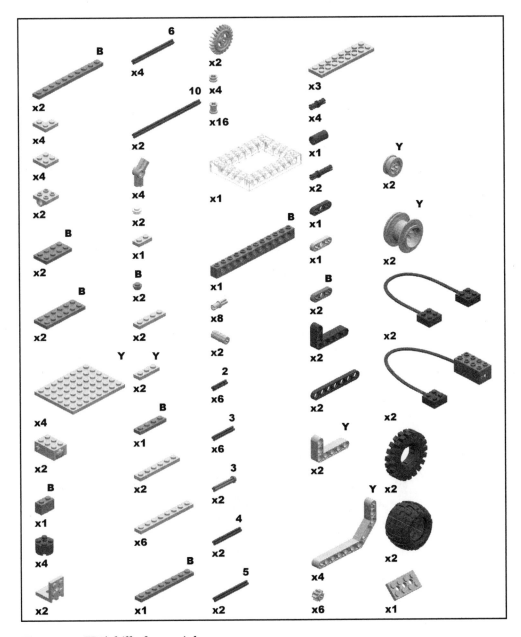

Figure 7-2. ZR2's bill of materials

NOTE *Although the RSEP isn't vital to ZR2, there are some pieces we use from it that aren't common. If you happen to have the same parts that are used from the RSEP (they don't have to be in the same color), you can use those; otherwise, you'll need to acquire the parts or the RSEP itself. Like its ECEP companion, the RSEP has long been out of production. The best place to look for it is on eBay.*

You'll build six subassemblies for ZR2: a CRW subassembly, light sensor subassembly, light sensor mount subassembly, slope subassembly, and two eyes subassemblies. Additionally, you'll add a few pieces in the final assembly, but the majority of the piece-to-piece construction goes on in these subassemblies.

The CRW Subassembly

What you will soon notice is that the CRWs rotate in the opposite direction of ZR2's main wheels. That shouldn't be too surprising—these are *counter*-rotating wheels. But why make them rotate in the opposite direction? To repel the opponent? That's a possibility, but not the real purpose.

The answer is an explanation of another timeless robotic sumo trick. When two sumo-bots collide, and one of them has counter-rotating wheels like these, they can actually *flip* the opponent. The CRWs are rotating in the same direction that the opponent is pushing, meaning the opponent can actually be pushed upward by the wheels and eventually flipped—a great trick indeed!

Even though Figure 7-3 shows only two CRWs in this subassembly, there will be four. You will add the other two CRWs in the final assembly. This is necessary because of the cramped conditions. If you put the other two wheels on now, they will prevent you from adding other important pieces later during the final assembly.

Figure 7-3. The completed CRW subassembly

Step 1 begins the subassembly with four *3x5 L-shaped liftarms*, which can be found in the UBEP, and two long friction pins.

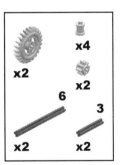

 CRW Subassembly Step 1

Step 2 adds two gears on each side—an 8t and a 24t crown gear—and their accompanying axles and bushings. Don't worry about the "loose" #3 axles—you'll strengthen them in the next step, and by the time ZR2 is completed, they'll be quite secure.

 CRW Subassembly Step 2

In step 3, take two of the RIS's *1x7 black half-liftarms* and place them across the axles. Then top off the ends of the axles with half-bushings. What you did in this step is highly important. And now I'll explain why.

You were probably thinking in step 2, "Why did he choose #3 axles to put the 24t crown gears on? These axles can easily fall out of the liftarms! There's a lot more room for longer axles." Well, in truth, there isn't a lot more room. When you've attached this assembly to the chassis, there will be another liftarm directly in between each pair of 3x5 L-shaped liftarms; those "in between" liftarms hold *axle holes*, and those axle holes happen to be directly behind the #3 axles with a 24t crown gear. Of course, an axle hole is a hole for axles that prohibits any movement or rotation. If you lengthened the #3 axles, they would go into these holes and wouldn't be able to rotate! This is *part* of the reason why you're using #3 axles.

> **NOTE** *The 1x7 half-liftarms we use here are a little long for their purpose, as there will be an unused hole on the front and back end; a 1x5 half liftarm would actually be the best fitting piece. However, the RIS has only four 1x5 half-liftarms, and all of them are currently being used by the Brain-Bot chassis. The 1x7 half-liftarms are substitutes for 1x5 half-liftarms, but if you have additional ones, you can use those.*

The other part has to do with the fact that you still need to properly secure these axles to the subassembly. You'll notice that two-thirds of these #3 axles are "used," but there is still one-third "unused." These unused portions will work with other pieces to keep the 24t crown gears and essentially the #3 axles themselves in place. What you see in step 3 is responsible for securing the #3 axles: 1x7 half-liftarms and half-bushings that go *onto* the unused thirds.

You might think this setup is a little weak, but don't worry; when you do the final assembly, you will add another axle through each half-liftarm. Once that piece is added and when the final assembly is complete, the 1x7 half-liftarms will prove their worth. Overall, this setup greatly increases the gear's ability to withstand high levels of pressure.

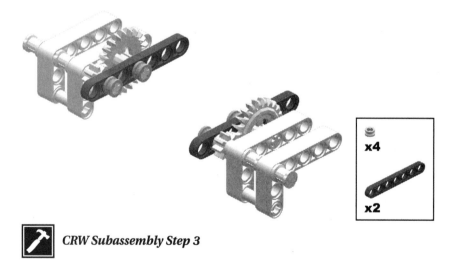

x4

x2

🔨 *CRW Subassembly Step 3*

In step 4, you add the actual #10 axles that the CRWs will go on, bushings, and two 8t gears. These 8t gears transfer the power down one stud's space on the assembly, which is good since you want the CRWs to be positioned a little lower.

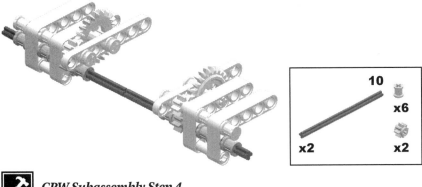

CRW Subassembly Step 4

Step 5 adds a set of wheels (the CRWs) from the RIS and more bushings. These wheels possess an interesting property: they can slip! Once a certain amount of pressure has been applied to them, the yellow center rotates, and the black tire can stay still. However, if *all* the CRWs on this assembly had the ability to slip, they would stop counter-rotating very quickly and prove to be inefficient. To prevent this, the other two wheels (which you'll add in the final assembly) do not have the ability to slip. In other words, 50 percent of the CRWs slip and 50 percent don't!

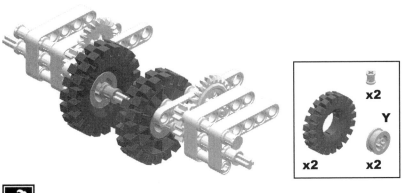

CRW Subassembly Step 5

The *pin joiner* we add in step 6 is intended to, as its name suggests, join the two sides of the assembly. Right now, the two sides could easily separate from each other. But once ZR2 is finished, they will *not* be doing any separating. However, there is more to this assembly technique than just joining sides together.

Consider what would happen if you placed all the CRWs on only one axle. The CRWs are connected to the wheel's power, and the wheels aren't always going in the same direction. With the CRWs on one axle that is plugged into the wheel's power, what will happen when the right side is in forward and the left side is in reverse? It hurts just to think about it! ZR2 couldn't turn, and you would hear the most horrendous, axle-wrenching, beam-snapping sound.

On the other hand, you don't want to use two separate axles for the CRWs. That would result in "axle droop," or axles protruding into midair—inefficiency at its worst. The solution is to use two separate axles and then join them together to act like one axle, using a pin joiner. This pin joiner allows the two axles to rotate in different directions at the same time.

x1

CRW Subassembly Step 6

That completes the CRW subassembly construction. It should look like the one shown in Figure 7-3, at the beginning of this section.

The Light Sensor Subassembly

The light sensor subassembly, shown in Figure 7-4, is a reminder of an impending issue: if we have two touch sensors and two light sensors, we have ourselves a "more sensors than input ports" problem. But there's no need to worry—a solution is just around the corner.

Figure 7-4. The completed light sensor subassembly

Do we use the light-sensor-and-touch-sensor-on-the-same-input-port trick? No, that setup won't work with ZR2. Because of his special setup, which we'll examine in the final assembly, each of ZR2's touch sensors must have their own input port. Although there may be more than one way to work this problem out, the most obvious thing to do then is this: put both light sensors on the *same* input port. Does this work? Actually, it does! When we do this, the reading comes in a little higher than normal, but we can still easily detect the line.

Construction for the light sensor subassembly is simple, quick, and composed of two steps. I threw in a few blue pieces from the RSEP, but you can easily substitute them with any other color you like.

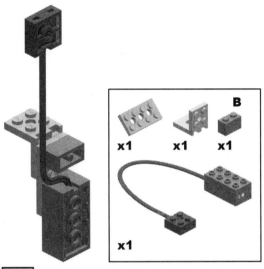

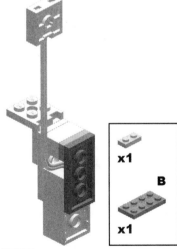

Light Sensor Subassembly Step 1

Light Sensor Subassembly Step 2

The Light Sensor Mount Subassembly

The light sensor mount subassembly, shown in Figure 7-5, is based around a transparent 6x8 brick with an open center. It contains—as the title alludes—a light sensor, but it also contains a 1x12 blue beam, which is braced with 1x3 half-liftarms. This beam has a slightly unusual but important purpose. This purpose has to do with ZR2's slope, which you will be building in a moment, so we're going to quickly discuss slopes and how you will attach ZR2's slope to the chassis.

Figure 7-5. The completed light sensor mount subassembly

Slopes are great fun, but they aren't exactly great fun when you're trying to build them. All too often, they result in "builder's block." Slopes are at (or are supposed to be at) slightly slanted angles—angles (almost) unprecedented to the LEGO world. The only way to get these crucially important angles is with unique and often hard-to-use techniques.

The 1x12 blue beam, and other pieces you'll add later, sandwiches the slope firmly together, allowing practically no breathing room. The bracing is there to prevent the beam from breaking off. It might sound a little crazy that this beam is going to "sandwich" a slope, but it's true; you'll see it happen in the final assembly.

In step 1, pull out and position the 6x8 transparent brick with an open center, found in the UBEP, two friction pins, and four corner plates.

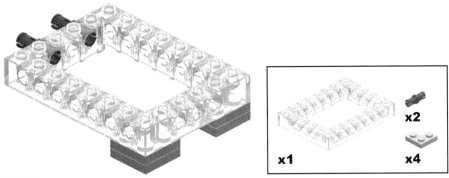

 Light Sensor Mount Subassembly Step 1

Step 2 adds the 1x12 blue beam (from the RSEP) we just talked about and two axle pins.

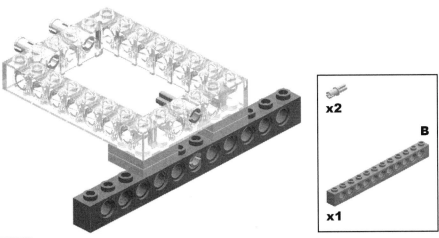

Light Sensor Mount Subassembly Step 2

In step 3, you do the bracing with two half-liftarms. You can actually use any color of liftarm you like; blue and gray are the colors I picked.

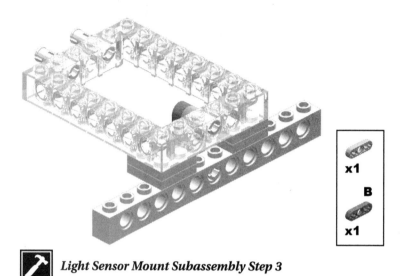

Light Sensor Mount Subassembly Step 3

Step 4 completes the assembly with several plates, including an angle plate, and a light sensor.

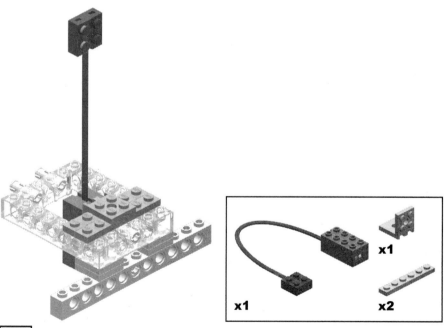

Light Sensor Mount Subassembly Step 4

The Slope Subassembly

It is here, in the slope subassembly section, that the RSEP comes in handy with its diverse 6x8 yellow plates. Sometimes nothing but large-sized plates will do, and this is definitely one of those times. Figure 7-6 shows the slope subassembly with these big plates.

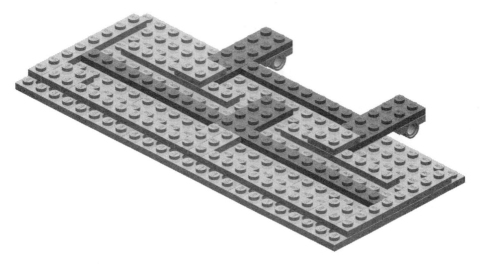

Figure 7-6. The completed slope subassembly

> **NOTE** *Back in February 2003, I undertook my largest LEGO MINDSTORMS project ever: Chameleobot the Quadruped. Four and a half feet long, with two RCXs, five motors, and more pieces than one would like to think about, Chameleobot was amazingly gigantic. This robot even went on to win an official Special Mention Award from the LEGO MINDSTORMS web site in the Inventions section. That was a case when large plates—including the 6x8 yellow plates from the RSEP—came in handy. If you would like to see some pictures of Chameleobot, visit* www.brickshelf.com/cgi-bin /gallery.cgi?f=45946. *Brickshelf is a fan-created web site for LEGO builders to post pictures of their LEGO creations, at no charge. Be sure to check Brickshelf out, too, at* www.brickshelf.com.

In step 1, position all four of the large, yellow plates and three 2x8 TECHNIC plates as shown, and then add all the different (much smaller) plates. These smaller plates begin the process of properly strengthening the larger plates.

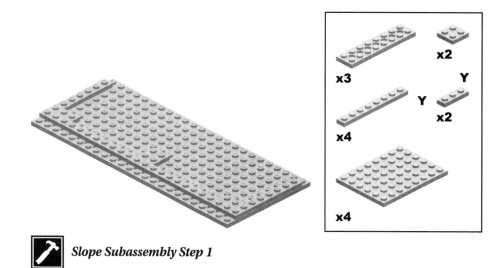

Slope Subassembly Step 1

Step 2 adds many more plates, which do a great deal of strengthening. Some of these plates are from the RIS, and some are from the RSEP.

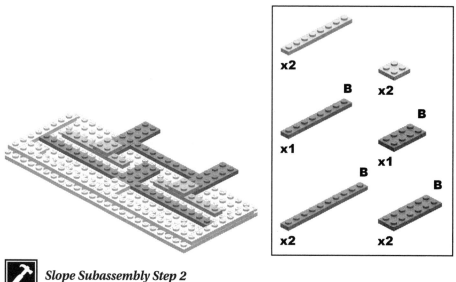

Slope Subassembly Step 2

Finally, in step 3, turn the model around to the other side and add a few plates to the bottom side. Also, add two *2x2 plates with holes*, which are found in the RIS. The 2x2 plates with holes will be your means of attaching the slope subassembly to the chassis.

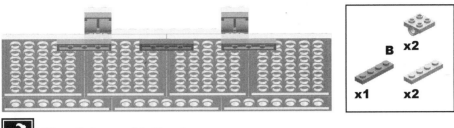

Slope Subassembly Step 3

The Left Eyes Subassembly

As usual, we want to add some characteristic features, such as some eyes. If the back of ZR2 is going to be the front, and the front the back, then the sumo-bot should have eyes in the front and back as well! The left eyes subassembly, shown in Figure 7-7, and right eyes subassembly accomplish this with a unique design, as I think you'll agree.

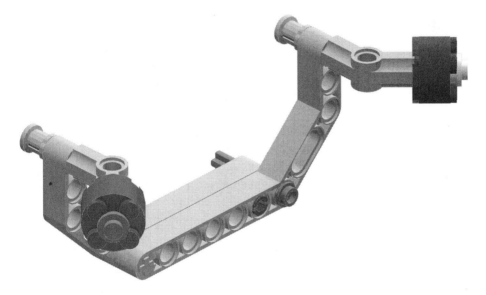

Figure 7-7. The completed left eyes subassembly

In step 1, pull out one of the large, yellow liftarms from your RIS and the pins and axle designated, and position them as shown. Step 2 adds another liftarm, another pin, and two #3 axles.

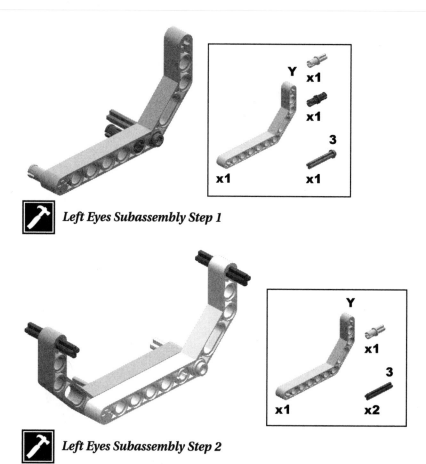

Left Eyes Subassembly Step 1

Left Eyes Subassembly Step 2

Using #4 angle connectors from the RIS, steps 3 and 4 position the eyes in a very "eye-like" way. The eyes consist of 2x2 round bricks and 1x1 round plates, like XK2's eyes. You are now finished with the left eyes subassembly and ready to move on to the right eyes subassembly.

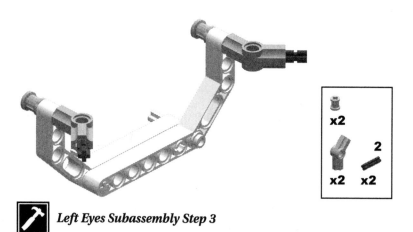

Left Eyes Subassembly Step 3

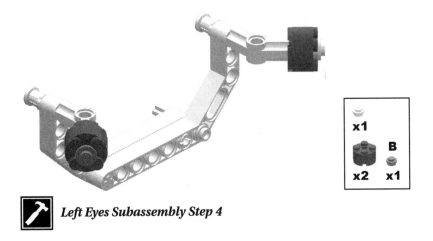

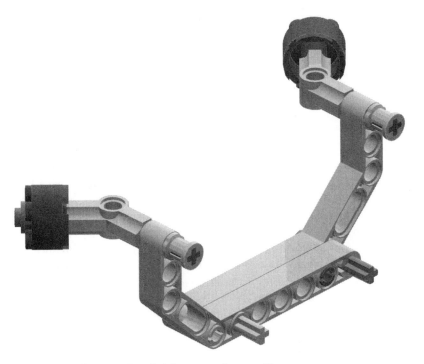

Left Eyes Subassembly Step 4

The Right Eyes Subassembly

The right eyes subassembly, shown in Figure 7-8, is a mirror image of the left eyes subassembly, and consists of the same pieces and steps. Follow the building instructions shown in the left eyes subassembly section to build this assembly, but switch the orientation of the pieces while you're building, so that your completed assembly looks like Figure 7-8.

Figure 7-8. The completed right eyes subassembly

Putting ZR2 Together

You are now ready to put this monstrous machine (which is actually a 2- to 3-pound LEGO sumo-bot) together. In step 1, take out the Brain-Bot chassis. For this version, you need to modify the chassis a bit.

Do you see the axles closest to the front of the chassis—the ones 40t gears are on? The axles there aren't long enough for the CRWs, and these are what you need to modify in step 1. Temporarily remove the 2x4 yellow plates above those axles and pull out the #6 axles that are in the blue axle extenders. Unfortunately, this isn't exactly easy to do. You'll probably need to pull out the 1x15 blue straight liftarms on the side of the chassis out a little to be able to yank the #6 axles out of there. Once you have successfully done so, replace them with #4 axles and put an axle extender on the end of each #4 axle.

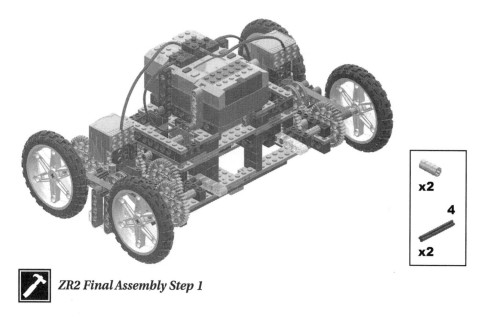

ZR2 Final Assembly Step 1

In step 2, replace the 2x4 yellow plates. Then pull out the **CRW subassembly** and position it as shown. There are two important parts to this step. First, slide #6 axles into the new axle extenders you added in step 1; these axles will also go through the 1x7 black half-liftarms on the CRW subassembly. And when they do go through, position an 8t gear in their way, so that the drivetrain is complete. Also, instead of pushing the #6 axles all the way in, push them *almost* all the way in, leaving just enough of the axle to stay inside the 1x7 half-liftarms. Next, take notched #2 axles and slide them through the outer 3x5 L-shaped liftarms on the CRW subassembly and into the transparent liftarm's axle holes. The CRW subassembly is now properly attached.

In the event that any of the CRWs that do not have the ability to slip are subjected to extremely high amounts of pressure—so high that they can't rotate—during a collision with the opponent, the corresponding 24t crown gear will pop out just a little. It will pop out to where the main 8t gear can rotate, but the 24t crown gear won't transfer that power. This is good, because it will prevent an "overload" of the gears. And, after the confrontation, the 24t crown gear will *come back*, so that everything is positioned about the same as it was before the collision. Because of the 1x7 half-liftarm and the half-bushings, the 24t crown gear and its #3 axle are drawn back.

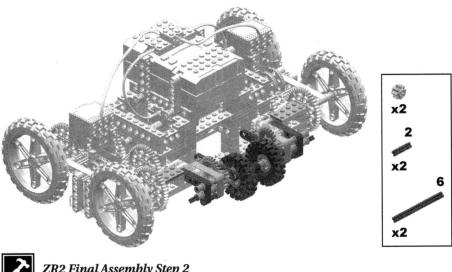

ZR2 Final Assembly Step 2

Step 3 adds the other two wheels onto the CRW subassembly's #10 axles, the **light sensor subassembly**, and a touch sensor with its electrical wire. The wheels you add in this step can be found in the RSEP or the Exploration Mars Expansion Pack (EMEP). The touch sensor, which is right up against a 40t gear, is your sumo-detection system; in other words, it allows ZR2 to detect the opponent.

Like 24t gears, 40t gears contain holes in their "faces," and in ZR2, these holes cause the touch sensors to be pressed and released as the 40t gear is rotating. If the touch sensor's clicker is directly in the middle of one of these holes, the touch sensor is in the "unpressed" state, as the hole provides sufficient room for the clicker to protrude outwards. However, if the hole is *not* directly in front of the touch sensor's clicker, the 40t gear itself forces the sensor's clicker inwards, and thus places the sensor in the "pressed" state. This is how the touch sensor can be pressed and released by the 40t gear.

When ZR2 has run into the opponent, the number of times the touch sensor is clicked reduces, since the 40t gear isn't rotating as fast. Using some programming, we can detect this difference and then react to it. Actually, this is a kind of makeshift rotation sensor; you *could* use a rotation sensor instead of this touch sensor, but touch sensors work well, too. Incidentally, some MINDSTORMS fans state that "bumpers" of this type are better than "traditional" bumpers, such as the ones you saw in Chapters 4 and 5, because they can detect hits from virtually anywhere, not just where the bumper is positioned.

Attach the light and touch sensor's electrical wires to the RCX like this:

- The **light sensor** goes on **input port 2**.

- The **touch sensor** goes on **input port 3**.

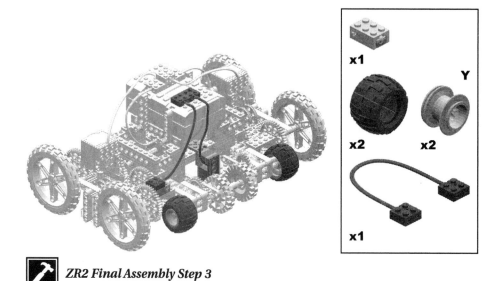

🔨 *ZR2 Final Assembly Step 3*

For step 4, turn the model around to the back and attach the **light sensor mount subassembly** as shown. At the heart of the chassis are two 1x4 beams, into which you snap this subassembly's friction pins. Once you have the subassembly in place, attach the light sensor's electrical wire to **input port 2**.

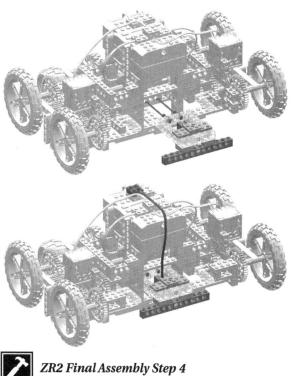

🔨 *ZR2 Final Assembly Step 4*

In step 5, add a second touch sensor for the sumo-detection system. By using two touch sensors, you can get maximum efficiency and ensure that you can detect a hit from either side of the sumo-bot. Attach the touch sensor's electrical wire to **input port 1** on the RCX.

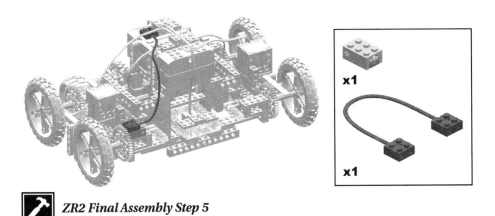

ZR2 Final Assembly Step 5

Step 6 attaches the **slope subassembly**. There is a little trick to this step, involving the assembly's 2x2 plates with holes. First, flip the back slope subassembly upside down. Next, position the 2x2 plates with holes as shown in the image: in between the transparent liftarms and the large, transparent brick with an open center. Then, and only then, attach the assembly. Take #5 axles and push them through the axle holes of the transparent liftarms, through the 2x2 bricks with holes, and into the transparent brick with an open center.

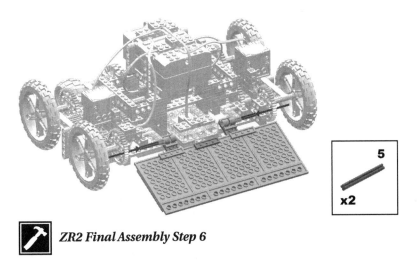

ZR2 Final Assembly Step 6

Right now, the slope can freely rotate. You need to prevent that, which you'll do by sandwiching it in between pieces, as mentioned earlier in the "Light Sensor Mount Subassembly" section. The assembly currently has pieces underneath the slope that prevent it from moving downward, but not pieces above it. You take care of this in steps 7 and 8 with two 1x3 half-liftarms and two axle pins. What you're going to do is push these pieces onto the back end of the transparent brick with an open center. But realize that this seemingly small task is far from ordinary. Read the following instructions carefully, because you are positioning these pieces in a very particular way.

First, push two axle pins into the transparent brick with an open center. Then push the half-liftarms onto the axle pins. Now comes the unordinary part: pull out the half-liftarms and axle pins just a little, but far enough that the outer half-liftarm is directly over the upside-down 1x4 blue plate on the slope subassembly. With these pieces pulled out only a minute amount, the slope subassembly is completely sandwiched. If the half-liftarms and axle pins were pushed in all the way, the slope subassembly would be free to move upwards.

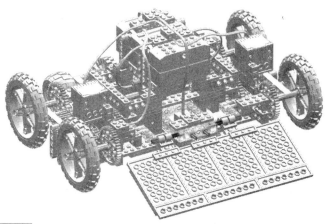

x2

 ZR2 Final Assembly Step 7

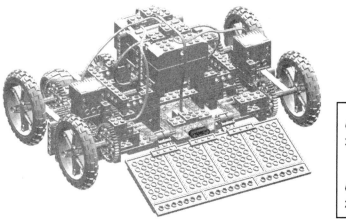

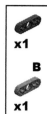
x1

B

x1

 ZR2 Final Assembly Step 8

Step 9 is the final one. Pull out your **left eyes subassembly** and the **right eyes subassembly**, and push them into the blue pins with a stop bush that are part of Brain-Bot's RCX subassembly.

 ZR2 Final Assembly Step 9

You're finished! You're completed ZR2 should look like the one shown in Figure 7-1 at the beginning of this chapter.

Formulating a Solid Programming Solution for ZR2

As mentioned in Chapter 6, Brain-Bot is a really smart bot. And we make it smart with the program presented in this chapter. For this program, we're still going to be using NQC's access control feature. This works so excellently and smoothly, we'll keep it. (If it's not broken, don't fix it—right?) You may be wondering, if we use access control again, does that mean this program will be just the same old thing? By no means; because of its special features, access control provides us with a chance to create programs that were otherwise difficult or impossible to make. Okay, we have a slope, CRWs, a line to detect… how many tasks do we need? More than we've used in previous chapters, that's for sure! Take a look:

- **Line-detection task:** If you're worried that this task is going to be "boring" and "simple" because we have this same task in all our programs, well, no need to worry about that! Due to the combination of variables we are using, the line-detecting task comes in at number 1 in the list of most complex tasks in this program.

- **Sumo-detection task:** This task receives information from two other tasks that monitor the touch sensors. Using that information, it can determine if ZR2 has made contact with the opponent. If contact has been made, this task will switch ZR2 to slow speed.

- **Touch-sensor-registry tasks:** Actually, there are two tasks here, but they both have the same job: monitoring a touch sensor. These are the tasks that provide the sumo-detection task with its information.

- **Maneuvering task:** Unlike all our previous maneuvering tasks, this one actually does maneuver the robot. This task uses small, but effective, turns to maneuver ZR2 over the arena, and is noticeably longer than the maneuvering task in Chapter 5. This task must now be able to tell if the sumo-bot is traveling in forward or reverse, and this generates more code.

- **NQC header:** In reality, this isn't a task, but that doesn't mean it's not important. Do you remember using headers in the previous chapter? We'll be doing that in this chapter as well, for the reasons mentioned in Chapter 6.

Before we go any further, let's talk about the speed theory and direction theory I mentioned at the beginning of the chapter. And let's begin with speed theory and a scenario: ZR2 has just found the opponent, switched to slow speed, and is gleefully shoving the other sumo-bot forward. Suddenly, the opponent slips out of ZR2's grasp, and at that very same moment, ZR2 detects the line encircling the arena. Since the line-detecting task has the highest priority, it gets control immediately. But wait! ZR2 is still on slow speed! Yes, it still sees the line, and yes it still avoids the line, but in the aftermath, ZR2 is still on slow speed. How can we prevent this? How can ZR2 know when to switch to fast speed when it sees the line, and know when not to change speed?

One word sums up the answer: variables. We will keep track of ZR2's current speed with a variable named speed. If ZR2 is in fast speed, speed is 0. If it's in slow speed, speed is 1. Every time ZR2 changes speed, the speed variable is updated; in this way, we always know which mode ZR2 is in. With this surprisingly pain-free system, we can tell ZR2 to get back in fast speed if it goes over the line while on slow speed.

Now let's talk about direction theory and begin with another scenario: ZR2 is going along, minding its own business, when it detects the line—for ZR2, no big deal. It reverses direction and starts heading the other way. After going in reverse for a little while, ZR2 detects the line again with its other light sensor. What happens? It goes straight over the line! Why would this happen? The line-detecting task tells ZR2 to go in reverse once it has seen the line. However, ZR2 is *already* going in reverse. The results are, obviously, disastrous. What should we do?

The solution is to use the direction theory. This is based on essentially the same concept as the speed theory. To keep track of ZR2's direction of travel, we are going to use two variables: fwd (for forward) and rvs (for reverse). Every time ZR2 changes its direction, the program updates these variables. Using these variables, ZR2 will always know if it is traveling in forward or reverse; consequently, ZR2 will always know if it should go forward or reverse when it detects the line.

And exactly how will ZR2's program be able to tell that it has rammed the opponent or the opponent rammed it? Well, as I stated earlier, it's going to take some programming smarts, and you'll see what they are soon.

Programming ZR2 with the Solution

You can probably guess the first part of the program we will examine: the NQC header. Then we will proceed with the programming for the calibration function and tasks.

Creating the NQC Header

Do you remember what the header back in Chapter 6 looked like? This one is pretty similar, at least in the sense of its organization. Take a look at the header in Listing 7-1.

Listing 7-1. Brain-Bot-ZR2.nqh

```
/* Brain-Bot-ZR2.nqh - A file holding important
* instructions for Brain-Bot version ZR2.
* To be included in ZR2's main program */

// motors
#define Left OUT_A
#define Right OUT_C
#define Switch OUT_B

// constants
#define CHANGE 85
#define CHANGER 45
#define CALIBRATION 50
#define SEARCH  100
#define SPIN 65
#define GO 565
#define AMOUNT 3
#define TOUCH 3

// sensors
#define Clicker SENSOR_1
#define See SENSOR_2
#define Clicker2 SENSOR_3

// go forward
void Forward()
{
   OnFwd(Left+Right);
}

// go in reverse
void Reverse()
{
   OnRev(Left+Right);
}

// switch gears to fast speed
void SwitchF()
{
   OnRev(Switch);
   Wait(CHANGER);
   Off(Switch);
}
```

```
// switch gears to slow speed
void SwitchS()
{
   OnFwd(Switch);
   Wait(CHANGE);
   Off(Switch);
}

// spin in place
void Turn()
{
   Rev(Left);
   Fwd(Right);
   Wait(SPIN);
}
```

NOTE *All the following code makes use of the constants presented in this header. Instead of adding all the definitions of the constants again in each code example, you can go back to the header here to determine each constant's value.*

What you might have noticed was that the gear-switching functions, SwitchF() and SwitchS(), use different constants for the period of time the switching motors are powered. The reason for this is a mechanical one. By the time ZR2 has finally recognized it has run into the opponent, it has been slowed down considerably, and extra stress is being exerted on its motors. When it attempts to switch gears, using the basic 0.35 second power time, the attempt will usually fail.

You can see why this happens by taking a closer look into the process of switching gears. When switching gears, the teeth must always match up—if there's no match, there's no switch. Cars use special mechanics to deal with teeth matching, but in the LEGO MINDSTORMS world, you must have all the gears running when activating the gear switch. If everything is sitting still, and you activate the transmission, there's absolutely no guarantee that the teeth will match up. When you have all the gears constantly rotating, the transmission can easily do its job, because at some point, the gears *will* match up.

When ZR2 has run into the opponent and slowed down considerably, it's a little difficult for the gears to switch speeds; their chance of matching up with the other gears has been reduced because ZR2 has slowed down. However, their chance of meshing properly with the other gears hasn't disappeared—everything is still moving, just at a slower pace. What we need is for the program to give the switching motors more time to switch the gears to slow speed; more time means more chances to properly make the switch. Therefore, the CHANGE constant in SwitchS() has been raised to 0.85 second.

NOTE *The* SwitchF() *function uses the* CHANGER *constant, which has a value of 0.45 second. Switching to fast speed remains pretty easy, so 0.45 second is sufficient for the* SwitchF() *function.*

That covers the NQC header. Now we can turn our attention to the calibration function.

Programming the Calibration Function

The calibration function actually won't contain anything different from what we have been doing. We only need to tailor it to this program.

```
/* This function calibrates the
 *  "line searching" light sensors */
void Calibrate()
{
    until(Clicker2==1);
    line=See;
    threshold=line+AMOUNT;
    until(Clicker2==0);
    PlaySound(SOUND_CLICK);
    until(Clicker2==1);
    until(Clicker2==0);
    PlaySound(SOUND_CLICK);
    Wait(CALIBRATION);
}
```

Other than the fact that we use the touch sensor on the front of ZR2 in this function (I'll explain how to do the calibration in the "Testing ZR2" section later in this chapter), this function is similar to ones you've seen in earlier chapters.

Programming the Line-Detection Task

What's next? We tackle the line-detecting task, as shown here:

```
// Task that watches for the line
task LWatch()
{
    // highest priority
    SetPriority(0);

    while(true)    // infinite loop - always check for line
    {
        until(See<=threshold); // until light sensor detects line

            acquire(ACQUIRE_USER_1)  // get control
            {
                if(speed == 1)    // if in slow speed..
                {
                    if(fwd == 1)    // if going forward...
                    {
                    SwitchF();    // switch to fast
```

```
        speed = 0;    // tell program we're on fast speed
        Reverse();    // go the other way!
        Wait(SEARCH);
        fwd = 0;      // update variables!
        rvs = 1;
        PlaySound(SOUND_UP);
        }

        else      // if we're in reverse
        {
        SwitchF();    // switch to fast
        speed = 0;    // tell program we're on fast speed
        Forward();    // go the other way!
        Wait(SEARCH);
        fwd = 1;        // update variables
        rvs = 0;
        PlaySound(SOUND_UP);
        }
    }

    else      // this is if we're already on fast speed
    {
      if(fwd == 1)    // if we're going forward
      {
      Reverse();          // go the other way!
      Wait(SEARCH);
      fwd = 0;            // update variables
      rvs = 1;
      PlaySound(SOUND_UP);  // end of this task...
      }

      else      // if we're going in reverse
      {
      Forward();  // go the other way!
      Wait(SEARCH);
      fwd = 1;      // update variables
      rvs = 0;
      }
    }
  }
  }
}
```

Things were looking pretty normal for the first ten lines of code, and then suddenly it happens: we do not have two main divisions after the acquire statement, but *six*. There are now several variations of situations ZR2 could encounter because of the speed, fwd, and rvs variables. Better put, the combination of the speed theory and the direction theory is responsible for this. For instance, the sumo-bot could be going slow while on reverse, going fast in the forward direction, or going slow in the forward direction. The task has a certain method that it uses to find ZR2's current situation. Here's a summary of how the task works:

1. The program asks the robot's current speed. If the robot is on slow speed, the program goes on through the `if` statement. If the robot is on fast speed, the program goes on through the `else` statement.

2. After figuring out the speed, the program asks another question: Is the robot going in the forward direction or in reverse? After determining the answer, with the `fwd` and `rvs` variables, the program goes through another `if` or `else` statement.

3. With the speed and direction determined, the robot switches to fast speed, if needed, runs the motors in the opposite direction, and updates the variables.

4. Once all physical actions have been completed, the task is exited.

As you can see, this line-detection task is the most complex task you've come across so far in this book. Line-detection tasks aren't so boring after all!

Programming the Touch-Sensor-Registry and Sumo-Detection Tasks

We need to work on two more tasks that are closely related to each other: the touch-sensor-registry tasks. These are the tasks that contain the "special code," or more appropriately, a "special method." The code in the touch-sensor-registry tasks is neither complex nor lengthy; the method itself that allows ZR2 to detect the opponent is what can be considered special.

What we know for sure is that the touch sensors are constantly being pressed and released by the 40t gears, and that the consistency of the pressing and releasing action will decrease when ZR2 has run into the opponent. There must be a way to detect this decrease, and task `Spin()` shows you the technique:

```
// This task watches the touch sensor on input port 1
task Spin()
{
    while(true)      // infinite loop - continually check
    {
        until(Clicker==1); // until sensor clicked...
        until(Clicker==0); //...until sensor unclicked...
        ClearTimer(0); // ...clear timer 0
    }
}
```

What exactly is this task doing? Not much—all it does is wait until a specified touch sensor has been pressed and released, and then it clears a specified timer. But we need to take a look at the rest of the picture: another task will monitor the timer that Spin() is constantly clearing, and when that timer exceeds a set amount of time, the program *knows* that ZR2 has run into the opponent. For example, if it takes only 0.2 second to click and unclick the touch sensor—and thus clear the timer—and if the timer hasn't been cleared in 0.9 second, we know without a doubt that ZR2 has run into the opponent.

For ZR2's program, we also have an additional task named Spin2(), which is identical to Spin() in every respect except that it's named Spin2() and clears a different timer. In other words, Spin() is for one of the touch sensors, and Spin2() is for the other one.

These are the tasks that monitor the touch sensors. What about that other task that receives and processes the information provided by Spin() and Spin2()? That would be the task Crash(). Try to pick out the code in this task that watches the timers that are cleared by Spin() and Spin2() to see if they have exceeded a set amount of time:

```
// This is the "attacking" task
task Crash()
{
    // second highest priority
    SetPriority(1);

    while(true)   // infinite loop - continually check
    {
        // until timer 0 > than .3 seconds or timer 1 > .3 seconds
        until(Timer(0)>TOUCH || Timer(1)>TOUCH);

            acquire(ACQUIRE_USER_1)    // get control
            {
                if(fwd == 1)  // if going forward
                {
                    SwitchS();    // attack!
                    speed = 1;    // update speed variable
                    OnFwd(Left+Right); // go forward
                    Wait(1000);    // wait 10 seconds
                    SwitchF();     // switch to fast speed
                    speed = 0;     // update variable
                    ClearTimer(0);
                    ClearTimer(1);  // clear timers
                }

                else    // if going in reverse
                {
                    SwitchS();    // attack!
                    speed = 1;    // update speed variable
                    OnRev(Left+Right); // go in reverse
                    Wait(1000);    // wait 10 seconds
                    SwitchF();      // switch to fast speed
```

```
        speed = 0;      // update variable
        ClearTimer(0);
        ClearTimer(1);  // clear timers
      }
    }
  }
}
```

The specific time period in this task that, when exceeded, will cause the program to put ZR2 into "attack mode" is 0.3 second. We use the constant TOUCH to represent 0.3 second in the program. Here is the line of code, which is near the top of the Crash() task, that watches the timers and also uses the TOUCH constant:

```
// until timer 0 > than .3 seconds or timer 1 > .3 seconds
until(Timer(0)>TOUCH || Timer(1)>TOUCH);
```

When either touch sensor has not been pressed and released in more than 0.3 second, the task determines first if ZR2 is going forward or in reverse, and then switches to slow speed and turns on the motors in that direction for 10 seconds.

CAUTION *Depending on your RCX's battery power, the 0.3-second time period for the TOUCH constant may or may not work. RCXs with a relatively low battery power level will definitely not work. RCXs with a relatively new set of batteries most likely will work. If 0.3 second doesn't appear to be working, you have two options. First, you can put fresh batteries in your RCX. Alternatively, raise the value of TOUCH in 0.1-second increments, but realize that the performance will decrease proportionally. The larger TOUCH is, the longer it takes ZR2 to detect a hit; the longer it takes ZR2 to detect a hit, the harder and more inefficient it is for ZR2 to switch to slow speed. A value of 0.4 for TOUCH works pretty well, but if you go much beyond that, ZR2's performance will decrease noticeably.*

"Only 10 seconds?" Yes, just 10 seconds. We have ourselves another "MINDSTORMS problem," and I had to combat it with those 10 seconds. Here is the problem: after detecting the opponent, when should ZR2 switch back to fast speed? Let's say we had ZR2 switch to slow speed upon detection of the opponent and stay that way. If the opponent gave ZR2 just a tiny jolt and then moved away, ZR2 would be left on slow speed until it reached the line. ZR2 being on slow speed—unnecessarily—for 20 seconds doesn't sound too appealing.

For ZR2, the issue of trying to decide when to switch back to fast speed on the basis of touch sensor clicks is a somewhat difficult one. I wanted a simple solution, so I used the following plan: after detecting the opponent, wait 10 seconds and then switch back to fast speed. If ZR2 is still pushing the opponent, it can switch back to slow speed and wait another 10 seconds. If it isn't pushing the opponent, then it's back on fast speed, as it should be.

Programming the Maneuvering Task

I mentioned that the maneuvering task would need to be able to determine whether ZR2 was traveling in forward or reverse. Here's the reason: if the maneuvering task simply told ZR2 to go forward for a certain amount of time and then execute a turn, what would happen when ZR2 starts heading in reverse after it detected the line? It would almost immediately begin going forward again because of the maneuvering task! What the maneuvering task needs is a section for when the sumo-bot is going in reverse. And that's exactly what ZR2's maneuvering task does.

```
// Our maneuvering task
task Maneuver()
{
   // third highest priority
   SetPriority(2);

   while(true)   // infinite loop - continually do this
   {
        acquire(ACQUIRE_USER_1) // get control
        {
          if(fwd == 1)  // if going forward
          {
          while(true)   // infinite loop - continually do this
          {
          OnFwd(Left+Right);
          Wait(GO);         // go straight for a while
          stop Crash;       // turn off the Crash task
          Turn();        // make a turn
          Fwd(Left+Right);
          Wait(SEARCH);     // go forward for a second
          ClearTimer(0+1);  // clear the timers
          start Crash;      // start Crash back up
          }
          }

          else      // if going in reverse
          {
            while(true)    // infinite loop - continually do this
            {
            OnRev(Left+Right);
            Wait(GO);         // go straight for a while
            stop Crash;       // turn off the Crash task
            Turn();        // make a turn
            Rev(Left+Right);
            Wait(SEARCH);     // go forward for a second
            ClearTimer(0+1);  // clear the timers
            start Crash;      // start Crash back up
            }
        }
     }
   }
}
```

If ZR2 is going forward, the program goes through the if statement; if ZR2 is going in reverse, the program goes through the else statement. What you might have noticed was that there was a lot of stopping and starting of Crash() in this task. Why do we do this? Consider what might happen when ZR2 makes a turn. One or both of the touch sensors might not get pressed and released within the 0.3-second time period, because the wheels would be in the process of changing direction, starting up again, and so on. Then, of course, Crash() will kindly step in with its higher level 1 priority and take complete control. To prevent this from happening, we actually turn off Crash() with the stop command, and then start it back up again at the very end of the task. For extra precaution, near the end of the task we have several lines of code that make ZR2 go straight for just a little while, and then clear the timers.

This approach of turning off Crash() does have its disadvantages, since the opponent might ram ZR2 during this maneuvering phase. However, we must ensure that the maneuvering task can take control at some point, as it is ZR2's only means of making turns on the arena. Speaking of turning, the maneuvering task does this with the Turn() function, which provides ZR2 with small but effective turns that will eventually sweep most of the arena's surface.

> **NOTE** *You might need to modify the power level for the switching motors. For instance, I have the switching motors on power level 4, but you might need it on 5, or possibly just 3; it all depends on the current battery power in your RCX. You will find the command for changing the power level of* OUT_B *near the top of the program shown in Listing 7-2.*

Putting the Program Together

You are now ready to see the entire program, shown in Listing 7-2. Don't forget to look back at the header for this program when you need to determine a constant's value.

> **NOTE** *Remember that you don't need to retype the programs in this book into BricxCC. All of the programs for this book are available from the Downloads section of the Apress web site (*www.apress.com*).*

Listing 7-2. ZR2_Access_Control.nqc

```
// ZR2_Access_Control.nqc
// A sumo-bot program for Brain-Bot Version ZR2

#include "Brain-Bot-ZR2.nqh"    // include our header

// set some variables
int line,threshold,fwd = 1,rvs = 0,speed = 0;
```

```
task main()
{
  SetSensor(See,SENSOR_LIGHT);      // let's not forget to
  SetSensor(Clicker,SENSOR_TOUCH);  // initialize our
  SetSensor(Clicker2,SENSOR_TOUCH); // sensors!

  SetPower(Switch,4);  // putting OUT_B at the correct power level

  Off(Switch);  // make sure these motors are in brake mode

  Calibrate();    // calibrating light sensor...

  OnFwd(Left+Right);    // get moving forward...

  ClearTimer(0);      // clear the timers
  ClearTimer(1);

  start LWatch;   // turn on all five tasks!
  start Maneuver;
  start Spin;
  start Spin2;
  start Crash;
}

// Task that watches for the line
task LWatch()
{
  // highest priority
  SetPriority(0);

  while(true)   // infinite loop - always check for line
  {
    until(See<=threshold); // until light sensor detects line

      acquire(ACQUIRE_USER_1)  // get control
      {
        if(speed == 1)   // if in slow speed..
        {
          if(fwd == 1)   // if going forward...
          {
          SwitchF();   // switch to fast
          speed = 0;   // tell program we're on fast speed
          Reverse();   // go the other way!
          Wait(SEARCH);
          fwd = 0;     // update variables!
          rvs = 1;
          PlaySound(SOUND_UP);
          ClearTimer(0+1); // clear the timers
          }

          else     // if we're in reverse
          {
```

```
            SwitchF();    // switch to fast
            speed = 0;    // tell program we're on fast speed
            Forward();    // go the other way!
            Wait(SEARCH);
            fwd = 1;        // update variables
            rvs = 0;
            PlaySound(SOUND_UP);
            ClearTimer(0+1); // clear the timers
            }
         }

      else     // this is if we're already on fast speed
      {
        if(fwd == 1)   // if we're going forward
        {
        Reverse();        // go the other way!
        Wait(SEARCH);
        fwd = 0;          // update variables
        rvs = 1;
        PlaySound(SOUND_UP);
        ClearTimer(0+1);  // clear the timers
        }

         else      // if we're going in reverse
         {
         Forward();  // go the other way!
         Wait(SEARCH);
         fwd = 1;    // update variables
         rvs = 0;
         PlaySound(SOUND_UP);
         ClearTimer(0+1);  // clear the timers
         }
        }
      }
    }
}

// This is the "attacking" task
task Crash()
{
   // second highest priority
   SetPriority(1);

   while(true)   // infinite loop - continually check
   {
      // until timer 0 > than 0.3 seconds or timer 1 > 0.3 seconds
      until(Timer(0)>TOUCH || Timer(1)>TOUCH);

         acquire(ACQUIRE_USER_1)    // get control
         {
           if(fwd == 1)  // if going forward
           {
```

```
                    SwitchS();   // attack!
                    speed = 1;   // update speed variable
                    OnFwd(Left+Right); // go forward
                    Wait(1000);    // wait 10 seconds
                    SwitchF();     // switch to fast speed
                    speed = 0;     // update variable
                    ClearTimer(0);
                    ClearTimer(1); // clear timers
                 }

               else   // if going in reverse
               {
                    SwitchS();   // attack!
                    speed = 1;   // update speed variable
                    OnRev(Left+Right); // go in reverse
                    Wait(1000);    // wait 10 seconds
                    SwitchF();     // switch to fast speed
                    speed = 0;     // update variable
                    ClearTimer(0);
                    ClearTimer(1);  // clear timers
               }
         }
      }
}


// Our maneuvering task
task Maneuver()
{
   // third highest priority
   SetPriority(2);

   while(true)   // infinite loop - continually do this
   {
         acquire(ACQUIRE_USER_1) // get control
         {
           if(fwd == 1)  // if going forward
           {
            while(true)   // infinite loop - continually do this
            {
            OnFwd(Left+Right);
            Wait(GO);          // go straight for a while
            stop Crash;        // turn off the Crash task
            Turn();         // make a turn
            Fwd(Left+Right);
            Wait(SEARCH);      // go forward for a second
            ClearTimer(0+1); // clear the timers
            start Crash;       // start Crash back up
            }
           }

           else       // if going in reverse
           {
```

```
            while(true)    // infinite loop - continually do this
            {
            OnRev(Left+Right);
            Wait(GO);          // go straight for a while
            stop Crash;        // turn off the Crash task
            Turn();         // make a turn
            Rev(Left+Right);
            Wait(SEARCH);      // go forward for a second
            ClearTimer(0+1);  // clear the timers
            start Crash;       // start Crash back up
            }
        }
    }
  }
}


// This task watches the touch sensor on input port 1
task Spin()
{
   while(true)       // infinite loop - continually check
   {
      until(Clicker==1); // until sensor clicked...
      until(Clicker==0); //...until sensor unclicked...
      ClearTimer(0); // ...clear timer 0
   }
}


// This task watches the touch sensor on input port 3
task Spin2()
{
   while(true)       // infinite loop - continually check
   {
      until(Clicker2==1); // until sensor clicked...
      until(Clicker2==0); //...until sensor unclicked...
      ClearTimer(1); // ...clear timer 1
   }
}


/* This function calibrates the
 * "line searching" light sensors */
void Calibrate()
{
    until(Clicker2==1);
    line=See;
    threshold=line+AMOUNT;
    until(Clicker2==0);
    PlaySound(SOUND_CLICK);
    until(Clicker2==1);
    until(Clicker2==0);
    PlaySound(SOUND_CLICK);
    Wait(CALIBRATION);
}
```

With the entire program observed, explained, and scrutinized, you are ready to do some testing!

Testing ZR2

Compile ZR2_Access_Control.nqc and download it to your RCX (following the procedure outlined in Chapter 3, in the "Downloading Programs to the RCX" section).

The good news is that you can do the calibration in the same way that you have for previous sumo-bots. Although there are two light sensors on ZR2, you need to put only one on the line when doing the calibration. If you have only one light sensor viewing the line during calibration, you will get a value of, for example, 75. Since you add 3 to that using the AMOUNT constant, you get 78 as your final value for triggering the line-detection task. During play, ZR2 will go over the line with *one* light sensor, read the value of 75 for the line, call <=, and detect the line. Because you calibrate ZR2 with *one* light sensor viewing the black line, it takes only *one* light sensor to activate the line-detection task.

Here is how you can calibrate ZR2:

1. Place ZR2 in such a way that its front light sensor is viewing the line.

2. Remove ZR2's front touch sensor and hold it in your hand. You'll be using this touch sensor to tell the RCX when to take the reading of the line and when to end the calibration function.

3. Press the Run button on the RCX to start the program.

4. Press and release the touch sensor's clicker. You should hear a click, indicating that the light sensors have now been calibrated.

5. Still holding the touch sensor in your hand, pick up ZR2 and position it in your arena.

6. Place the touch sensor back on the chassis. Several things could happen at this point. The touch sensor could immediately get pressed and released in the process, and you would hear a click. Make sure you get the touch sensor firmly on the chassis fast enough if this happens, because after the click, you have only a short amount of time before ZR2 starts up! Another scenario is that, after placing the touch sensor back on the chassis, nothing happens. To press and release the touch sensor, twist the wheel adjacent to it until the RCX emits a click. After you have the light sensors calibrated and the touch sensor pressed and released a second time, ZR2 should start moving.

Let's begin testing with the sumo-detection system. While ZR2 is moving along, firmly press its CRWs with your hand. In just a moment, it should switch to slow speed. Notice how the middle two CRWs have the ability to slip, as pointed out earlier. When activating the Crash() task, also try applying pressure to only one or two CRWs, ZR2's back slope, side, and anywhere else you might feel like, and watch its response.

Next, test the line-detection and maneuvering tasks. Line detecting isn't too hard to test, but it is interesting to watch because of ZR2's unique tactic. Something important to mention is the fact that after ZR2 has detected the line, it will execute the Turn() function *before* it reaches the other side of the line. If it didn't, ZR2 would always be going back and forth in a straight line on the arena!

ZR2 eventually makes a little turn after each time it detects the line and can therefore effectively maneuver the arena. All you need to do to see this happen after activating ZR2 is sit back and watch. ZR2 will detect the line, avoid it, and execute Turn() all by itself (sumo-bots are autonomous you know!).

Take those objects you have been using to test the other sumo-bots you've made, and get ready to test ZR2 with them. Use one to firmly press its CRWs; use another to press—or slide on—its slope; and take several and push ZR2 from the side. Also, place some of the objects on the arena and let ZR2 find them and push them out of the arena. Be creative! Try out as many situations as you can think of to get a feel for what ZR2 can do.

Considering the Pros and Cons of ZR2's Design

As usual, we need to do a summary of the results of all our building, programming, and testing. And again, we'll do this by summarizing the pros and then the cons.

The Pros

Here are the advantages of ZR2's design:

- The two-speed system makes ZR2 very efficient; it can go fast while searching and slow while pushing.

- The CRWs have the potential to flip the opponent.

- The slope can run underneath opponents.

- ZR2's "the back is the front and the front is the back" approach decreases chances of being pushed off the arena near the line.

- ZR2 can detect opponents without needing to use a bumper.

The two-speed system, CRW, slope, and specific strategies give ZR2 a fighting edge. Its unique "back is the front and front is the back" approach eliminates the need to make large turns upon detection of the line, and therefore greatly reduces its vulnerability when "escaping" from the line. In addition, the sumo-detection system ZR2 uses has particular advantages. Regardless of whether ZR2 is being pushed from the back, front, side, or at virtually any angle, ZR2 can detect the contact.

The Cons

The following are some disadvantages of ZR2's design:

- There are some instances where ZR2 can accidentally switch to slow speed.

- ZR2's switching subassemblies can get knocked off chassis.

- The extra wide structure causes ZR2 to sag a little in the middle.

- ZR2's wheels are vulnerable to a hit.

There are a few rare instances where ZR2 might accidentally switch to slow speed. The majority of these instances are caused by the battery power level in the RCX. If you have TOUCH on 0.3 second when you start ZR2, and then proceed to run ZR2 for 30 minutes, the battery power could drop enough so that 0.3 second wouldn't work. In this case, you should raise the value of TOUCH or put fresh batteries in your RCX. But even if ZR2 does accidentally switch to slow speed, it can get back on fast speed within 10 seconds.

There is one undesirable situation that is possible that I didn't include on the cons list, because it's rare. But I'm going to tell you about it, since you never know what can happen. This is the situation of an opponent with a slope going under ZR2's CRWs when ZR2 is going *away* from the opponent. Since ZR2 is going away from the opponent, its CRWs will be rotating in such a way that they would actually help the slope go under it. Many different conditions would need to be present for this to happen, but it is a possible disadvantage.

Concerning the switch subassemblies, there isn't quite as much strength as would be optimal in the connection between the 3/4 pins and the 1x7 blue liftarms. A direct hit to a switch subassembly could possibly separate the motor and its pieces from its 1x7 liftarm attached to the chassis. If you are fascinated by transmissions, gears, and switching subassemblies, feel free to modify or even reconstruct the switch subassemblies and to experiment with different ways to attach them to the chassis.

An obvious characteristic of Brain-Bot is its great width. This has the advantage of increased finding abilities: when you have a sumo-bot that wide, it's easier to run into the opponent. On the other hand, the super-width of Brain-Bot combined with its unique design causes it to sag a little in the middle. The bottom bracer subassembly helps to reduce this sag, but there will always be some sagging in this model. Fortunately, sagging isn't a serious problem.

The final disadvantage of the ZR2 is its unprotected wheels. They are open to getting rammed and pushed. Having the wheels protected is beneficial, of course, but leaving them unprotected won't cause any major problems. The seriousness of a side hit—hitting the wheels—is really based on the type of sumo-bot giving the hit. ZR2 has excellent traction, and, after a few seconds, should be able to get away from a side-pushing sumo-bot.

The wheels are also vulnerable because they have a slightly weak connection to the chassis. Although the connection they do have works fine, there are a few situations where problems could arise (for example, a wheel might get pulled out). You could fix this by protecting the wheels. When you have a beam (or liftarm, axle accessory, and so on) on one side of the wheel and another on the other side—and also all the proper bushings and other pieces in place—that wheel is not going to come out. Brain-Bot would need to be radically changed to switch over to protected wheels, but it is possible—that's another idea for modifying the Brain-Bot chassis.

Conclusion

ZR2 is quite different from XK1, isn't it? Now you can clearly see how different the M-class strategy is from the small-and-fast strategy. And after constructing and programming ZR2, you can also see how to build an M-class sumo-bot that can fight a round and come out on top.

This chapter wraps up the coverage of the M-class strategy—not for you, for this book. After building and programming the Brain-Bot chassis and then the full-fledged sumo-bot ZR2, you now have a working knowledge of the M-class strategy. Using your newfound knowledge and this book as a guide, it's up to you to create your own M-class sumo-bots.

I'd like to leave you with one last thought before you leave the M-class section of this book. This is that there is a feature that M-class sumo-bots can use—and which other sumo-bots can use as well—that can be quite beneficial: searching abilities. That is, using various methods and means to actively search for the opponent. The bonus chapter, "Brain-Bot Version ZR1," discusses this concept and shows you how to give the Brain-Bot design a searching ability. You can download this bonus chapter from the Downloads section of the Apress web site (www.apress.com).

And now let's sum up some of the important and useful points about the M-class strategy:

- Speed is important, but pushing power is important as well; either find the fine line between the two or use a transmission.

- Traction is extremely important—use good wheels on your sumo-bots.

- The ability to search for the opponent, with light sensors, custom sensors, and so on, is very advantageous.

- Don't design your sumo-bot and its program around a defensive program; go on the offensive.

- Keep your sumo-bots low to the ground. Slopes are quite common in this strategy.

- Don't be limited to the three input ports on the RCX—the more sensors, the more power. You saw just one way to go beyond that limitation in this chapter.

We're at the end of Chapter 7, and you've learned quite a bit: first, robotic sumo basics, then the small-and-fast strategy, and now the M-class strategy. You can now consider yourself an experienced and capable LEGO MINDSTORMS robotic sumo competitor. Go ahead and pat yourself on the back! With this knowledge, you can go on to make amazing sumo-bots. But that isn't all there is to robotic sumo. There is something else: *the big-sumo strategy*. For what calculus does for math, the big-sumo strategy does for robotic sumo! Gargantuan-Bot beckons from the next page.

Part Four

The Third Approach: The Big-Sumo Strategy

CHAPTER 8

The Gargantuan-Bot Chassis

MANY PEOPLE GET hung up on one idea when they first start doing LEGO MINDSTORMS robotic sumo: pushing power, strength, and toughness are what matter most. As I've stressed in the previous chapters, these are not the deciding factors. You must take many other factors into account to make a successful and realistic sumo-bot.

However, with the big-sumo strategy, things are different: *pushing power, strength, and toughness are what matter most!* Now please don't get me wrong; there are many other aspects that are quite important in the big-sumo strategy. But, overall, the big-sumo strategy is so much different than the previous strategies that we have covered that this common "rule" has been overruled.

Going with the toughness approach, the Gargantuan-Bot chassis, shown in Figure 8-1, uses four motors, all of which are for powering the wheels. All of the motors are put on just two output ports of the RCX—the left side's motors on one output port, the right side's motors on another—which leaves a free output port for later use. Gargantuan-Bot has many other interesting features, as you'll discover during the construction process.

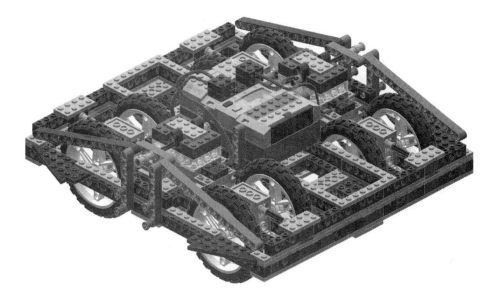

Figure 8-1. Completed Gargantuan-Bot chassis

Why Cover the Big-Sumo Strategy?

Whenever people think about LEGO MINDSTORMS robotic sumo, they often imagine the sumo-bots to be something like the Zip-Bam-Bot series presented in Part Two of this book: small, fast, and relatively simple. Indeed, most LEGO MINDSTORMS robotic sumo events revolve around sumo-bots like Zip-Bam-Bot. They are engaging to make, fun to watch, and usually easy to program. But then there are those other events: ones where serious MINDSTORMS fans who own thousands of parts, have years of experience, and are familiar with many programming languages make macho sumo-bots and duke it out.

Does this mean only a handful of people can make and compete with *big* sumo-bots? No, anyone with enough parts can make a big sumo-bot. It is true that the more experienced and serious fans are the ones who make huge sumo-bots and host events for them, but that doesn't mean you can't join in on the fun!

But why even cover the big-sumo strategy if it's not quite as common as other forms of robotic sumo? After all, as I pointed out, most people will be doing robotic sumo on a smaller scale. The reason is that *people like seeing huge robots, and they like seeing them fight each other.* There is something awe-inspiring in seeing a four-pound LEGO MINDSTORMS sumo-bot, and there is an unforgettable excitement that only the big-sumo strategy holds. Not only is it fun to watch huge robots, building your own gargantuan sumo-bot is special and exhilarating. It all goes back to *bigness*—people simply like big robots.

My hope is that Gargantuan-Bot will inspire you, even if you won't be able to build it due to lack of parts. Whatever your situation, get ready to see one big LEGO MINDSTORMS sumo-bot!

Building the Gargantuan-Bot Chassis

Gargantuan-Bot: the very name evokes an image of a colossal monstrosity. And that's exactly what Gargantuan-Bot is and what the big-sumo strategy is all about. Since this sumo-bot is so large, we'll need a very organized construction.

The Gargantuan-Bot chassis is much like a square. If that's the case, why not make four little squares that snap together to make the one big square, the chassis? That's exactly what we'll do, and I'll call these four little squares *quarter subassemblies* since they each make up a quarter of the model. We also have two motor bulk subassemblies, two key subassemblies, two middle connector subassemblies, and two side frame subassemblies. You'll see exactly what they are and what they do in their construction sections.

Gargantuan-Bot is constructed out of pieces from two RIS sets, two Exploration Mars Expansion Packs (EMEP), and the Ultimate Builders Expansion Pack (UBEP). Its bill of materials is shown in Figure 8-2.

NOTE *As you know from building the Brain-Bot chassis, it is safe to put more than one motor on an output port of the RCX; this is called* coupling motors. *What you may not know is that you're not getting twice the power by using two motors on one port. The RCX puts out a specified level of power for each output port. Therefore, the two motors on the one port* share *the allotted power. The benefit of coupling motors is that the motors don't need to work as hard when under strain (pushing a sumo-bot). In short, they share the load. This makes the sumo-bot more efficient and, in one sense, more powerful.*

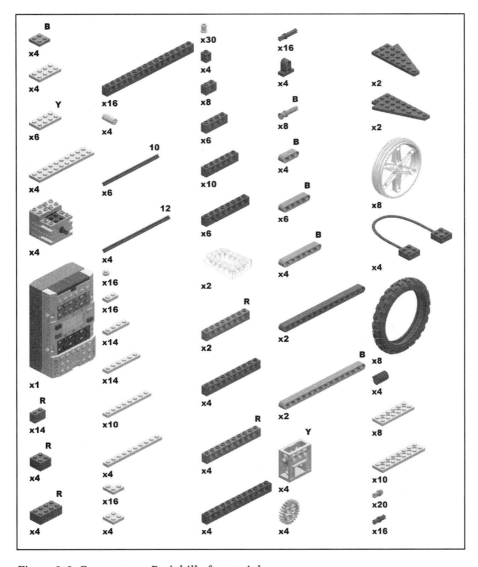

Figure 8-2. Gargantuan-Bot's bill of materials

Before you become convinced that you don't have all these pieces, look carefully at the bill of materials. We don't use every single part in the two RISs; we use *some* of the parts. The same is true for the expansion packs. So if you don't have all these sets, you still might have the pieces.

Before diving into the building instructions, let's take a look at two important design details.

Some Notes on Gear Ratios and Traction

The most important concept to begin with is the *gear ratio*, which will directly affect the speed. What gear ratio should Gargantuan-Bot possess? Gear switches are a possibility, but they generally bring along a lot of gears and, in turn, great complexity (you saw that firsthand in Chapter 6). If we're not using a gear switch, we're going to need to find the fine line between speed and push. This is extremely important; too slow is not good (if it's your only speed), but too fast means too little pushing power. So what speed does Gargantuan-Bot use? Figure 8-3 shows the gearing: a 1:24 ratio. Note that Figure 8-3 is a "cut-away" image—meaning there are many additional pieces to hold everything in place—and also that the axle the 24t gear is on is also the same axle the wheels will be on.

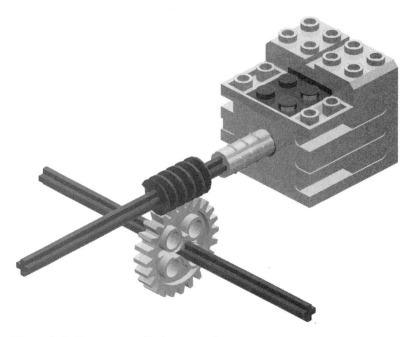

Figure 8-3. Gargantuan-Bot's gear ratio

"If Brain-Bot's slow speed was 1:75, isn't 1:24 going to be insufficient for Gargantuan-Bot?" Not really, as 1:24 offers a lot of pushing power and will suit our needs just fine. "Aren't there any other gears in the gear train besides the two in the image?"

Except for the other quarter assemblies, which have their own sets of gears, there aren't any other gears. Whenever possible, simplicity is often the best choice. (Of course, that doesn't rule out complexity, if it's used carefully and necessary for the results you wish to achieve.) The Gargantuan-Bot chassis as a whole (and the entire full-fledged sumo-bot in the next chapter) may not be simple, but its gear train can be considered simple. These two gears—a *worm gear* and a 24t gear—give just the ratio we need, so that's just what we'll use.

> **TIP** *There is another reason for using worm gears: they cannot be turned by external sources. This means* only *the motor can turn the worm gear. If you try to turn the 24t gear (which is on the same axle as the wheels) meshing with the worm gear, it won't work! This means the opposing sumo-bot can't budge Gargantuan-Bot's wheels, which is a great protective device!*

Another important concept in robotic sumo is *traction*. Someone once said, "If you forget traction for your sumo-bot, you can forget success for yourself." How true! After a side hit, a front slam, a rear-ending, or any other collision, if you don't have traction, your sumo-bot will be speedily pushed off the arena. Your sumo-bot must be able to get a *good* grip on the arena's surface. So what does Gargantuan-Bot do about it? By using *eight* of the large, black-and-white wheels that come directly from the RIS, we ensure that Gargantuan-Bot has a very high amount of traction. All those wheels make turning a little difficult, but Gargantuan-Bot *can* turn. The tradeoff between traction and turning abilities is, I believe, well worth it. Okay, enough talk. Let's build and think *big* while we're doing it!

> **CAUTION** *Never, ever, in any circumstances whatsoever, use tank treads for your sumo-bot's means of mobility. Out of all the methods of mobility, treads have the least traction. As soon as a sumo-bot with treads starts to get pushed, it will give way and eventually land outside the arena. Treads aren't useless—they are one of the best choices for rough terrain in non-sumo-bot applications. Just don't make the mistake of putting treads on your* sumo-bots*!*

The Left Quarter Subassembly

You will build *two* left quarter subassemblies; what's ironic is that one of the *left* quarter subassemblies goes in the back, on the *right* (well, it's on the right when you're attaching it, not when you're viewing the sumo-bot from the front).

As shown in Figure 8-4, the left quarter subassembly holds, among other pieces, two wheels, a motor, two gears, and a *gearbox*. Gearboxes are one of a MINDSTORMS fan's best friends. They completely encase a worm gear and a 24t gear, and they can easily attach to beams.

Figure 8-4. Completed left quarter subassembly

> **TIP** *Gearboxes are found in two expansion packs: the EMEP and UBEP. The EMEP includes two gearboxes, and the UBEP has a clear, transparent gearbox. As of this writing, you can purchase gearboxes from* www.plestore.com.

In step 1, we begin with a gearbox. Not only a gearbox, but also a worm gear and four 3/4 pins. Take that worm gear and push it into that little empty space in the gearbox; after a little squeeze, it should pop into the space and stay there. The pins will be your means of attaching the gearbox to the main structure of the subassembly, which you will be, by the way, building *onto* the gearbox. That's what step 2 is about: grab two 1x16 beams and snap them onto the 3/4 pins.

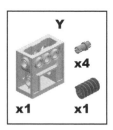

 Left Quarter Subassembly Step 1

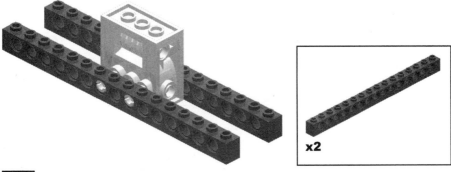

 Left Quarter Subassembly Step 2

Steps 3 and 4 add a motor, a 24t gear, and two long (and important) axles. The longer #12 axle goes on the bottom and holds the 24t gear, and the #10 axle goes on the motor's shaft and powers the worm gear. The #12 axle is also the axle the wheels will be going on.

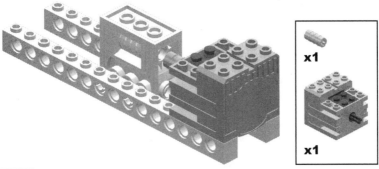

 Left Quarter Subassembly Step 3

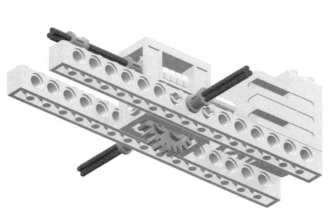

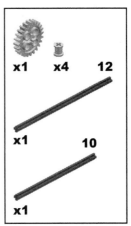

 Left Quarter Subassembly Step 4

Step 5 slides the wheels onto the subassembly. They are, once again, the wheels we have been using throughout the book: the large "motorcycle" wheels.

Left Quarter Subassembly Step 5

In step 6, turn the model around and add two 1x16 beams and two 2x6 TECHNIC plates to hold the beams together and two long friction pins.

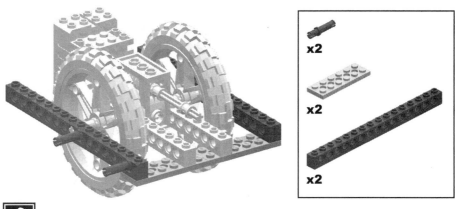

Left Quarter Subassembly Step 6

Step 7 adds a number of bricks and one 2x2 plate. One of the bricks you add in this step is quite important, but you won't find out why until the next chapter!

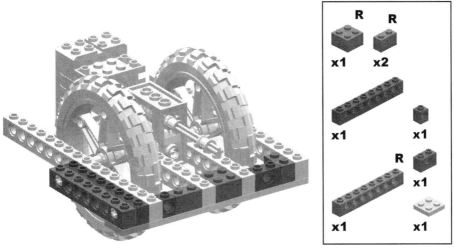

 Left Quarter Subassembly Step 7

Steps 8 through 11 build up the front section of this assembly with plates, bricks, and beams. Notice how you direct the axle on the motor's shaft into a 1x2 beam. This prevents the axle from sagging at one end.

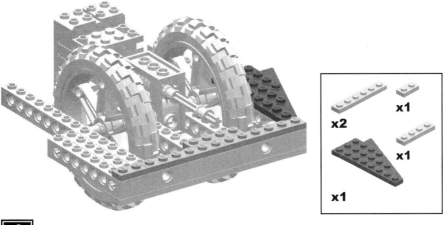

Left Quarter Subassembly Step 8

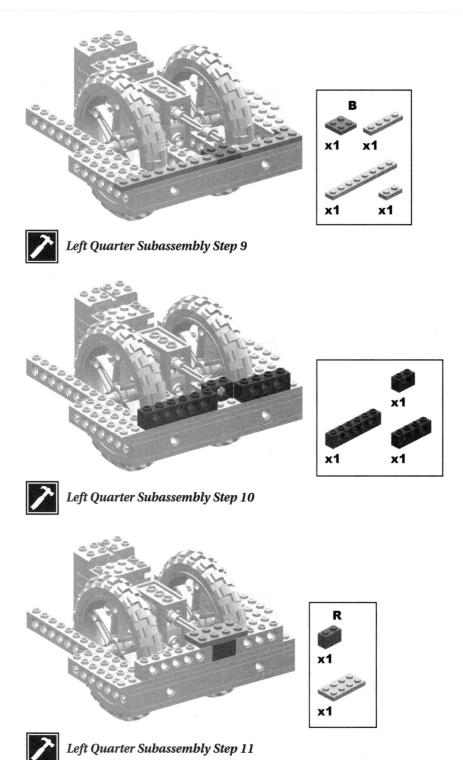

B

x1   x1

x1   x1

Left Quarter Subassembly Step 9

x1

x1   x1

Left Quarter Subassembly Step 10

R

x1

x1

Left Quarter Subassembly Step 11

Turn the model around to the back, so you can do some work there. Steps 12 and 13 attach a 1x12 beam and some plates, including a yellow 2x4 plate and four corner plates.

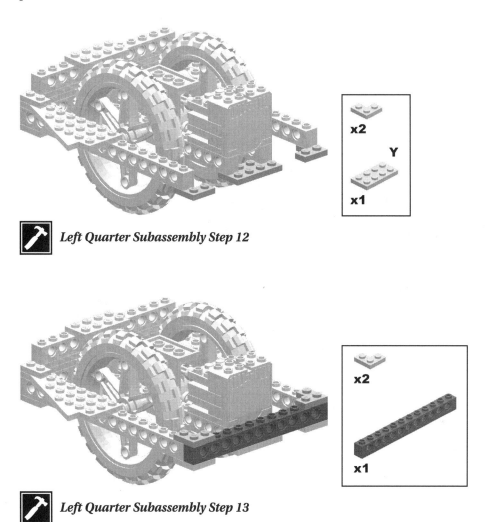

x2

Y

x1

Left Quarter Subassembly Step 12

x2

x1

Left Quarter Subassembly Step 13

That completes the first left quarter subassembly. It should look like the one shown in Figure 8-4, at the beginning of this section. You need to build one more left quarter subassembly, and then you're finished and ready to start on the next quarter subassembly.

The Right Quarter Subassembly

The right quarter subassembly, shown in Figure 8-5, is a mirror image of the left quarter subassembly. Construction takes place in 13 steps, and, as with the previous subassembly, you need to build *two* right quarter subassemblies. To build this subassembly, simply follow the instruction steps shown for the left quarter subassembly, but switch the orientation of the pieces while you're building so that your completed assembly looks like Figure 8-5. (Not all of the pieces will have a different orientation; some will be oriented in the same way.)

Figure 8-5. Completed right quarter subassembly

The Motor Bulk Subassembly

When you attach the four quarter subassemblies together, the motors on each subassembly will be close together. Perhaps there's a way you can connect them together to strengthen the model? Yes, there is a way, and that is to use motor bulk subassemblies, of which we'll need *two*. These go right on top of the motors and make a direct stud-to-stud classic connection—no unusual or roundabout connections here. On the other hand, this assembly, shown in Figure 8-6 serves a threefold purpose. You'll see exactly what these purposes are in this and the next chapter.

For the motor bulk subassembly, there are only two steps, which include a transparent brick with an open center from the UBEP and a handful of other pieces. If you're this far in the book, you won't need me to tell you how to put them together! However, I do have one comment: those odd-looking black pieces are called *1x2 x 1 & 2/3 TECHNIC pin joiner plates*. With these pieces, you can perform a variety of jobs. You'll see what purpose they serve for this project in the final assembly of the chassis.

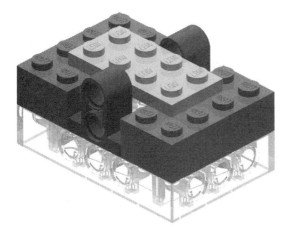

Figure 8-6. Completed motor bulk subassembly

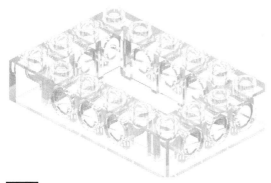

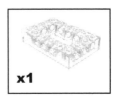

x1

 Motor Bulk Subassembly Step 1

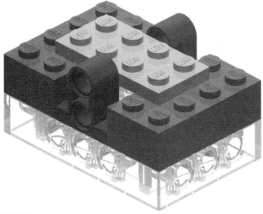

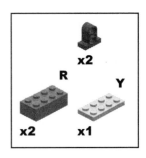

R

Y

x2

x2

x1

 Motor Bulk Subassembly Step 2

The Key Subassembly

This subassembly is the key to attaching the left and right sides of the chassis together—okay, not *the* key, but it does help, and it begins the process of securing the two sides together. You will need to build *two* key subassemblies.

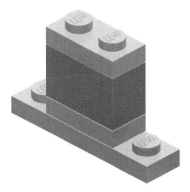

Figure 8-7. Completed key subassembly

Building this subassembly also requires only two steps.

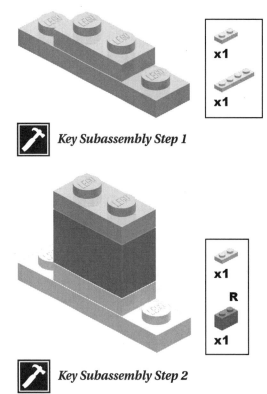

Key Subassembly Step 1

Key Subassembly Step 2

The Middle Connector Subassembly

To properly strengthen the chassis, you'll need plates going from the left side to the right side, and that is what the middle connector subassembly accomplishes. You will need to build two of these subassemblies, shown in Figure 8-8.

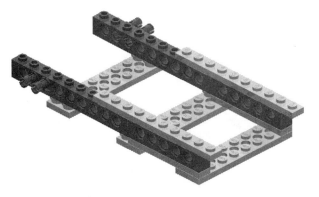

Figure 8-8. Completed middle connector subassembly

This is a simple, two-step subassembly.

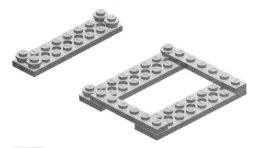

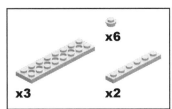

 Middle Connector Subassembly Step 1

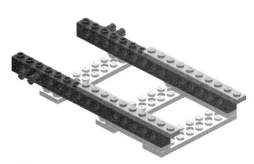

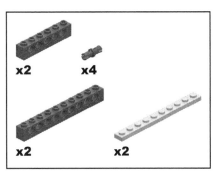

 Middle Connector Subassembly Step 2

The Left Side Frame Subassembly

After the robot has been assembled—or the majority of the robot anyway—there seems to be something missing on the left and right sides of the chassis. What should you do? You can add side frame subassemblies. You'll build one for the left side and one for the right side. The completed left side frame subassembly is shown in Figure 8-9.

Figure 8-9. Completed left side frame subassembly

The side frame subassemblies rely heavily on the UBEP. In fact, they can be built entirely from the UBEP. So pull out your UBEP and follow these two steps to build a left side frame subassembly.

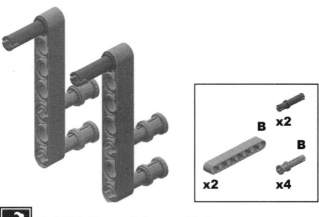

Left Side Frame Subassembly Step 1

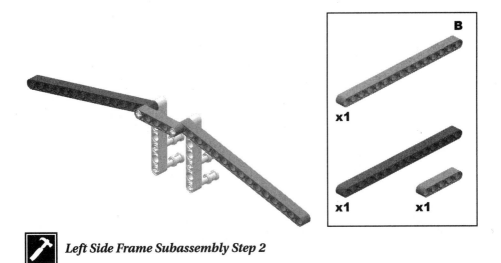

Left Side Frame Subassembly Step 2

The Right Side Frame Subassembly

The corresponding side frame subassembly for the right side of the chassis is shown in Figure 8-10. To build this subassembly, follow the instruction steps presented for the left side frame subassembly, but switch the orientation of the pieces so that the completed assembly looks like Figure 8-10.

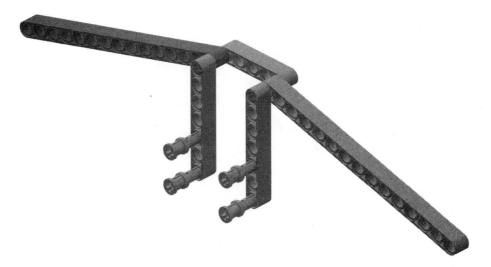

Figure 8-10. Completed right side frame subassembly

Putting Gargantuan-Bot Together

Now it's time to transform that pile of subassemblies into a sumo-bot chassis. The first task is connecting the "little squares" to make the big square (that is, the chassis).

Begin in step 1 by making the two sides—the left and right sides—of Gargantuan-Bot. You do this by taking all of your **quarter subassemblies**, adding four friction pins, positioning the assemblies as shown, and then snapping them together.

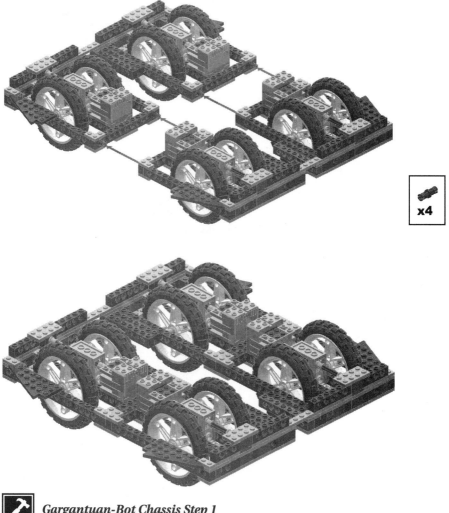

x4

Gargantuan-Bot Chassis Step 1

In steps 2 and 3, you strengthen the connections between the quarter subassemblies, add a few more pieces to the edges of the model, and attach the **motor bulk subassemblies**.

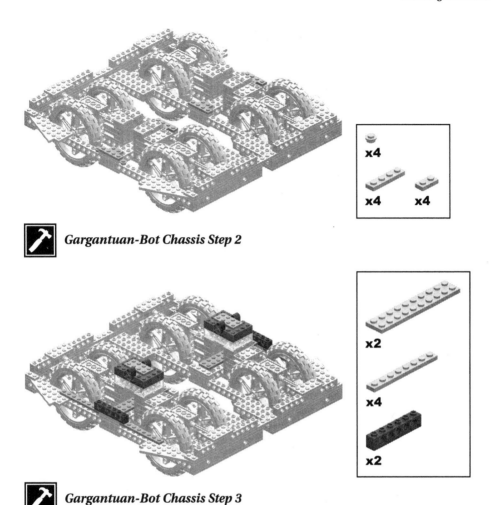

Gargantuan-Bot Chassis Step 2

Gargantuan-Bot Chassis Step 3

The chassis needs to be widened a bit, so in steps 4 and 5 you attach friction pins, then beams on those friction pins, and finally you begin attaching the two sides together by adding the **key subassemblies**. The long friction pins you add in step 4 are, obviously, for the beams, but the regular friction pins you add in this step are for something quite different: bracing. You'll be doing that a little later.

When you add the regular friction pins, take careful notice of where they are positioned. It might appear that they are all positioned in the same way, but this is not the case. Starting from the center of the model, the front two friction pins are in the first hole of the 1x16 beams they are on, but the back two friction pins are in the second hole of the 1x16 beams they are on.

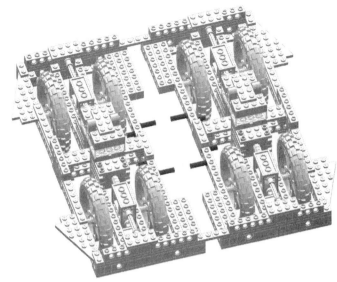

 Gargantuan-Bot Chassis Step 4

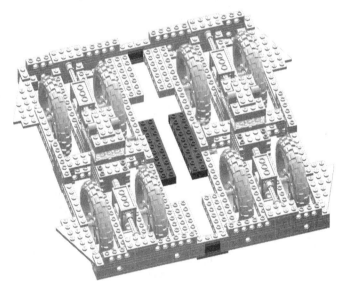

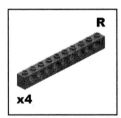

 Gargantuan-Bot Chassis Step 5

Steps 6 and 7 do some serious strengthening. First, turn the model upside down and attach all the plates as shown. Then flip the model right side up and attach both **middle connector subassemblies**. Step 8 adds a few beams and plates to help finish up the chassis.

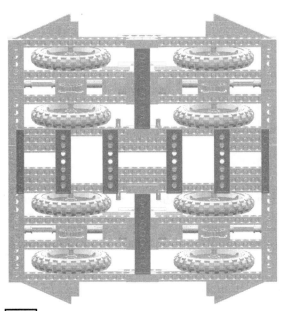
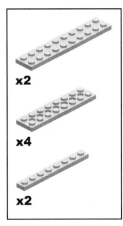

 Gargantuan-Bot Chassis Step 6

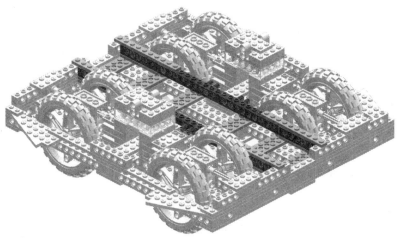

 Gargantuan-Bot Chassis Step 7

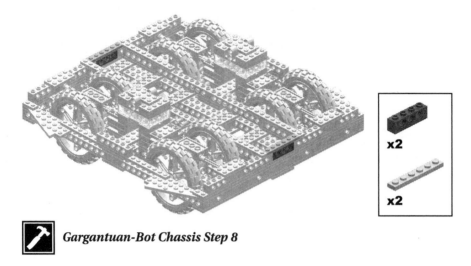

![hammer icon] **Gargantuan-Bot Chassis Step 8**

Step 9 does bracing. Remember earlier when you added four friction pins? You're going to use those and four 1x3 blue straight liftarms from the UBEP to do this bracing.

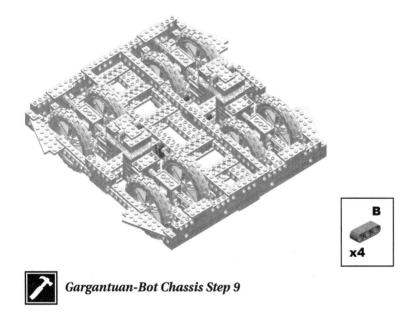

![hammer icon] **Gargantuan-Bot Chassis Step 9**

Now you add the side frames. In steps 10 through 15, you attach the **left side frame subassembly** and the **right side frame subassembly**, along with some additional pieces to strengthen their attachment to the chassis. The method of attaching both of these subassemblies is the same: first, properly align the subassembly, push in the blue pins, and in the following steps run a #10 axle through the assembly and into those odd-looking black pieces mounted on the motor bulk subassemblies. That is one of the three purposes the motor bulk subassemblies provide. Don't forget to top the ends of the #10 axles off with bushings.

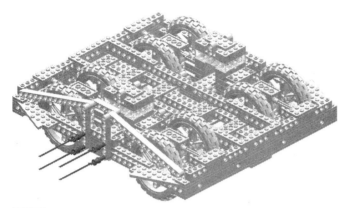

 Gargantuan-Bot Chassis Step 10

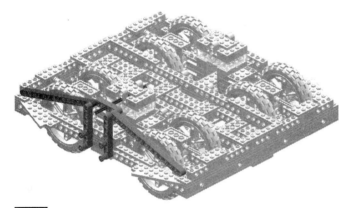

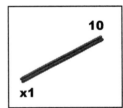

 Gargantuan-Bot Chassis Step 11

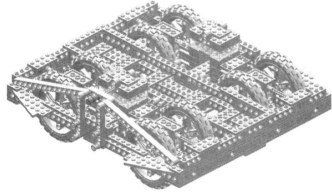

 Gargantuan-Bot Chassis Step 12

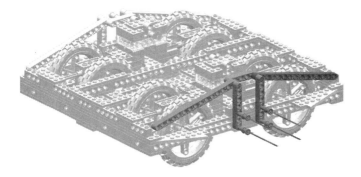

 Gargantuan-Bot Chassis Step 13

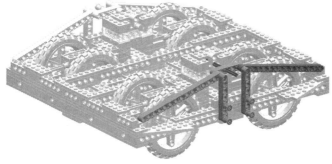

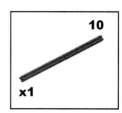

 Gargantuan-Bot Chassis Step 14

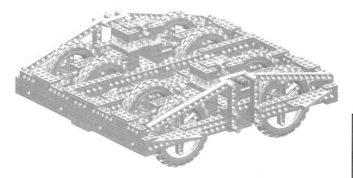

 Gargantuan-Bot Chassis Step 15

The chassis is nearing completion! In step 16, take your RCX and place it on the chassis, also snapping four 3/4 pins into the RCX as well.

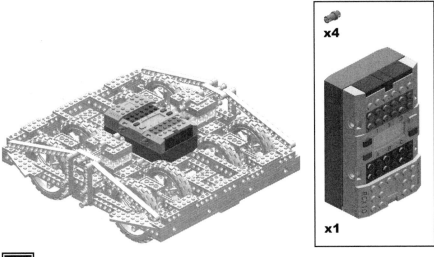

 Gargantuan-Bot Chassis Step 16

Step 17—the last step—braces the RCX to the chassis with 1x5 blue straight liftarms and adds all the electrical wires:

- All **motors** on the **right side** go on **output port C**.

- All **motors** on the **left side** go on **output port A**.

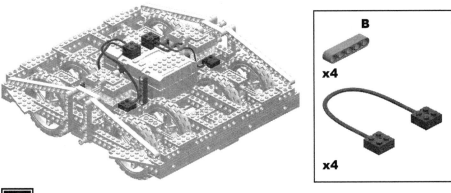

Gargantuan-Bot Chassis Step 17

Wow! You're finally finished with this hunk of machinery (see Figure 8-1, at the beginning of this chapter). Now let's move on to programming the Gargantuan-Bot chassis.

Programming the Gargantuan-Bot Chassis

The Gargantuan-Bot chassis currently doesn't possess any sensors. Does that mean programming is going to be exceedingly boring? No, if you look hard enough, you can *always* find something interesting to do with your programming. We will be using the header scheme we've used in the past several chapters, variables, and a lot of random movement to make some interesting programs with which to test the Gargantuan-Bot chassis.

Creating the Gargantuan-Bot Header

After all the headers you've seen by now, and all the programming we've done, this should be as easy as putting two bricks together. We have something new in this header though, shown in Listing 8-1. You'll see how it works and exactly what it does in just a moment, when we test the first program.

Listing 8-1. Gargantuan-Bot.nqh

```
/* Gargantuan-Bot.nqh - A file holding important
 * instructions for the Gargantuan-Bot chassis.
 * To be included in Gargantuan-Bot's main program */

// motors
#define Left OUT_A
#define Right OUT_C

// constants
#define SEARCH  100
#define SPIN 300
#define GO 500
#define TIME 50

// go forward
void Forward()
{
    OnFwd(Left+Right);
}

// go in reverse
void Reverse()
{
    OnRev(Left+Right);
}
```

```
// play a song
void PlaySong()
{
   PlayTone(450,50);
   PlayTone(220,70);
   PlayTone(655,35);
   PlayTone(700,35);
   PlayTone(750,35);
   PlayTone(440,50);
   PlayTone(800,100);
}

// spin in place
void TurnL()
{
   Rev(Left);
   Fwd(Right);
   Wait(SPIN);
}

// spin in place in a different way
void TurnR()
{
   Rev(Right);
   Fwd(Left);
   Wait(SPIN);
}
```

Programming the Gargantuan-Bot Chassis with the Direction Theory

Remember how we used the direction theory to keep track of ZR2's direction (in Chapter 7)? Let's do that again, but in a different way. To begin with, we'll use only one variable, fwd, and make it 1 when the robot's in forward, and 0 when the robot's in reverse. Secondly, with the previous program that used the direction theory, we couldn't really see what was going on. So this time, why not make it *visual*? We'll push the fwd variable right onto the RCX's LCD, do some interesting maneuvers with Random(), and even compose a little song. Take a look at the Gargantuan-Bot-One.nqc program in Listing 8-2.

Listing 8-2. Gargantuan-Bot-One.nqc

```
// Gargantuan-Bot-One.nqc
// A program for the Gargantuan-Bot Chassis

#include "Gargantuan-Bot.nqh" // include our header

int fwd = 0;  // our fwd variable
```

```
// main task
task main()
{
    // set the display to our "fwd" variable
    SetUserDisplay(fwd,0);

    // head forward for while, then reverse for a while
    Forward();
    fwd = 1;
    Wait(GO - Random(SEARCH));
    Reverse();
    fwd = 0;
    Wait(SPIN);

    TurnL();  // turn left

    Forward();  // head forward again
    fwd = 1;

    // wait for specified amount of time + random amount
    Wait(SPIN + Random(SEARCH));

    PlaySong();  // play a song

    // go in reverse for a little while
    Reverse();
    fwd = 0;
    Wait(SPIN + Random(SEARCH));

    TurnR(); // turn right

    // go forward for a little while then stop
    Forward();
    fwd = 1;
    Wait(100);
    Off(Left+Right);

    // play a song and a sound
    PlaySong();
    PlaySound(SOUND_DOUBLE_BEEP);
}
```

A Quick Test of Gargantuan-Bot-One.nqc

Fire up your computer (if it isn't already on), download the program to slot 1 of your RCX (following the procedure outlined in Chapter 3, in the "Downloading Programs to the RCX" section), put Gargantuan-Bot in your arena, and press the Run button on the RCX. The value of fwd, which begins on 0, should instantly appear on the LCD. Then Gargantuan-Bot will go forward, reverse, or turn, and each time it does, the fwd variable is updated—and you can actually see it happening!

NOTE *Remember that you don't need to retype the programs in this book into BricxCC. All of the programs for this book are available from the Downloads section of the Apress web site (*www.apress.com*).*

At the very end of the program, we get to try out that song. While the RCX speaker may not be an orchestra, it can create interesting and recognizable tunes. After the little song, a DOUBLE_BEEP is played, and the program stops.

Understanding Gargantuan-Bot-One.nqc

Sure enough, we sent the fwd variable right to the LCD at the beginning of the program. We did this with the SetUserDisplay() command, which we first used in Chapter 6. You've seen how this command can be quite useful. Next, we use our Forward() function, located in the header, then update the variable and, well, let's observe the next line of code again:

```
Wait(GO - Random(SEARCH));
```

GO equals 5 seconds, but how much does the rest equal? The answer: we'll never know! It's random! SEARCH equals 1 second, so the random amount can be anywhere from 0 to 1 second. This amount is actually *subtracted* from the GO amount with, understandably, the - operator.

The majority of the program reflects this type of behavior (going forward or reverse for random amounts of time). However, we also have the TurnL() and TurnR() functions, which are located in the header, and the very special ending to the program: the song. Let's look at one of the lines of code that makes up the song:

```
PlayTone(450,50);
```

Actually, instead of calling it a sound, *tone* would probably be more accurate. The PlayTone() command takes two arguments: *frequency* and *duration*. Thus, the proper way to set up a tone is like this: PlayTone(frequency, duration). The duration is in hundredths of seconds, so our example plays the frequency 450 for one-half second. By using strings of these commands, you can come up with almost anything! This song is just one out of endless possibilities.

> **TIP** *If you would like to pursue "RCX music" further, BricxCC has a feature that provides a great starting point. This feature is a virtual piano: click the keys of the piano and the IR tower sends the corresponding tone to the RCX, which then proceeds to play the tone (you can, of course, control the duration of the tone). Using this piano, you can play an entire song, and then save the code that plays the song. To find the virtual piano in BricxCC, open the Tools menu and choose Brick Piano. You must first make contact with the RCX using the IR tower before you can access this feature.*

Programming the Gargantuan-Bot Chassis with Random Turning

NQC seems to have one strike against it: limited randomness. It's easy to get random numbers, as we have been doing all along, but when it comes to getting something like random motors (such as, use OUT A *or* OUT C), NQC doesn't appear to have it.

Wait a second! RCX code has many random features—including random motors—and NQC uses the same firmware, so the functionality *is there*. So NQC doesn't really have limited randomness. But how do we get to these "random features" such as random motors? We just need to do some work.

We'll begin with a variable named x. This x has everything to do with randomness, because without x, we wouldn't be able to get random turning. Take a look at the second program—a random turning program—for the Gargantuan-Bot chassis, shown in Listing 8-3.

Listing 8-3. Gargantuan-Bot-Two.nqc

```
// Gargantuan-Bot-Two.nqc
// A program for the Gargantuan-Bot Chassis

#include "Gargantuan-Bot.nqh" // include our header

int x = 0;  // our x variable

// main task
task main()
{
    // set the display to our "x" variable
    SetUserDisplay(x,0);

    // start task that constantly updates "x" variable
    start X;

    while(true) // infinite loop
    {
        // clear timer and go forward...
        ClearTimer(0);
        Forward();
        until(Timer(0) > TIME); // ...until timer is > TIME
```

```
    // if x is less than 31, turn left
    if(x < 31)
    {
      TurnL();
    }

    // if x is more than 30, turn right
    else if (x > 30)
    {
      TurnR();
    }

    // clear timer and go in reverse...
    ClearTimer(0);
    Reverse();
    until(Timer(0) > TIME); //...until timer is more than TIME

    // if x is less than 31, turn left
    if(x < 31)
    {
      TurnL();
    }

    // if x is more than 30, turn right
    else if (x > 30)
    {
      TurnR();
    }

    PlaySong();  // play a song
  }
}

// this task constantly updates the "x" variable
task X()
{
  while(true) // infinite loop - constantly update
    {
      x = Random(60);  // x = anything 0 to 60
    }
}
```

A Quick Test of Gargantuan-Bot-Two.nqc

Once again, download the program, but this time to program slot 2 on the RCX. Pick up the Gargantuan-Bot chassis and place it on your arena, press the Run button, and see x on the LCD! (Actually, not x but the *value* of x.) Notice that x is constantly changing. This is what should happen: Gargantuan-Bot will go forward until Timer(0) is more than a predefined constant. Watch carefully at this point, since it will make a turn. What direction will the turn be? We don't know until it happens.

After the turn—whatever it may be—has been executed, Gargantuan-Bot will go in reverse, wait until the timer exceeds the constant, and execute another random turn. At this point in the program, our little tune plays. What happens after this? The same process, again and again and again. As a matter of fact, it's eternal! There is an infinite loop near the beginning of the code that is responsible for this. Don't worry; you don't need to wait for eternity for Gargantuan-Bot to finish. Just press the Run button on the RCX when you're finished.

Understanding Gargantuan-Bot-Two.nqc

Wow, real random movement! How did the program manage to do that? As I said earlier, it all goes back to that single letter variable, x. But it *also* goes back to the X() task. Look at this task again, and you'll see something interesting: x is in an infinite loop that constantly changes its value. This random value can be anywhere from 0 to 60, courtesy of Random(60);.

Back at the top of the program, after the task has been started, the x variable is pushed to the LCD, the infinite loop is initiated, and the program clears the timer and moves the robot forward until the timer is more than TIME. At this point, things really get interesting. The program has an if statement and an else if statement here that ask questions about the x variable (remember that x is constantly being changed). The program reads this variable and looks at the questions being asked: if x is less than 31, turn left; if x is more than 30, turn right. *This* is how we get randomness in our turning.

After this episode, the program repeats the same set of actions, but with the sumo-bot going in reverse. At the end of the program, the whimsical little tune is played, and everything starts all over again.

Testing the Gargantuan-Bot Chassis

All right, you've got one big LEGO sumo-bot, so let's do some sumo-oriented testing! With both of the programs we just observed loaded in your RCX, place the Gargantuan-Bot chassis on your arena. Along with Gargantuan-Bot, you should place several different objects. How big should they be? The Gargantuan-Bot chassis weighs about three pounds; therefore, the objects should be around that weight. Items like the RIS box, thick books, and canned food will work well.

Begin with the first program: Gargantuan-Bot-One.nqc. Place your objects around Gargantuan-Bot and start the program with the Run button on the RCX. First, let Gargantuan-Bot push something by itself off the arena (don't let it fall off the arena—it doesn't have a light sensor yet). After watching the "pushing show" to your satisfaction, step up to the arena and get involved. Grab one of your objects, because you are the opposing sumo-bot now!

Hmmm…how about a side hit? Go ahead, give Gargantuan-Bot a nice little shove in the side. And a back slam? Try shoving and pushing Gargantuan-Bot from many different angles and in many different ways.

You need to try out the second program: Gargantuan-Bot-Two.nqc. This program does a bit more going back and forth, so it will be a great chance to experiment with the back and front of the Gargantuan-Bot chassis. Switch the program to slot 2 and press the Run button, and you have some random turning! As Gargantuan-Bot is going back and forth, do some more testing (pushing, ramming, and so on) on its front and back sides.

How did Gargantuan-Bot do in your testing? You probably saw right away how much traction the eight wheels provide, and the very durable structure it has. Remember also that it's not a real sumo-bot yet; the next chapter will take care of that with some real programming, an additional motor, sensors, and more subassemblies.

Conclusion

The Gargantuan-Bot chassis accurately portrays what a chassis from the big-sumo strategy should look like, but only in its own uniqueness. The big-sumo strategy contains an extremely large variety of sumo-bots, and you can try just about any type of building methodology, mechanics, color schemes, and much more on them. When you have sumo-bots that big, there's a lot you can do. In the next chapter, you will build onto the Gargantuan-Bot chassis to create a full-fledged sumo-bot: BL58. You'll find out very quickly how it takes advantage of what the big-sumo strategy has to offer!

CHAPTER 9

Gargantuan-Bot Version BL58

YOU'VE PROBABLY BEEN waiting for this moment all throughout the first eight chapters—if you haven't already peeked. (Actually, peeking is just fine because you don't *have* to do the projects in this book in order.) We're ready to discuss *bigness*; you could also call it *gargantuaness*. Take a look at Figure 9-1 to see this gargantuaness, which is BL58.

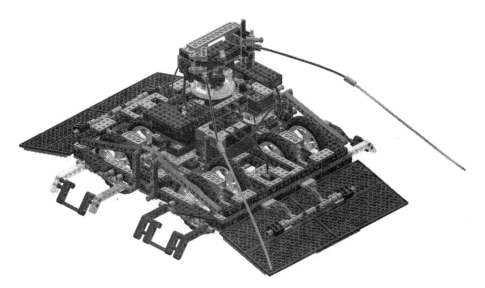

Figure 9-1. Completed Gargantuan-Bot Version BL58

Now, let's take a look at one of the most exciting and interesting parts: BL58's substrategy. Its substrategy mixes ZR2's and also (of course) some of its own smarts. As you'll notice, BL58 has a large slope on its front and back end. ZR2 took the "back is the front and the front is the back" approach, with a slope for one end and counter-rotating wheels for another. BL58 takes a similar but more parallel approach: *both* sides have slopes, so that the back really is the front and the front really is the back. Also like ZR2, BL58 has two light sensors; this means it can simply switch direction upon seeing the line, as opposed to turning.

"How can the back be the front and the front be the back if that 'head thing' is facing in one direction?" Well, this brings up two points. The first point is that the "head thing" (which is, in fact, a head) can turn; upon seeing the line, BL58 turns its head in the opposite direction, making the other side the front. To properly align the head, we use a *rotation sensor*.

The second point is that BL58 searches for the opponent using antennae. Two long antennae—each with their own touch sensor—are mounted on the head we have been talking about and protrude about a foot out into space in an attempt to find the opponent.

"Wait a second! Doesn't that add up to *five* sensors? Two touch sensors, two light sensors, and a rotation sensor? We can't fit all that on the RCX, can we?" Believe it or not, we can, as you'll see when we construct this sumo-bot.

In addition to all the mechanics, we have several new programs—the longest programs in this book. *That's* something to be excited about!

Constructing Subassemblies for BL58

BL58 will be constructed with pieces from the same sets you used for the chassis: the UBEP, two EMEP, and two RIS (there are plenty of pieces left to build with in these sets). Even though we are using the same sets, there are a lot of new pieces to talk about. Take a look at the bill of materials for BL58 in Figure 9-2.

> **NOTE** *The rotation sensor is one of the most versatile LEGO sensors available, and it's highly recommended that you get this type of sensor, if you don't already have one. The rotation sensor can be found in the Ultimate Accessory Expansion Pack,* www.plestore.com, *and auction sites like eBay and* www.bricklink.com. *By itself, it retails for around $16 to $20.*

You need to build 11 subassemblies, but not 11 *different* subassemblies—we're going to be duplicating a number of the assemblies. Here's a list of all the subassemblies that you will need to build: two slope subassemblies, two type 1 and type 2 side protector subassemblies, two light sensor subassemblies, a head base subassembly, a head bracer subassembly, and two different antenna subassemblies. Building all those subassemblies should keep you busy; it certainly kept me busy!

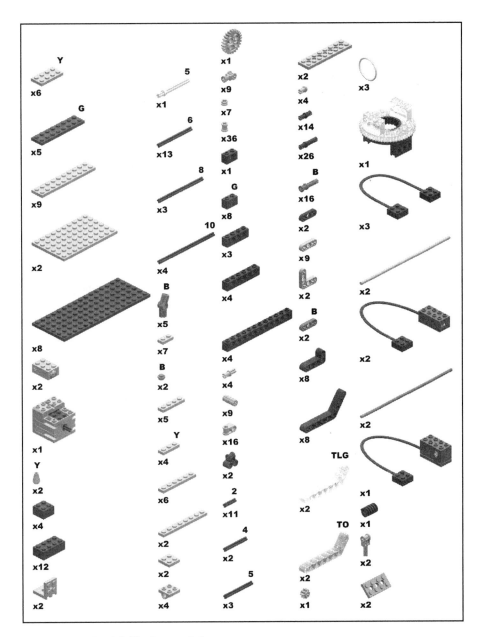

Figure 9-2. BL58's bill of materials

The Slope Subassembly

This slope subassembly, shown in Figure 9-3, is the *biggest* one we have made in this book, and we're going to be constructing *two* of them. One will go on the front and the other on the back (with the intention, of course, that these will go right underneath the opponent).

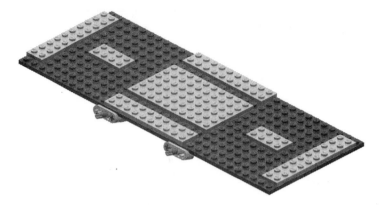

Figure 9-3. Completed slope subassembly

The main part of the slope is constructed from four of the EMEP's super-size 6x16 black plates. You connect this assembly to the chassis by means of two blue pins with a stop bush. This is where those 1x1 bricks with a hole in the chassis come into the picture. As I said in the previous chapter, these bricks have a special purpose, and that purpose is to provide a place for the blue pins in this subassembly to snap into.

We begin in step 1 with nothing but plates, but that's exactly what we want for a slope. Position the four 6x16 plates as shown, and then place the other plates on top; these hold everything together.

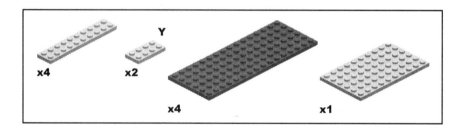

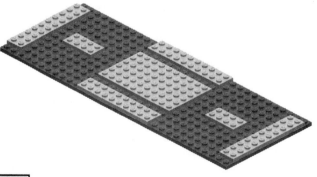

Slope Subassembly Step 1

Steps 2 through 6 construct the section that will attach to the chassis. Begin by turning the model upside down and pushing four 1x2 green axle bricks and two 2x2 plates with holes into the large, black plates. The next two steps run axles through these pieces, with an axle extender in the middle and an axle on each side. Once you've completed these steps, add the remaining pieces, in steps 5 and 6, which include #3 axle connectors, #2 notched axles, half-liftarms, and blue pins with a stop bush. The angle the #3 axle connectors possess makes them a perfect choice for using in a slope; these pieces are responsible for putting the slope at an angle.

> **NOTE** *Unfortunately, the RIS, UBEP, and EMEP do not contain #3 angle connectors. However, the RSEP contains two #3 angle connectors, and the Extreme Creatures Expansion Pack (ECEP) has four of these connectors.*

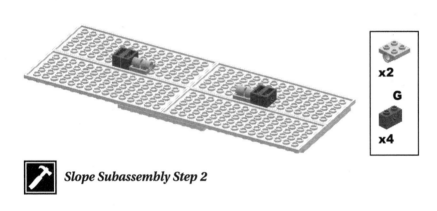

 Slope Subassembly Step 2

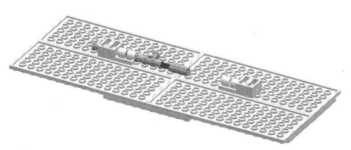 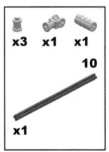

Slope Subassembly Step 3

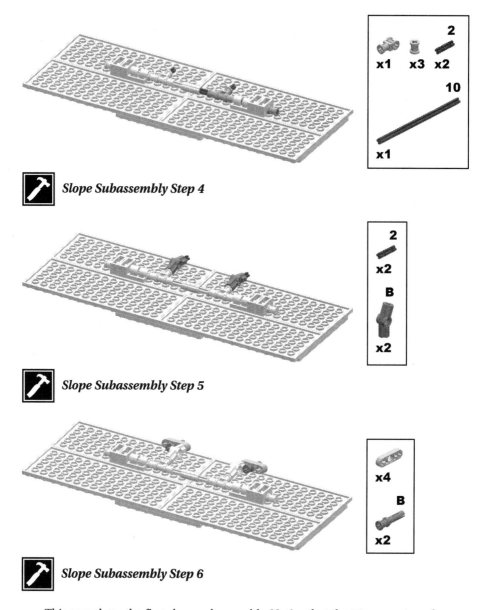

Slope Subassembly Step 4

Slope Subassembly Step 5

Slope Subassembly Step 6

This completes the first slope subassembly. Notice that the #3 connectors slope inwards, but since the plates are there, they jut upwards a little. This is okay; no harm comes from this. You could position the entire section you just built forwards several studs, but this comes at the price of protruding the slope subassembly outwards that same amount of studs.

Be sure to build *two* slope subassemblies.

The Type 1 Side Protector Subassembly

You may be wondering just what the "type 1" and "type 2" is all about. The reason for these two types is a strictly mechanical one: to avoid excessive use of specific pieces. For example, it's possible that you don't have 10 or 12 of one type of liftarm, so you wouldn't have enough of them to build four of one type of subassembly that uses that type of liftarm. To avoid that situation, you'll build two of one type of side protector subassembly and two of another type, using some different pieces for each type. In the following steps, you'll build the first type, shown in Figure 9-4.

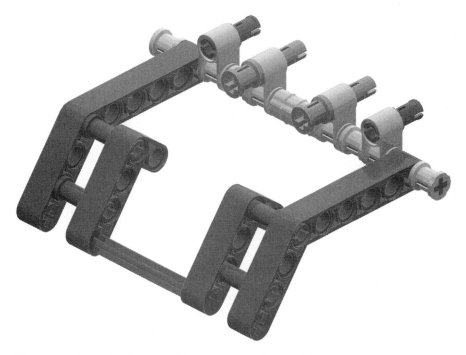

Figure 9-4. Completed type 1 side protector subassembly

"What is a side protector subassembly and why use them?" BL58's front and back ends are protected by the large slopes positioned there, but what about the sides? There is a noticeable gap between the ground and chassis that some sneaky opponent might use to its advantage. You need to protect the sides of BL58, even if only partially, to prevent this from happening. The side protector subassemblies provide this protection by getting in the way of the opponent.

Step 1 begins with a #6 axle, a few axle accessories, and a black liftarm from the RIS. Step 2 places another crossblock and an axle extender on the end of the #6 axle.

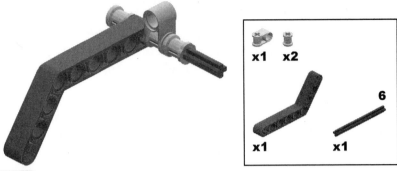

 Type 1 Side Protector Subassembly Step 1

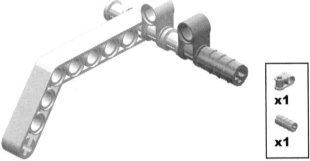

 Type 1 Side Protector Subassembly Step 2

Steps 3 and 4 are like steps 1 and 2, but for the right side. However, step 4 also adds various pins. Some of these pins snap into the crossblocks and will also snap into the chassis in the final assembly; the other ones, which are long friction pins, provide a place to attach other pieces.

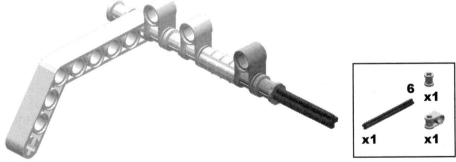

 Type 1 Side Protector Subassembly Step 3

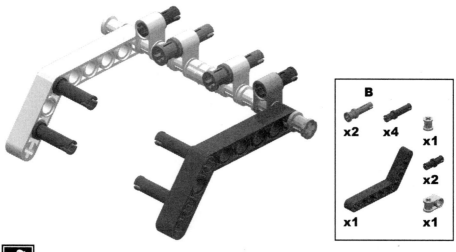

 Type 1 Side Protector Subassembly Step 4

Step 5 finishes the middle of the subassembly by snapping two L-shaped liftarms onto the long friction pins and sliding a #6 axle through the liftarms.

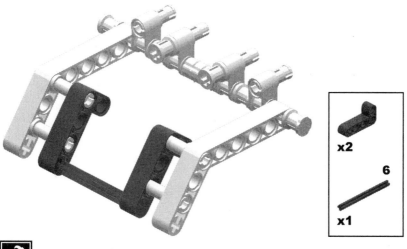

 Type 1 Side Protector Subassembly Step 5

Now that you're finished with this side protector subassembly, build another one.

The Type 2 Side Protector Subassembly

The type 2 side protector subassembly, shown in Figure 9-5, is almost identical to the previous side protector subassembly. The only differences are the type of liftarm used and the positioning of the smaller black liftarms. As with the other type, you'll need to build *two* of these.

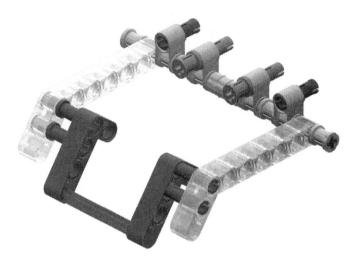

Figure 9-5. Completed type 2 side protector subassembly

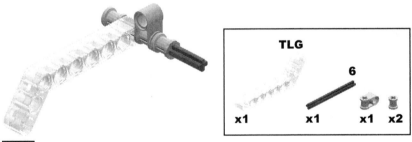

 Type 2 Side Protector Subassembly Step 1

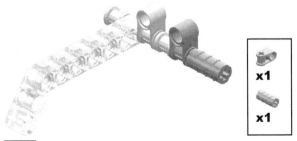

 Type 2 Side Protector Subassembly Step 2

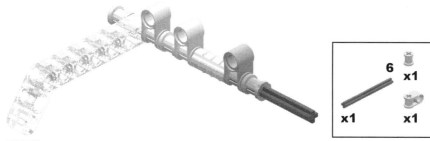

 Type 2 Side Protector Subassembly Step 3

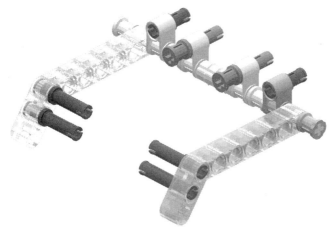

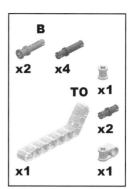

 Type 2 Side Protector Subassembly Step 4

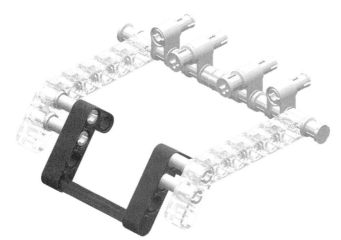

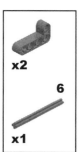

 Type 2 Side Protector Subassembly Step 5

The Light Sensor Subassembly

Most of the light sensor subassemblies in this book haven't been too hard to build, and this one, shown in Figure 9-6, continues with that trend. You'll be constructing *two* of these: one for the front and one for the back. When you attach the electrical wires to the RCX, both will go on the same input port. This is the same little trick you used with ZR2; it's a great way to save an input port.

Figure 9-6. Completed light sensor subassembly

This light sensor subassembly consists of the usual light sensor and angle plate, but that's not all. An additional brick and a few other plates make an appearance in this subassembly, too; these will conform to the shape of the chassis and ensure a firm connection.

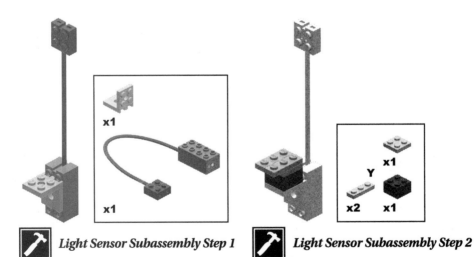

The Head Base Subassembly

You might be wondering what the head base subassembly, which is shown in Figure 9-7, is supposed to do. Well, when you add that head with those two super-long antennae to the chassis, you can't just slap it onto the RCX, because a hit from the opposing sumo-bot would send it rocketing into space. You need a sort of base for the head—a head base—that is firmly attached to the chassis. The actual head with antennae can then be connected to that base. With this setup, you won't need to worry about BL58 using its head to practice aeronautics!

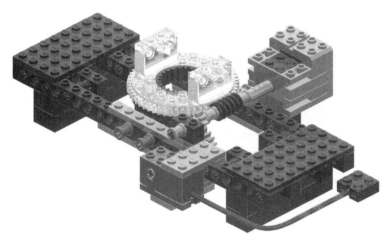

Figure 9-7. Completed head base subassembly

This head base is more than just bricks and plates. It also has a motor, rotation sensor, and *turntable*. We'll talk about how these pieces work during construction of this subassembly. Steps 1 and 2 begin construction with beams, long friction pins, and plates.

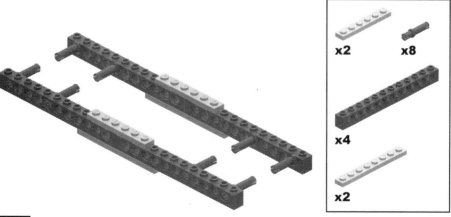

 Head Base Subassembly Step 1

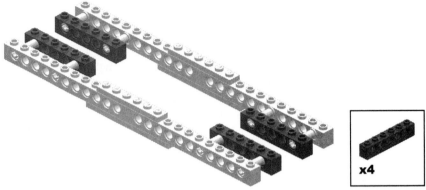

 Head Base Subassembly Step 2

The head base subassembly will be running all the way across from one motor bulk subassembly (located on the chassis) to the other. In between is the RCX, and stacked up on that RCX are three electrical wires. (You'll see why and what they're for later.) For this reason, you need to add some height to the head base subassembly. It must be elevated at the left and right extremes to be able to make contact with the motor bulk subassemblies. So in step 3, you add a number of 2x4 black bricks. You also add two 2x2 bricks and four 2x8 green plates.

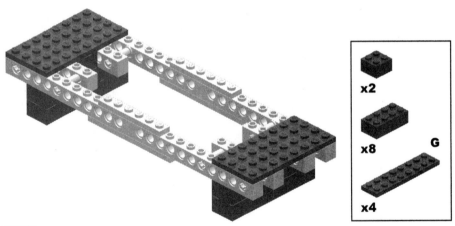

 Head Base Subassembly Step 3

In step 4, you add two friction pins, which you'll use in the next step, and a turntable (from the UBEP). Turntables are extremely useful, efficient, and effective pieces. They are easily powered by worm gears and give pinpoint precision when turning. In addition, turntables can hold up under a lot of weight. Entire sections of a robot can be built on top of a turntable (observe the Disc Shooter robot on the back of the UBEP box). When building large creations (and small ones, too), the turntable is your friend!

TIP *Turntables come in other colors besides clear transparent and black. You can find turntables in the Spare Parts section of* www.plestore.com, *which offers a package containing two turntables. You can also do a search on eBay or* www.bricklink.com *for turntables.*

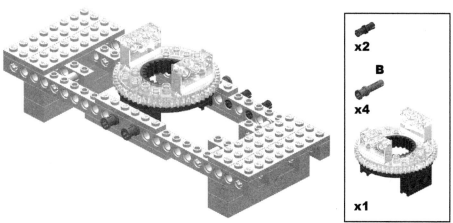

 Head Base Subassembly Step 4

Steps 5 does some preparatory work necessary for adding a motor and rotation sensor. Before you can attach these important pieces, you need to add several plates and a 1x4 beam—this beam goes onto the pins you added in the previous step.

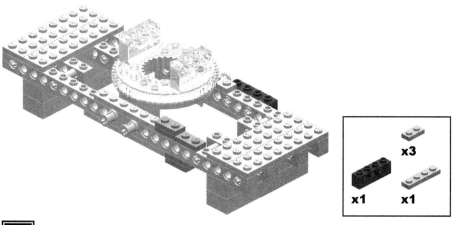

 Head Base Subassembly Step 5

Step 6 adds the motor and a host of other pieces, most of which go on the motor's shaft. Among these pieces is a worm gear, which will turn the turntable, and an 8t gear. As you can see from the image, the 8t gear meshes with the 24t gear also added in this step, and with these pieces you gear down. This provides us with a 1:3 ratio (the ratio between the worm gear and turntable is a different one).

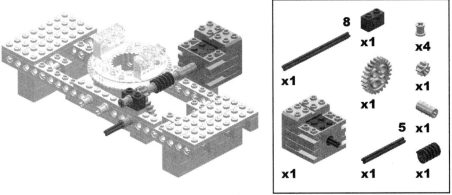

 Head Base Subassembly Step 6

You extend the gear train all the way over here to go through the rotation sensor, which you add and secure with two plates in step 7. Why use this specific ratio for the rotation sensor? The reading the rotation sensor returns depends on the gear ratio. LEGO MINDSTORMS fans have found that a rotation sensor that goes too fast can read incorrectly, as can one that goes too slowly. A 1:3 ratio for a rotation sensor gives good results and is commonly used.

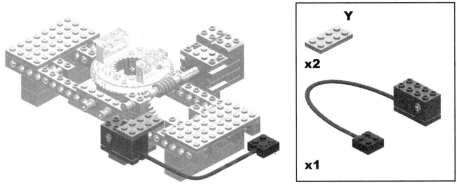

 Head Base Subassembly Step 7

The Left Antenna Subassembly

The left antenna subassembly, shown in Figure 9-8, brings us to the discussion of how you can attach *five* sensors to the RCX's *three* sensor ports. As you know, you are going to have two light sensors on one port. Well, you will add a touch sensor to that as well! Wouldn't that just screw things up? No, not necessarily—we can use a special method that can help us to save an input port. This method works by putting a light sensor and a touch sensor on the same input port and then configuring the port as a light sensor. When set up this way, the light sensor reads as it normally would, and when the touch sensor is pressed, the input port reads 100. Since the light sensor will practically never read 100 (unless you hold it right up to a light), we can safely say the touch sensor has been pressed if the input port reads 100; therefore, we can distinguish between the light sensor's readings and the touch sensor's readings. In this case, there are *two* light sensors on the port, but it doesn't really matter.

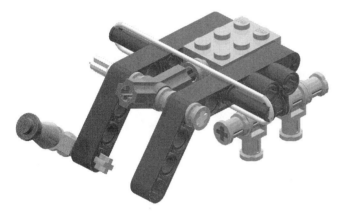

Figure 9-8. Completed left antenna subassembly

Now let's consider the possible bumper types for our antennae. For Zip-Bam-Bot XK1 and XK2 (built in Chapters 4 and 5), we used *press-type* bumpers, which are activated when they press the touch sensor. On the other hand, *release-type* bumpers are activated when they are *no longer* pressing on the touch sensor's clicker. In other words, release-type bumpers are constantly pressing down the touch sensor's clicker, and when the bumper is pressed, the touch sensor's clicker becomes released or "unpressed"—this is what activates a release-type bumper. Release-type bumpers are more sensitive, safer for the sensor, and all around more efficient than press-type bumpers, so we want to use them for BL58. However, we have a problem: if we use a release-type bumper on a port that is using the special sensor method to save an input port, then that input port will always return 100. For this reason, one of the sumo-bot's antennae will be a release-type bumper (this one), and the other will be a press-type (the next one). The press-type bumper will be the one going on the same port as the light sensors, the release-type bumper will have its own port, and the rotation sensor will have its own port as well. In this way, you can fit five sensors on just three input ports.

Step 1 begins with a bent 1x9 black liftarm from the RIS, a #4 axle and a touch sensor on the axle. Step 2 connects another black liftarm and several pins. Do you see the long friction pins? These are going to hold the rubber bands.

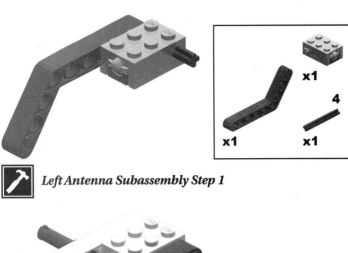

 Left Antenna Subassembly Step 1

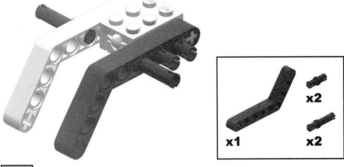

 Left Antenna Subassembly Step 2

In step 3, you add the actual piece that will activate the touch sensor: yet another #3 axle connector. There's another very interesting piece you use in this step: a *white #5.5 axle with a stop*—this piece can be found in the UBEP. You start from the left with this piece and push towards the right, sliding the various axle accessories onto it as you go along. Step 4 snaps a double crossblock with a #5 axle through its axle hole onto the two friction pins at the right.

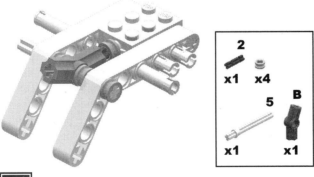

 Left Antenna Subassembly Step 3

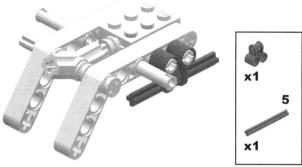

 Left Antenna Subassembly Step 4

In step 5, you add a number of axle accessories onto the #5 axle, and begin construction of a funny looking eye. Believe it or not, the axle accessories you add in this step will be the pieces that attach to the Gargantuan-Bot chassis. Step 6 finishes the eye and adds a white rubber band. The rubber band comes from the RIS and slips into the little notches in the long friction pins. It takes a little effort to stretch the rubber band that big, but it shouldn't snap.

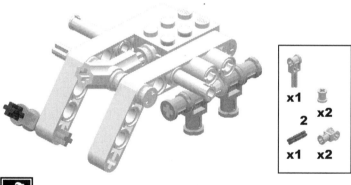

 Left Antenna Subassembly Step 5

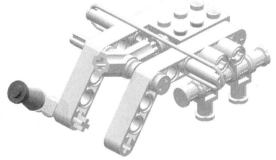

 Left Antenna Subassembly Step 6

You are now finished with the left antenna subassembly. You'll be adding the actual antenna in the final assembly.

The Right Antenna Subassembly

What's better: an antenna that doesn't work very well or no antenna? Truthfully, the right antenna subassembly, shown in Figure 9-9, works a lot better than "not very well." I needed to design this antenna with the ability to detect a hit from either the left or right side, and the solution I came up with is successful, but the antenna must be moved quite a bit before it can detect anything. What's important is that it does work!

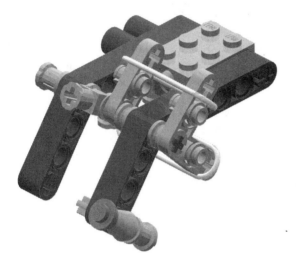

Figure 9-9. Completed right antenna subassembly

You'll notice the similarities between the two antennas, but the unique parts of this subassembly are quite obvious as well. Steps 1 and 2 are identical to those for building the left antenna subassembly, except that this subassembly doesn't have any long friction pins.

 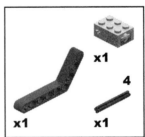

 Right Antenna Subassembly Step 1

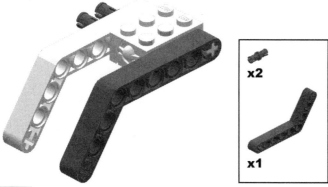

 Right Antenna Subassembly Step 2

Step 3 stays parallel with the left antenna subassembly's step 3, but not all the pieces are the same. Instead of a #3 axle connector, you use a catch and also two 3x3 L-shaped half-liftarms. These L-shaped half-liftarms are the key pieces to the right antenna subassembly. If a hit comes from the left, one side of the L-shaped liftarm presses the touch sensor; if a hit comes from the right, the other side of the L-shaped liftarm presses the touch sensor.

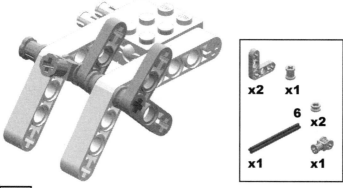

 Right Antenna Subassembly Step 3

Steps 4 through 6 are nearly parallel to the left antenna subassembly's steps 4 through 6. There may be a different piece here and there, but the main difference is in the rubber band, or actually rubber *bands*. You now use *two* rubber bands, and each one loops around an arm of each L-shaped liftarm. Also on those L-shaped liftarms are *half-pins*. These prevent the rubber bands from slipping back too far.

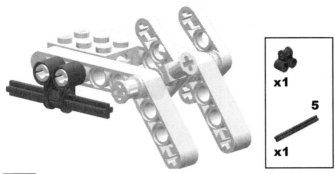

 Right Antenna Subassembly Step 4

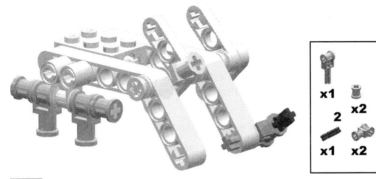

 Right Antenna Subassembly Step 5

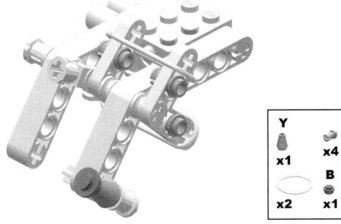

 Right Antenna Subassembly Step 6

You've finished building this subassembly. Feel free to play around with it a bit so you can see exactly how it can detect hits from the left and right and how the rubber bands work. You'll also be doing plenty of testing with the bumpers at the end of this chapter in the "Testing BL58" section.

The Head Bracer Subassembly

The head bracer subassembly, shown in Figure 9-10, will make up part of the head, and its purpose is to give the head bulk and strength.

Figure 9-10. Completed head bracer subassembly

It consists of only a handful of pieces and is easy to make—just two steps (bricks and plates aren't rocket science!).

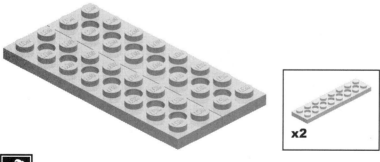

 Head Bracer Subassembly Step 1

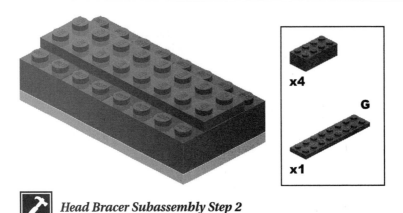

 Head Bracer Subassembly Step 2

That completes all of your subassembly construction. Now it's time to put BL58 together.

Putting BL58 Together

You are now ready to assemble the *last* sumo-bot in this book (well, of course, you can always go back and build the sumo-bots again).

In step 1, pull out the chassis, two **light sensor subassemblies**, and an extra electrical wire. The light sensor subassemblies are easy to attach—simply push them down onto the chassis where directed. Both light sensor's electrical wires go on **input port 2**, and *then* you place one end of the extra electrical wire on top of those, making a grand total of three electrical wires on input port 2. Although you aren't going to use the extra electrical wire at the moment, it works much better to add it now rather than later. And as I mentioned earlier, when you add the head base subassembly, it will go on top (and thus attach to) these three electrical wires.

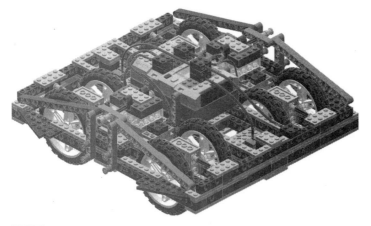

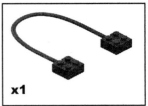

 BL58 Final Assembly Step 1

Next, in step 2, you add the **slope subassemblies**, **side protector subassemblies**, and some height to the motor bulk subassemblies on the chassis; this height is necessary for the head base subassembly, which you'll add in the next step.

To add the slope subassemblies, simply turn them upside down (with the studs facing upside down) and push the blue pins into the 1x1 holes built into the chassis.

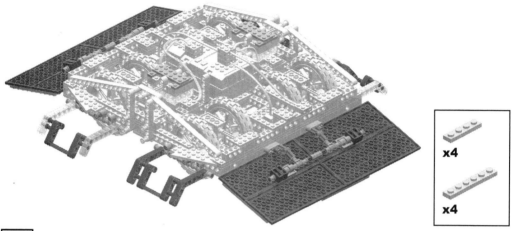

x4

x4

 BL58 Final Assembly Step 2

In step 3, you add the **head base subassembly**, and an electrical wire for it's motor, four 1x2 plates, two 1x4 beams, and four axle pins, all of which you build onto the head base subassembly's turntable. The head base subassembly should be positioned directly in the middle of the model, with the left and right sides connecting into the plates added in step 2, and the front beam attaching to the three electrical plates stacked up on input port 2. Here is how you should attach the motor and sensor's electrical wires to the RCX:

- The **rotation sensor** goes on **input port 3**.

- The **motor** goes on **output port B** (the orientation should be as if it were coming in from the back of the RCX).

NOTE *In this final assembly, you are placing the head base subassembly and the head itself directly in the middle of the model. Doing this helps to keep the COG (center of gravity) in the middle of BL58, and it also keeps the model's excellent symmetry. However, there is a disadvantage to placing everything in the middle: it blocks access to the RCX. It doesn't block the RCX's IR port, but it does make it somewhat difficult to get to the buttons on the RCX and the RCX in general. It doesn't completely block the buttons; it is still possible to push them. And, in reality, the RCX can be easily accessed: simply pull off the head base subassembly.*

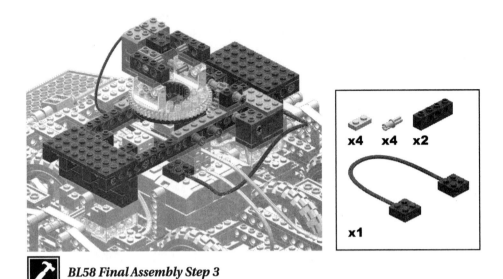

BL58 Final Assembly Step 3

Step 4 braces the just-added beams and plates with half-liftarms.

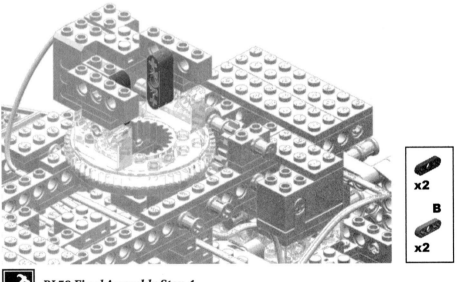

BL58 Final Assembly Step 4

Step 5 attaches the **head bracer subassembly** and slides two #8 axles through the 1x4 beams. As its name implies, the head bracer subassembly gives strength to the two sides of the head (although the head isn't in its full form at this point). This assembly also adds some bulk, which will give the head more of a finished appearance.

 BL58 Final Assembly Step 5

Step 6 adds the **antenna subassemblies**. Push their connectors with an axle hole into the #8 axles added in step 5. Attach the electrical wires (using the extra electrical wire from step 1 for the press-type bumper) to the RCX in this way:

- The **press-type bumper's touch sensor** goes on **input port 2**.

- The **release-type bumper's touch sensor** goes on **input port 1**.

> **NOTE** *If you are using the regular-length electrical wires that come with the RIS, you will need to use two for each bumper; the head needs some "spare" wire when it is turning a full 180 degrees. Some sets, like the ECEP or UBEP, contain a longer electrical wire, which works very well for this setup. Alternatively, you can use the RIS's extra-long electrical wires; however, there will be a lot of extra wire hanging around, so you'll probably need to tie it up in a bundle.*

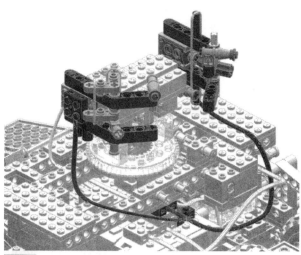

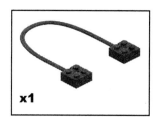

 BL58 Final Assembly Step 6

Step 7 puts some finishing touches on the head. By inverting several plates, you can push them into the antenna subassembly's liftarms and create a "bridge" going from one side of the head to the other. Step 7 also adds the antennae. Simply push the *flexible hosing* into the antenna subassembly's catch and #3 axle connector. There are many ways to orient the hosing—some are good, and some are not so good. I have found that slightly "twisting" the hosing outwards away from the robot and downward toward the floor works well for "feeling" for the opposing sumo-bot.

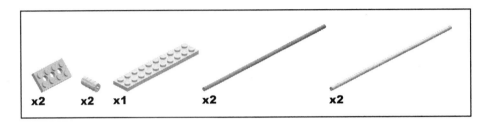

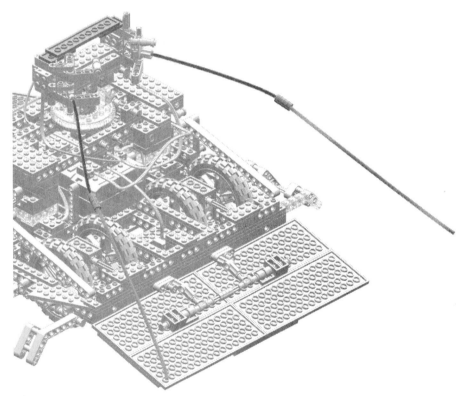

 BL58 Final Assembly Step 7

You're finished! Your Gargantuan-Bot Version BL58 should look like the one shown in Figure 9-1 at the beginning of this chapter. With the construction finally completed, let's begin working on the biggest programs in this book.

Formulating a Solid Programming Solution for BL58

You can do a lot with five sensors, but there's a lot you *shouldn't* do with five sensors. In other words, in a program using five sensors, there are many things you can do that will cause a lot of problems. We're going to need to carefully think this program through. We will be using the direction theory as we did in Chapter 7, since BL58 uses "the back is the front and the front is the back" approach like ZR2, but we won't need the speed theory since BL58 doesn't switch speeds. Let's examine the task lineup:

- **Line-detection task:** Just like ZR2, BL58 simply goes in the opposite direction when it detects the line. And like ZR2's line-detection task, BL58's line-detecting task is somewhat complex.

- **Dual-bumper task:** Since BL58 will be programmed to turn once a bumper has been pressed, what happens when both bumpers are activated? I found this out the hard way: BL58 reverses! This odd behavior can be avoided with a dual-bumper task. If both bumpers are activated, this task takes over, and keeps the robot moving forward until both bumpers have been de-activated.

- **Right bumper task:** If the right bumper gets pressed, this task will turn the robot to the right.

- **Left bumper task:** If the left bumper gets pressed, this task will turn the robot to the left.

- **Maneuvering task:** This task faces a difficult problem: BL58 (seemingly) can't detect when it has run into the opponent, so when should it execute random turns? As you'll see in a moment, I came up with an original solution to address that question.

- **NQC header:** This header boasts a new feature: *smart functions*. These are functions that don't just execute, but actually think for themselves! You'll see what I mean when we look at the header.

To illustrate BL58's issue of deciding when to execute a random turn, imagine this scenario: BL58 is pushing the other sumo-bot, but since BL58 can't detect when it has run into the opponent, the maneuvering task kicks in and executes a turn. BL58 is (literally) turning away from success! How can we avoid this? Well, it takes a complex maneuvering task to accomplish the job. Here's the trick: BL58 turns its head a little to the right—just a little, but far enough so that its left antenna is placed directly in front. If it detects something (BL58 is pushing the other sumo-bot), it will turn its head back and keep going forward. If it doesn't detect something (BL58 is not pushing the other sumo-bot), it turns its head back and executes a turn.

Programming BL58 with the Solution

Now we are ready to delve into the code. For this project, we will make an optimized, improved version of this program after we finish making the first one. Creating improved code is always good practice!

Creating the NQC Header

As I stated earlier, this will be different from our other headers in that it has "smart" functions. In addition, the variables for the program are declared here instead of in the main program. The header is shown in Listing 9-1.

Listing 9-1. Gargantuan-Bot-BL58.nqh

```
/* Gargantuan-Bot-BL58.nqh - A file holding important
 * instructions for Gargantuan-Bot version BL58.
 * To be included in BL58's main program */

// set some variables
int line,threshold,fwd = 1,rvs = 0, check = 0;

// motors
#define Left OUT_A
#define Right OUT_C
#define Head OUT_B

// constants
#define CALIBRATION 50
#define GO 500
#define PUSH 800
#define TURN 300
#define AMOUNT 2

// sensors
#define See SENSOR_2
#define LBump SENSOR_1
#define Rotate SENSOR_3

// go forward
void Forward()
{
   OnFwd(Left+Right);
}

// go in reverse
void Reverse()
{
   OnRev(Left+Right);
}

/* smart function for turning right - can
 * turn right regardless of BL58's current direction*/
void TurnR()
{
   if(fwd == 1)
   {
```

```
    Rev(Right);
    Wait(TURN);
    Fwd(Right);
    }

    else
    {
    Fwd(Left);
    Wait(TURN);
    Rev(Left);
    }
}

/* smart function for turning left - can
 * turn left regardless of BL58's current direction*/
void TurnL()
{
    if(fwd == 1)
    {
    Rev(Left);
    Wait(TURN);
    Fwd(Left);
    }

    else
    {
    Fwd(Right);
    Wait(TURN);
    Rev(Right);
    }
}

// basic turning fuction
void Turn()
{
    Rev(Left);
    Fwd(Right);
    Wait(TURN);
}
```

Why were the variables declared in the header? The smart functions use variables, so we need the variables *here*. Are the variables also in the main program? Yes, what's in the header gets put into the main program.

Now about these smart functions: what do they do and why are they necessary? Think about this: if the robot is in reverse—instead of going forward, which it previously was—what happens when you call a "generic" turn right function? The robot would actually turn left! To prevent this from happening, the program needs to determine the robot's current direction, and then execute special code for turning right when the robot is going in that particular direction. All this is accomplished by the smart functions, which can figure out BL58's current direction—by using the variables declared in the header—and execute the appropriate code. Now we can simply call TurnR() or TurnL() anywhere in the main program without having to worry about BL58 making incorrect turns.

With the header behind us, we need to start working on that main program. We'll begin with the calibration function.

Programming the Calibration Function

Take a look at BL58's customized calibration function:

```
/* This function calibrates the
 *  "line searching" light sensors */
void Calibrate()
{
    until(LBump==0);
    line=See;
    threshold=line+AMOUNT;
    Wait(CALIBRATION);
    until(LBump==1);
    PlaySound(SOUND_CLICK);
    Wait(CALIBRATION);
    until(LBump==0);
    Wait(CALIBRATION);
    until(LBump==1);
    PlaySound(SOUND_CLICK);
    Wait(CALIBRATION);
}
```

This calibration function is about the same as the others we've worked on, but notice all the pauses. We're using BL58's release-type bumper for the calibration process, and this specific bumper can be prone to rapid bumper clicks; that is, the touch sensor can be rapidly pressed and released by just barely touching the antenna. The pauses in the calibration function are in between each time the antenna needs to be pressed or released, and they practically eliminate the problem of rapid bumper clicks.

We've taken care of the calibration function. Now we need to begin working on the task that uses information from the calibrating function: the line-detecting task.

Programming the Line-Detection Task

Some of the unique aspects of BL58's line-detection task are the use of a moving head and a rotation sensor. These make the task quite interesting but more complex. When BL58 detects the line, it simply switches direction and begins heading in reverse. But what about its head? It's facing in the opposite direction! We need to turn the head all the way around now and end up in a *specific* position. Using timing, we might be able to get the head in the general direction of where we want it to be, but it would soon be out of whack, and the program wouldn't have any idea of the head's position. With a *rotation sensor*, we can get the head in virtually the same place every time! Here is the line-detection task:

```
// clear the rotation sensor
ClearSensor(Rotate);

// Task that watches for the line
task LWatch()
{
    // highest priority
    SetPriority(0);

    while(true)   // infinite loop - always check for line
    {
        until(See<=threshold); // until light sensor detects line

            acquire(ACQUIRE_USER_1)  // get control
            {
                check = 0;   // allow antennae to detect

                if(fwd == 1)   // if going forward...
                {
                Reverse();   // go the other way!
                OnRev(Head);
                until(Rotate==150); // move head 180 degrees
                Off(Head);
                fwd = 0;      // update variables!
                rvs = 1;
                PlaySound(SOUND_UP);
                }

                else    // if we're in reverse
                {
                Forward();   // go the other way!
                OnFwd(Head);
                until(Rotate==0);   // move head 180 degrees
                Off(Head);
                fwd = 1;       // update variables
                rvs = 0;
                PlaySound(SOUND_UP);
                }
            }
    }
}
```

NOTE *Every time you begin a program that uses a rotation sensor, you need to clear the rotation sensor's reading. I included the line of code that is responsible for this above the line-detection task, but in reality, it will be somewhere in the main task. I included it here only for illustrative purposes.*

Before we go any further, we need to discuss how to use a rotation sensor. First, when we clear the rotation sensor, it equals 0. Every time we start the program, we will make sure the head is facing exactly straight, and then clear the rotation sensor; this position equals 0. What is the value of the rotation sensor when the head is facing in the opposite direction? Through testing, I determined 150 to be a good value.

Another important point to note is that when making large turns, such as a 180-degree turn, the head will be turning only to the right. We're not doing this because we have trouble keeping track of the head's position; we're doing this because we have problems with the electrical wires. If we start turning the head left and right, and 180 degrees here and 360 degrees there, before you know it, the head will be one tangled mess! The head *can* move left and right, but when turning it all the way towards the back, it will be traveling by means of a right turn *only*.

Let's get back to the line-detection task. First, the check variable is something for the antennae, which we will be discussing later. Second, we have two general sections: one for when BL58 is going forward, and another for when BL58 is going in reverse. In each section, BL58 changes its current direction and then turns its head 180 degrees to the other side. Here is one example of how this is accomplished:

```
Reverse();   // go the other way!
OnRev(Head);
until(Rotate==150); // move head 180 degrees
Off(Head);
```

We use an until statement to indicate when to stop the head. At the bottom of each of these sections, we update the direction-theory variables and play a sound for confirmation that the task is completed.

Programming the Dual-Bumper Task

Now we need to work on the dual-bumper task. Now actually, the chances of *both* antennae, which are widely separated, getting pressed at the same time are very low indeed. However, if both *did* get pressed, the sumo-bot would experience that erratic behavior I mentioned—suddenly going in reverse. To be on the safe side, we will create the BPressed() task:

```
// Task Both Pressed
task BPressed()
{
   // second highest priority
   SetPriority(1);

   while(true)  // infinite loop - always check
   {
      until(LBump==0&&See==100);  // until both sensors activated

      acquire(ACQUIRE_USER_1)  // get control
        {
```

```
            if(fwd == 1)      // if we're going forward
            {
            Forward();         // keep going forward
            until(LBump==1&See<100); // until both sensors not pressed
            PlaySound(SOUND_UP);
            }

            else      // if we're going in reverse
            {
            Reverse();   // keep going in reverse
            until(LBump==1&See<100); // until both sensors not pressed
            PlaySound(SOUND_UP);
            }
        }
    }
}
```

The dual-bumper task is quite simple: if both bumpers are pressed simultaneously, continue going in the current direction. One part that deserves mention is this line:

```
until(LBump==0&&See==100);  // until both sensors activated
```

We're using our special sensor trick, so the touch sensor for the right bumper, See, reads 100 on the sensor input when activated. On the other hand, LBump equals 0 when pressed, since it is a release-type bumper. Therefore, this line of code says, "until the left bumper reads 0 and the right bumper reads 100." After both bumpers have been pressed, the task figures out whether BL58 is going in forward or reverse, and then continues going in that direction until both bumpers have been deactivated.

Programming the Bumper Tasks

The left and right bumper tasks are next on our agenda. These are extremely simple: if activated, they tell BL58 to turn in the direction of the bumper that was pressed. One example of a bumper task sufficiently explains how they operate:

```
// Task Bump Left Watch
task BLWatch()
{
   // third highest priority
   SetPriority(2);

   while(true)   // infinite loop - continually check sensor
   {
      // until LBump is released
      until(LBump==0&check == 0);

         acquire(ACQUIRE_USER_1)  // get control
         {
```

```
        TurnL();     // turn left
        PlaySound(SOUND_UP);
    }
  }
}
```

Notice that check variable is here again. This variable is, in fact, specifically for the bumper tasks. To understand its purpose, however, you first need to understand the maneuvering task.

Programming the Maneuvering Task

In our previous programs, the maneuvering task has usually been relatively simple and unimportant compared with crucial tasks such as those responsible for line and sumo detection. BL58 takes a different approach with its maneuvering task: here, it's complex and important. As described earlier in the chapter, BL58's maneuvering plan involves moving its head a little to the right, thus placing its release-type bumper directly in front, and checking to see if its left antenna (the release-type bumper) has detected anything. I call this action an *opponent check*.

We always wait a little while before making random moves, so that BL58 can make some simple forward progress. That's why an opponent check is spurred by the maneuvering task *after* a wait of five seconds. If BL58 really is pushing the opponent, it turns its head back and continues going forward for eight seconds, which we hope is enough time to push the opponent off the arena. If it's not, BL58 can always check again.

But the *real* purpose of checking is not for seeing if BL58 is pushing the opponent, but for flashing the green light for a turn. Why make a turn? BL58 doesn't make any turns when it detects the line, so another form of turning is needed, which is what the maneuvering task, shown next, accomplishes.

```
// Our maneuvering task
task Maneuver()
{
    // fourth highest priority
    SetPriority(3);

    while(true)   // continually ask for control
    {
        acquire(ACQUIRE_USER_1) // get control
        {
          Wait(GO); // wait a little while first

          if(fwd == 1)  // if going forward
          {
            check = 1;    // prevent BLWatch() and BRWatch() from taking over
            OnRev(Head);
            until(Rotate==40); // check to see if we're pushing the opponent

            if(LBump==0)    // if we are pushing opponent
            {
```

```
     Fwd(Head);
     until(Rotate==0);  // get head back in place
     Off(Head);
     Forward();   // continue pushing
     check = 0;   // allow BLWatch() and BRWatch() the ability to gain control
     Wait(PUSH);  // push for eight seconds
     PlaySound(SOUND_CLICK);
  }

   else if(LBump==1)      // if we aren't pushing opponent
   {
   check = 0;   // allow BLWatch() and BRWatch() the ability to gain control
   Fwd(Head);
   until(Rotate==0); // get head back in place
   Off(Head);
   Turn();        // turn a little
   Forward();     // then continue going forward
   PlaySound(SOUND_DOUBLE_BEEP);
   }
 }

   else   // if we're going in reverse
   {
    check = 1;   // prevent BLWatch() and BRWatch() from taking over
    OnRev(Head);
    until(Rotate==190); // check to see if we're pushing the opponent

    if(LBump==0)     // if we are pushing opponent
    {
      Fwd(Head);
      until(Rotate==150);  // get head back in place
      Off(Head);
      Reverse();    // continue pushing
      check = 0;    // allow BLWatch() and BRWatch() the ability to gain control
      Wait(PUSH);   // push for eight seconds
    }

    else if(LBump==1)   // if we aren't pushing opponent
    {
    check = 0;     // allow BLWatch() and BRWatch() the ability to gain control
    Fwd(Head);
    until(Rotate==150); // get head back in place
    Off(Head);
    Turn();          // turn a little
    Reverse();       // then continue in reverse
    }
   }
  }
 }
}
}
```

The large number of `if` and `else` statements can be attributed to the great variety of possible situations. Since there are so many situations BL58 might be in at this point, the maneuvering task asks one question, goes through one `if` or `else` statement, asks another question, goes through another `if` or `else` statement, and so on. There are a lot of subdivisions in this task!

Notice that `check` variable is here. Now you can understand what `check` is for, through an illustration. BL58 is moving along and decides it's going to do an opponent check. As it's doing this, its *right* bumper is pressed. What happens? The right bumper task gets control immediately and turns the robot to the right, but what about the head? It's not looking straight ahead anymore! If the left bumper got pressed during the opponent check, the same thing happens: the left bumper would take control, turn the robot to the left, and leave the head out of place. What can we do about this?

The solution is to use *limited accessibility*. In the world of access control, a task with a higher priority always gets control from a lower one no matter what, right? Wrong! We can manipulate the program so that specific higher priority tasks *cannot* take control at *certain times* in the program (we did a form of this in Chapter 7). We don't want either of the bumper tasks to be able to take control when we're doing the opponent check, so we make the `check` variable equal 1 (`check = 1`) while we're doing the opponent check.

A closer look at the bumper tasks reveals that not only must the proper sensor be pressed before its task can take control, but also `check` must equal 0. In this way, we can successfully prevent the bumper tasks from taking over when we're doing the bumper check. If the left antenna does detect the opponent when doing the opponent check, we want a different reaction than that of the left bumper's task, and we get this different reaction by making `check` equal 1. Finally, `check` is set back to 0 when the opponent check is finished, and, in case BL58 ran over the line while doing the opponent check, the line-detection task also sets `check` back to 0 upon detection of the line.

Now that you've seen all the parts and know what the `check` variable does, you're ready to see the entire program. See Listing 9-2 for a *big* program for a *big* sumo-bot!

Listing 9-2. BL58_Access_Control.nqc

```
// BL58_Access_Control.nqc
// A sumo-bot program for Gargantuan-Bot Version BL58

#include "Gargantuan-Bot-BL58.nqh"    // include our header

task main()
{
  SetSensor(See,SENSOR_LIGHT);    // initialize all the sensors
  SetSensor(LBump,SENSOR_TOUCH);
  SetSensor(Rotate,SENSOR_ROTATION);

  Calibrate();    // calibrating light sensors...

  OnFwd(Left+Right);    // get moving forward...

  ClearSensor(Rotate); // clear the rotation sensor
```

```
   start LWatch;    // turn on all five tasks!
   start BPressed;
   start BLWatch;
   start BRWatch;
   start Maneuver;
}

// Task that watches for the line
task LWatch()
{
   // highest priority
   SetPriority(0);

   while(true)   // infinite loop - always check for line
   {
      until(See<=threshold); // until light sensor detects line

         acquire(ACQUIRE_USER_1)  // get control
         {
            check = 0;    // allow antennae to detect

            if(fwd == 1)    // if going forward...
            {
            Reverse();    // go the other way!
            OnRev(Head);
            until(Rotate==150); // move head 180 degrees
            Off(Head);
            fwd = 0;      // update variables!
            rvs = 1;
            PlaySound(SOUND_UP);
            }

            else     // if we're in reverse
            {
            Forward();    // go the other way!
            OnFwd(Head);
            until(Rotate==0);    // move head 180 degrees
            Off(Head);
            fwd = 1;       // update variables
            rvs = 0;
            PlaySound(SOUND_UP);
            }
         }
      }
}

// Task Both Pressed
task BPressed()
{
   // second highest priority
   SetPriority(1);

   while(true)  // infinite loop - always check
```

```
     {
          until(LBump==0&&See==100);  // until both sensors activated

          acquire(ACQUIRE_USER_1)  // get control
             {
                   if(fwd == 1)      // if we're going forward
                   {
                   Forward();        // keep going forward
                   until(LBump==1&&See<100); // until both sensors not pressed
                   PlaySound(SOUND_UP);
                   }

                   else      // if we're going in reverse
                   {
                   Reverse();   // keep going in reverse
                   until(LBump==1&&See<100); // until both sensors not pressed
                   PlaySound(SOUND_UP);
                   }
             }
       }
}


// Task Bump Left Watch
task BLWatch()
{
   // third highest priority
   SetPriority(2);

   while(true)   // infinite loop - continually check sensor
   {
      // until LBump is released
      until(LBump==0&check == 0);

         acquire(ACQUIRE_USER_1)  // get control
         {
               TurnL();    // turn left
               PlaySound(SOUND_UP);
         }
   }
}

// Task Bump Right Watch
task BRWatch()
{
   // third highest priority
   SetPriority(2);

   while(true)   // infinite loop - continually check sensor
   {
      until(See==100&check == 0); // until RBump is pressed

         acquire(ACQUIRE_USER_1)  // get control
```

```
        {
            TurnR();    // turn right
            PlaySound(SOUND_UP);
        }
    }
}

// Our maneuvering task
task Maneuver()
{
    // fourth highest priority
    SetPriority(3);

    while(true)   // continually ask for control
    {
        acquire(ACQUIRE_USER_1) // get control
        {
          Wait(GO); // wait a little while first

          if(fwd == 1)  // if going forward
          {
           check = 1;    // prevent BLWatch() and BRWatch() from taking over
           OnRev(Head);
           until(Rotate==40); // check to see if we're pushing the opponent

           if(LBump==0)     // if we are pushing opponent
           {
             Fwd(Head);
             until(Rotate==0);  // get head back in place
             Off(Head);
             Forward();   // continue pushing
             check = 0;    // allow BLWatch() and BRWatch() the ability to gain control
             Wait(PUSH);  // push for eight seconds
             PlaySound(SOUND_CLICK);
           }

           else if(LBump==1)       // if we aren't pushing opponent
           {
           check = 0;    // allow BLWatch() and BRWatch() the ability to gain control
           Fwd(Head);
           until(Rotate==0); // get head back in place
           Off(Head);
           Turn();         // turn a little
           Forward();      // then continue going forward
           PlaySound(SOUND_DOUBLE_BEEP);
           }
          }

          else   // if we're going in reverse
          {
           check = 1;    // prevent BLWatch() and BRWatch() from taking over
           OnRev(Head);
           until(Rotate==190); // check to see if we're pushing the opponent
```

```
            if(LBump==0)      // if we are pushing opponent
            {
              Fwd(Head);
              until(Rotate==150);  // get head back in place
              Off(Head);
              Reverse();      // continue pushing
              check = 0;      // allow BLWatch() and BRWatch() the ability to gain control
              Wait(PUSH);     // push for eight seconds
            }

            else if(LBump==1)    // if we aren't pushing opponent
            {
            check = 0;      // allow BLWatch() and BRWatch() the ability to gain control
            Fwd(Head);
            until(Rotate==150); // get head back in place
            Off(Head);
            Turn();          // turn a little
            Reverse();       // then continue in reverse
            }
        }
      }
   }
}

/* This function calibrates the
 *  "line searching" light sensors */
void Calibrate()
{
    until(LBump==0);
    line=See;
    threshold=line+AMOUNT;
    Wait(CALIBRATION);
    until(LBump==1);
    PlaySound(SOUND_CLICK);
    Wait(CALIBRATION);
    until(LBump==0);
    Wait(CALIBRATION);
    until(LBump==1);
    PlaySound(SOUND_CLICK);
    Wait(CALIBRATION);
}
```

This program is great, but it's not perfect (but what program is?). There are several specific areas that need to be addressed, which we will do in the next section.

Creating an Improved Access Control Program for BL58

BL58 has the following blind spots when using BL58_Access_Control.nqc (Listing 9-2):

- While turning the head 180 degrees, the antennae are unable to detect the opponent. Since the line-detection task has ultimate authority, and since the 180-degree head turn is supervised by the line-detection task, the antennae can't detect anything when the head is turning all the way around—and that's a lot of lost opportunity for detecting the opponent!

- When executing an opponent check, the right antenna is unable to detect the opponent. We deliberately did this to prevent complications, but in reality, we should allow the right antenna to detect the opponent in this situation. If the other sumo-bot is there, BL58 should go after it!

Let's take these problems one at a time and see how to solve them.

The 180-Degree Head-Turn Problem

There is a simple solution to the first problem, but it is a little radical: give the bumper tasks a higher priority than the line-detection task! I know that I've stressed that you should *always* give line-detection tasks highest priority, but we can ignore that rule for right now, since we have a legitimate, specific reason. *The bumper tasks can't cause BL58 to accidentally run over the line.* The bumper tasks only execute turns; they do not make any physical progress other than turning. Therefore, BL58 can't accidentally run itself over the line, even though the line-detection task has a lower priority. So, we will change the LWatch() task's priority as follows:

```
SetPriority(2);
```

"A priority of 2!" That's right: one bumper gets a priority of 0, and the other a priority of 1. There is a reason for this: we can't have a dual-bumper task. If there were a dual-bumper task, it would need to possess a higher priority than that of the bumpers, and that priority would need to be the very highest one. This means that if both bumpers were pressed at the same time, the robot would have the potential to eventually run itself right off the arena! In the BL58_Access_Control.nqc program, we have a dual-bumper task to be on the safe side. For this program, we *don't* have a dual-bumper task to be on the safe side. Instead, to prevent erratic behavior, we give one bumper one priority and the other bumper another priority, thus making the line-detection task's priority 2.

> **NOTE** *Remember that the event of both bumpers getting pressed at the same time is extremely rare (with BL58). Giving the bumpers different priorities is safe and effective; it will not cause any problems.*

Now that the bumpers can detect a hit at any time, we need to see how that is accomplished. There are a number of situations that the bumper tasks must handle, so there's a lot of new code to observe. Let's look at the updated left bumper task:

```
// Task Bump Left Watch
task BLWatch()
{
   // highest priority
   SetPriority(0);

   while(true)   // infinite loop - continually check sensor
   {
      // until LBump is released
      until(LBump==0&check==0);

         acquire(ACQUIRE_USER_1)  // get control
         {
             if(fwd == 1)  // if we're going forward
             {
             if(Rotate == 0) // if head is aligned
             {
             TurnL();  // turn left
             PlaySound(SOUND_UP);
             }

             else      // if head isn't aligned
             {
             Off(Head);  // stop head from rotating immediately
             TurnR();    // turn right
             PlaySound(SOUND_UP);
             }
             }

             else    // if we're in reverse
             {
             if(Rotate == 150)  // if head is aligned
             {
               TurnL();     // turn left
               PlaySound(SOUND_UP);
             }

             else  // if head isn't aligned
             {
             Off(Head);  // stop head from rotating immediately
             TurnL();    // turn left
             PlaySound(SOUND_UP);
             }
             }
         }
   }
}
```

If the head is aligned, BL58 simply executes a turn. If the head isn't aligned, the task immediately stops the head from moving (if the head isn't aligned, it's moving) and then proceeds to execute a turn that will move the robot in the direction of the bumper that was activated. And, as you can see, this task is dependent on whether or not check equals 0 before it can take control. We still want this feature; when doing the opponent check, we want the maneuvering task to execute code different from the code here.

The Right Antenna Detection Problem

Next, we need to consider the second problem. The solution is, once again, rather simple: remove check from the right bumper task's statement that must be fulfilled before the task can take control. In other words, before we had:

```
until(See==100&check == 0);
```

And now we have:

```
until(See==100);
```

So when the opponent check has been activated, and check has been set to 1, the right bumper task can still be in "on" mode because it is no longer dependant on check to take control.

There is one problematic situation that this updated program brings up here in this task. Let's say BL58 has already detected the line once and has turned its head all the way around 180 degrees. After waiting a little while, it executes an opponent check. But suddenly, its *right bumper* detects the opponent. In the previous program, this situation wouldn't happen, since the right bumper was "turned off" during this period. However, with this program, the bumpers are virtually always active. So if the right bumper is activated in this particular situation, the code then proceeds to execute a *wrong* turn for the head—its head is past 150, so the program is confused. (Remember that the program turns the head in only one direction when making 180-degree turns, and thus, using the code from the previous program, doesn't work with values higher than 150.)

The solution is an extra else statement in the right bumper task to prevent something bad from happening during this specific (but rare) situation. See if you can find the extra else statement in the right bumper task:

```
// Task Bump Right Watch
task BRWatch()
{
    // second highest priority
    SetPriority(1);

    while(true)    // infinite loop - continually check sensor
    {
        // until RBump (under name of "See") is pressed
        until(See==100);

            acquire(ACQUIRE_USER_1)  // get control
            {
                if(fwd == 1)    // if we're going forward
                {
                if(Rotate == 0)  // if head is aligned
```

```
            {
            TurnR(); // turn right
            PlaySound(SOUND_DOWN);
            }

            else    // if head isn't aligned
            {
            Off(Head);  // stop head from rotating immediately
            TurnR();     // turn right
            PlaySound(SOUND_DOWN);
            }
            }

            else    // if we're in reverse
            {
            if(Rotate == 150)  // if head is aligned
            {
              TurnR();  // turn right
              PlaySound(SOUND_DOWN);
            }

            // if head is not aligned and slightly to the left
            else if(Rotate < 150)
            {
            Off(Head); // stop head from rotating immediately
            TurnR();    // turn right
            PlaySound(SOUND_DOWN);
            }

            // if head is not aligned and slightly to the right
            else
            {
            Off(Head);  // stop head from rotating immediately
            TurnR();    // turn right
            OnFwd(Head);        // reposition head
            until(Rotate==150);
            Off(Head);
            PlaySound(SOUND_DOWN);
            }
        }
      }
    }
}
```

The additional else statement is at the very bottom of the code: if the value of the rotation sensor is more than 150, stop the head, turn, and then reposition the head. This is the only code that we have seen so far that repositions the head, which brings up an important point: if the bumper tasks simply stop the head and leave it out of place, how will the head be repositioned?

Head Repositioning

We could put "head repositioning code" in the bumper tasks immediately after the code that turns BL58 as a whole, but this would bring back our problem of the antennae not being able to detect the opponent during certain periods of time. Since the bumper tasks are turning the head, and since the bumper tasks are responsible for responding to antenna hits, the antennae can't detect the opponent until the head has stopped turning.

What we'll do is put the repositioning code in the maneuvering task. Just as in the previous maneuvering task, the updated one is constantly asking for control, and the first thing this one does is it aligns the head if it is out of position; in other words, the repositioning code is at the very beginning of the maneuvering task. After the other tasks have finished their jobs but left the head out of position, this task takes over and repositions the head, if necessary. Once any aligning has been done, the maneuvering task does its regular maneuvering job. You can see the updated maneuvering task in the completed program, shown in the next section.

The Optimized Program for BL58

You are ready to see the new version of BL58's program. This version, BL58_Access_Control2.nqc, is shown in Listing 9-3.

Listing 9-3. BL58_Access_Control2.nqc

```
// BL58_Access_Control2.nqc
// A sumo-bot program for Gargantuan-Bot Version BL58

#include "Gargantuan-Bot-BL58.nqh"   // include our header

task main()
{
  SetSensor(See,SENSOR_LIGHT);      // initialize the sensors
  SetSensor(LBump,SENSOR_TOUCH);
  SetSensor(Rotate,SENSOR_ROTATION);

  Calibrate();    // calibrating light sensors...

  OnFwd(Left+Right);    // get moving forward...

  ClearSensor(Rotate); // clear the rotation sensor

  start BLWatch;    // turn on all four tasks!
  start BRWatch;
  start LWatch;
  start Maneuver;
}

// Task Bump Left Watch
task BLWatch()
```

```
{
    // highest priority
    SetPriority(0);

    while(true)   // infinite loop - continually check sensor
    {
        // until LBump is released
        until(LBump==0&check==0);

            acquire(ACQUIRE_USER_1)  // get control
            {
                if(fwd == 1)  // if we're going forward
                {
                if(Rotate == 0) // if head is aligned
                {
                TurnL();  // turn left
                PlaySound(SOUND_UP);
                }

                else      // if head isn't aligned
                {
                Off(Head);  // stop head from rotating immediately
                TurnR();    // turn right
                PlaySound(SOUND_UP);
                }
                }

                else    // if we're in reverse
                {
                if(Rotate == 150)  // if head is aligned
                {
                  TurnL();    // turn left
                  PlaySound(SOUND_UP);
                }

                else  // if head isn't aligned
                {
                Off(Head);  // stop head from rotating immediately
                TurnL();    // turn left
                PlaySound(SOUND_UP);
                }
                }
            }
    }
}

// Task Bump Right Watch
task BRWatch()
{
    // second highest priority
    SetPriority(1);
```

```
while(true)   // infinite loop - continually check sensor
{
    // until RBump (under name of "See") is pressed
    until(See==100);

        acquire(ACQUIRE_USER_1)  // get control
        {
            if(fwd == 1)   // if we're going forward
            {
            if(Rotate == 0)  // if head is aligned
            {
            TurnR(); // turn right
            PlaySound(SOUND_DOWN);
            }

            else    // if head isn't aligned
            {
            Off(Head);  // stop head from rotating immediately
            TurnR();    // turn right
            PlaySound(SOUND_DOWN);
            }
            }

            else    // if we're in reverse
            {
            if(Rotate == 150)  // if head is aligned
            {
              TurnR();  // turn right
              PlaySound(SOUND_DOWN);
            }

            // if head is not aligned and slightly to the left
            else if(Rotate < 150)
            {
            Off(Head); // stop head from rotating immediately
            TurnR();    // turn right
            PlaySound(SOUND_DOWN);
            }

            // if head is not aligned and slightly to the right
            else
            {
            Off(Head);  // stop head from rotating immediately
            TurnR();     // turn right
            OnFwd(Head);        // reposition head
            until(Rotate==150);
            Off(Head);
            PlaySound(SOUND_DOWN);
            }
        }
    }
```

```
    }
}

// Task that watches for the line
task LWatch()
{
    // third highest priority
    SetPriority(2);

    while(true)   // infinite loop - always check for line
    {
        until(See<=threshold); // until light sensor detects line

            acquire(ACQUIRE_USER_1)  // get control
            {
                // allow left bumper to gain control if needed
                check = 0;

                if(fwd == 1)   // if going forward...
                {
                Reverse();   // go the other way!
                fwd = 0;      // update variables!
                rvs = 1;
                OnRev(Head);   // turn head 180 degrees to other side
                until(Rotate==150);
                Off(Head);
                PlaySound(SOUND_UP);
                }

                else     // if we're in reverse
                {
                Forward();   // go the other way!
                fwd = 1;        // update variables
                rvs = 0;
                OnFwd(Head);  // turn head 180 degrees to other side
                until(Rotate==0);
                Off(Head);
                PlaySound(SOUND_UP);
                }
            }
        }
}

// Our maneuvering task
task Maneuver()
{
    // fourth highest priority
    SetPriority(3);

    while(true)   // infinite loop - continually check
    {
            acquire(ACQUIRE_USER_1) // get control
```

```
{
    // if we're going forward and head is not aligned
    if(fwd == 1 & Rotate!=0)
    {
    OnFwd(Head);      // properly align head
    until(Rotate==0);
    Off(Head);
    PlaySound(SOUND_CLICK);
    }

    // if we're going in reverse and head is not aligned
    else if(rvs == 1 & Rotate != 150)
    {
    OnRev(Head);      // properly align head
    until(Rotate==150);
    Off(Head);
    PlaySound(SOUND_DOUBLE_BEEP);
    }

    // once this is done, wait a little before "opponent check"
    Wait(GO);

    if(fwd == 1)  // if going forward
    {
     check = 1;  // prevent BLWatch task from interfering
     OnRev(Head);
     until(Rotate==40); // position head for a check

     // if we are pushing opponent
     if(LBump==0)
     {
       // align head and go forward
       PlaySound(SOUND_UP);
       Fwd(Head);
       until(Rotate==0);
       Off(Head);
       Forward();
       check = 0;  // allow BLWatch task to take over if needed
       Wait(PUSH); // push for eight seconds before checking again
     }

     // if we aren't pushing opponent
     else
     {
     // align head and turn
     Fwd(Head);
     until(Rotate==0);
     Off(Head);
     check = 0;  // allow BLWatch task to take over if needed
     Turn();
     Forward();
```

```
                PlaySound(SOUND_DOUBLE_BEEP);
                }
            }

            // if in reverse
            else
            {
            check = 1;   // prevent BLWatch task from interfering
            OnRev(Head);
            until(Rotate==190);   // position head for a check

            // if we are pushing opponent
            if(LBump==0)
            {
                // align head and go forward
                PlaySound(SOUND_UP);
                Fwd(Head);
                until(Rotate==150);
                Off(Head);
                Reverse();
                check = 0;   // allow BLWatch task to take over if needed
                Wait(PUSH); // push for eight seconds before checking again
            }

            // if we aren't pushing opponent
            else
            {
            // align head and turn
            Fwd(Head);
            until(Rotate==150);
            Off(Head);
            check = 0;    // allow BLWatch task to take over if needed
            Turn();
            Reverse();
            PlaySound(SOUND_DOUBLE_BEEP);
            }
        }
      }
    }
}

/* This function calibrates the
 *  "line searching" light sensors */
void Calibrate()
{
    until(LBump==0);
    line=See;
    threshold=line+AMOUNT;
    Wait(CALIBRATION);
    until(LBump==1);
    PlaySound(SOUND_CLICK);
```

```
    Wait(CALIBRATION);
    until(LBump==0);
    Wait(CALIBRATION);
    until(LBump==1);
    PlaySound(SOUND_CLICK);
    Wait(CALIBRATION);
}
```

Whew! That's a lot of code to put on paper! But, as you'll soon see, it operates better than the previous program.

> **NOTE** *Remember that you don't need to retype the programs in this book into BricxCC. All of the programs for this book are available from the Downloads section of the Apress web site (*www.apress.com*).*

Testing BL58

We're going to test both of the programs we made: the first one to see the basic idea of BL58's substrategy, and the second one to observe the improved sections of the previous program. Download both programs to your RCX—you can choose whichever program slots you would like.

Testing the First Version of the Program

Switch to the first program, BL58_Access_Control.nqc, and start it by pressing the Run button on the RCX. First, you need to perform the now-familiar chore of calibration. Position BL58 on your arena so that *both* of its light sensors are viewing the 2-inch-thick outer line (you'll need to hold the sumo-bot in this position). You get more efficient values for the line-detection task when you do this, rather than having just one light sensor viewing the outer line during calibration. After making sure that both light sensors are viewing the outer line, flick BL58's release-type bumper, or should I say antenna. The RCX should give a little beep, indicating that the proper readings have now been taken. Now place BL58 in the middle of your arena and, when you are ready, give the release-type antenna a little flick. With another little beep, BL58 should become alive.

The best way to start off is by activating BL58's various features (line detecting, touch sensor detecting, and so on), and then watching its responses. The first test is the simple touch sensor test: press either of BL58's bumpers (antennae). Activating the antenna on the right should result in a right turn, and activating the antenna on the left should result in a left turn. Now let BL58 find the line—it will promptly reverse and turn its head. As its head is executing the 180-degree turn, flick its antennae. What happens? Nothing! This is a problem that the updated program fixes, as you'll see when you test that program.

If you feel like pressing BL58's antennae again to see if it turns in the correct direction, go ahead. Even though it's traveling in a different direction, and even though it's using the same functions for turning right and left, BL58 will turn in the proper direction. All this is because of our smart functions (who doesn't like smart functions?).

To try out the dual-bumper task, press both antennae. At first, BL58 will begin to turn, but it will quickly start to go straight. And when it does go straight, that means the dual-bumper task has been activated. Notice that the chances of both bumpers being activated simultaneously are very unlikely!

Now let's observe that maneuvering task in action. Make sure BL58 has enough room to run for about five seconds, and sit back and watch. Sure enough, after five seconds, its head makes a slight turn to the right. Its left antenna should land right in front of the sumo-bot, and then its head should turn back. Since there wasn't anything in front of the sumo-bot (at the moment), it will execute a turn.

Let's go for another round of testing on that maneuvering task. Allow BL58 to go straight for another five seconds, but immediately before its head starts to turn, place your hand directly in front of the sumo-bot (hands come in handy don't they?). Once again, BL58 will execute an opponent check, but this time, it detects something is there, so it does just what its program tells it to do: go straight. The program will wait eight seconds before executing another opponent check.

Testing the Improved Version of the Program

Now let's move on to testing BL58_Access_Control2.nqc. After switching to this program on your RCX, and pressing the Run button on your RCX, do the calibration (this is the same as the last program's calibration), and then place BL58 on your arena. Flick the release-type antenna, and BL58 will become alive once again.

To observe the differences in the programming, begin by letting BL58 detect the line. As its head is turning, press either of its bumpers. *What happens?* BL58 will stop its head immediately, turn in the appropriate direction, and then continue to turn its head until it reaches the proper position. You can press the antennae as many times as you want when BL58 is turning its head, and it will always stop its head, make a turn, and resume turning its head until it has reached the proper position.

Do you remember this question: When BL58 does an opponent check, what happens if the right antenna gets pressed? The answer for the previous program was that it doesn't do anything! This is not the case with the updated and optimized program. With this program, the right antenna *can* detect opponents during an opponent check. To observe this in action, wait for BL58 to execute an opponent check, and then press its *right* antenna. BL58 will turn towards the right, align its head, and continue forwards. Now the right bumper can work in this situation! With these improvements, BL58 can be much more responsive and active in searching for the opponent, which is definitely something you want!

Now that we have tested all the individual actions BL58 provides, we need to let something else test BL58's actions. BL58 can push a maximum of approximately four pounds, so take anything within that weight range and place it in your arena. The typical large books and canned food work well for this purpose. Arrange everything to your liking in the arena and start up BL58 (not forgetting calibration). Sit back and watch the action as BL58 pushes objects off the arena.

NOTE *BL58's opponent check will not catch most books. This isn't an oversight. Just about any sumo-bot belonging to the big-sumo strategy will be taller than a one- or two-inch book.*

After watching to your satisfaction, grab some objects and do some pushing yourself. Push BL58 from the side and see how those eight wheels work together to provide a lot of traction. Push on the front, push on the back, push all you want, but don't be too rough—remember that you can push with a lot more strength than any LEGO MINDSTORMS sumo-bot!

Considering the Pros and Cons of BL58's Design

BL58 can undoubtedly be considered an intelligent sumo-bot. Its five sensors allow for extensive detecting and searching capabilities, and its five motors provide a great deal of power. But there are far more features and aspects of BL58. Let's quickly look into these features by observing the various pros and cons.

The Pros

Here are the advantages of BL58's design:

- BL58's mobility system, consisting of a motor for each wheel, is extra efficient.

- The worm gears contained in the mobility system give the positive side effect of not allowing the wheels to be rotated by external sources.

- The eight wheels provide great traction.

- The slopes play the dual role of offensive *and* defensive subassemblies.

- The rotation sensor gives pinpoint precision when aligning the head.

- BL58's multiple sensors, structural features, and program work together to provide an efficient and aggressive sumo-bot substrategy.

- The antenna-detection system allows for excellent searching and detecting capabilities.

Overall, BL58 makes for a highly efficient sumo-bot. It has a lot of motors, a lot of sensors, and efficient code. Out of all the sumo-bots I've made, BL58 is one of my top picks.

The Cons

The following are some disadvantages of BL58's design:

- The antennae can get pushed into different positions.

- The slope subassemblies have a somewhat weak connection to the chassis.

- Electrical wires might get caught when BL58's head is turning.

As you know from the final assembly, the antennae must be positioned in a particular way. If the opposing sumo-bot pushes BL58's antennae at just the right angle, they can get slightly out of position. Fortunately, this by no means stops them from working, but they are in a less desirable position.

Also, the slope subassemblies might get loosened during play or, in some rare cases, pulled off. This has to do with the slightly weak connection point to the chassis. For the greater part of the time however, the slopes should be just fine.

Lastly, when the head is making large turns, the 2x2x2/3 electrical connectors might get caught somewhere on the head base subassembly. In the ensuing event, the motor would detach itself from the chassis and fall off. Simply positioning the wires beforehand in places where they won't get caught can prevent this.

Conclusion

You have just completed the last sumo-bot project in this book (but not the book itself!). You've not only seen but also built small, medium, and large sumo-bots. I hope that you have come to an important conclusion: sumo-bots come in all shapes and sizes. I hope that you've come to another important conclusion: each of these sizes has specific approaches that work best in that situation. Each approach—small and fast, M-class, and big sumo—needs to be treated as a separate, distinct section of robotic sumo.

Speaking of what works best for a strategy, we need to sum up all the important points for the big-sumo strategy:

- Pushing power, "bigness," and plenty of motors are essential.

- The more sensors you can use, the better; sensors make your sumo-bot smart.

- Traction is particularly important for the big-sumo strategy.

- Multiple RCXs are encouraged (when allowed by rule sets). I didn't have multiple RCX sumo-bots in this book because I didn't want to have overwhelming requirements, but using more than one RCX on your sumo-bots belonging to the big-sumo strategy is extremely advantageous.

- Make your big sumo-bots especially attentive and aggressive. In a strategy like this one, those features pay off.

Now that you've completed Parts Two, Three, and Four—the sumo-bot chapters—the next step is creating your own sumo-bots. You might feel like starting from scratch and creating your own sumo masterpieces right away, or you might not be ready for that yet. Although building your own creations is an integral part of learning how to do MINDSTORMS, carefully observing other people's creations to learn from them is essential as well. Not only should you observe other people's creations, you should also take either the basic idea or actual sections of those creations and use them as springboards for your own robots. So, if you want to, you can take the chassis presented in this book and use them as starting points. You can also use my subassemblies, mechanisms, and substrategies for your sumo-bots.

Can you use BL58's antenna approach for Brain-Bot, or should all subassemblies, mechanisms, and substrategies shown in this book be used only in the strategy in which they were presented? While the different strategies are unique and should be considered as separate, distinct sections of robotic sumo, various tricks, subassemblies, and mechanisms *can be used throughout the strategies*. Could XK1's "claw approach" be applied to Gargantuan-Bot? Could BL58's "the front is the back and the back is the front approach" be applied to Zip-Bam-Bot? Could ZR2's CRW approach be applied to Gargantuan-Bot? *Absolutely!* Although you must take some care in applying certain approaches to certain strategies, many approaches and subassemblies do have the potential to be used in more than just one strategy.

Let's recap: you've learned all of the robotic sumo basics, built and programmed sumo-bots that cover the main types of sumo-bots that can be made, and have gained quite a bit of insight into LEGO MINDSTORMS and the NQC programming language. What you need to do now is participate in a robotic sumo event, and that's the subject of the next part of this book.

Part Five

Getting Involved in a Robotic Sumo Event

Participating in a LEGO MINDSTORMS Robotic Sumo Event

PARTICIPATING IN A ROBOTIC sumo event is perhaps the most exciting part of robotic sumo. After all your building and programming, you're finally able to put your creation to the real test. And getting to meet other people and their sumo-bots is an incredible, indescribable experience.

You can get involved in a robotic sumo event in two ways: find and attend a robotic sumo event or host your own robotic sumo event. We'll be looking at the first option in this chapter, and we'll discuss in detail how to host your own robotic sumo events in the following chapter. You'll probably want to gain some experience by participating in some robotic sumo events before hosting your own. However, if there aren't any events planned in your area, there is no reason why—with some help from this book—you can't host one.

Exactly how does a robotic sumo event operate? Can you reprogram your sumo-bots while participating? Can you bring more than one sumo-bot? Should you bring anything else? This chapter will answer these and other questions, and prepare you for some real robotic sumo action.

Another reason to learn about participating in a robotic sumo event is that it can help you *win* an event. So read on!

Finding a Robotic Sumo Event in Your Area

Checklist: you have a sumo-bot, programmed it, tested it, and are ready to bring it to an event. Now what? You need to *find* an event. Depending on where you live, you might think your chances are bleak indeed. "Come on, a robotic sumo event in my town?" That's right, there just might be one near where you live.

LEGO, in general, is very popular, and LEGO MINDSTORMS and the RIS are extremely popular. LEGO and LEGO MINDSTORMS fans have formed LEGO User Groups all across the world, and some of these groups organize robotic sumo events. Additionally, there are various other organizations that host LEGO MINDSTORMS robotic sumo events.

But if it turns out that there isn't an event in your area, that *doesn't* mean you will never be able to participate in an actual robotic sumo event. As noted at the beginning of this chapter, you can organize an event in your area, so you can always get in on the robotic sumo fun. You'll learn about hosting an event in the next chapter.

Here, we'll look at several ways to find robotic sumo events, starting with LEGO User Groups.

LEGO User Group's Robotic Sumo Events

All across America, and in other parts of the world, are numerous LEGO User Groups. These groups are not official; that is, LEGO neither founded nor operates LEGO User Groups. People like you and me formed these groups. Although LEGO may occasionally get involved in some of the User Groups' activities, all of them are completely unofficial. These groups are for LEGO fans that want to meet to talk about their common interests, show off their creations, and yes, to hold robotic sumo events (among other events, of course).

So, how do you find these LEGO User Groups? The answer is LUGNET: the LEGO Users Group Network. LUGNET, which is located at www.lugnet.com, is used and viewed by thousands upon thousands of LEGO fans all across the world. You can get an idea of its impact from its home page, shown in Figure 10-1.

LEGO fans can meet in the LUGNET forums to discuss their favorite LEGO themes, search the LUGNET set and part database, and much more. LUGNET has a membership available for a small price that gives you your own profile, web site, special privileges, and, of course, a password and member number. LUGNET has thousands of official members and continues to grow. In fact, LUGNET is so large that the LEGO Company posts messages on the forums there. If you have a question, you can find the related forum and post your question, and you should get a quick, friendly reply (LUGNET members are renowned for their friendliness).

But the LUGNET feature we're interested in now is the listing of LEGO User Groups and their web sites. To see this list, go to http://news.lugnet.com/org/. Another way to observe the various LEGO User Groups is with LUGMAP, which is LUGNET's map of the entire world. As shown in Figure 10-2, this map indicates where groups are located. You can go directly to the main map by visiting www.lugnet.com/map.

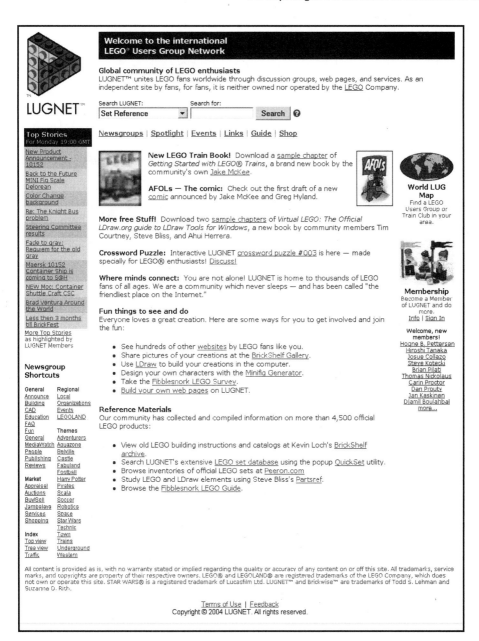

Figure 10-1. LUGNET's home page

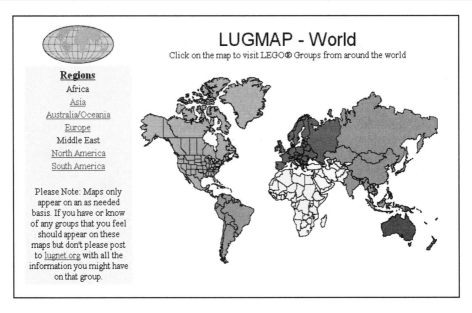

Figure 10-2. LUGNET's LUGMAP

To use this map, work through the submaps. For example, since it's possible for "general" LEGO User Groups to host LEGO MINDSTORMS robotic sumo events, you might do a search like this:

1. Click the continent of North America; doing so gives you additional information about that continent (see Figure 10-3).

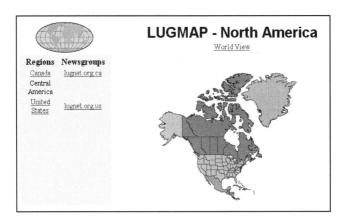

Figure 10-3. LUGNET's LEGO User Group Map centered on North America

2. Click United States to bring up another screen that narrows down the groups to General, LEGO Trains, and Robotics/MINDSTORMS, all of which have their own maps (see Figure 10-4).

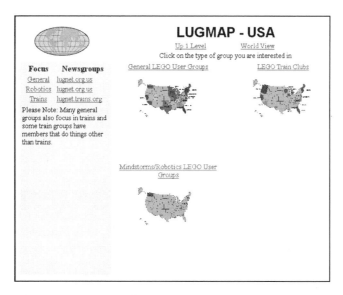

Figure 10-4. LUGNET's LEGO User Group Map showing the various types of LEGO Users Groups in the USA

3. Click the General LEGO User Groups map. That brings up the states and the various groups within those states (see Figure 10-5).

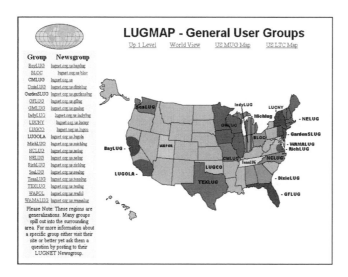

Figure 10-5. LUGNET's LEGO User Group Map showing general groups for the USA

4. Click a state that shows a group is there, and you will be taken to the group's web site.

However, you should be aware that LUGMAP, although it's quite useful indeed, is neither up-to-date nor complete. The LUGNET list of LEGO User Groups at http://news.lugnet.com/org/ is more complete than LUGMAP, but it doesn't list every single group in the world.

An example of a group that isn't listed in LUGMAP is the LEGO Robotics Group of Ann Arbor (LRGOAA). This group was founded and is headed by the technical reviewer of this book: Jona Jeffords. It is an incredible LEGO robotics-based group that hosts many challenging and exciting events. The web site for this group is www.24tooth.com, as shown in Figure 10-6.

The fact that this incredible group isn't listed in LUGMAP underscores the warning given on LUGMAP:

> *Please note: These regions are generalizations. Many groups spill out into the surrounding area. For more information about a specific group either visit their site or better yet ask them a question by posting to their LUGNET Newsgroup.*

So don't panic when you see a blank spot on the LUGMAP where you live. Head over to http://news.lugnet.com/org/ and look at this more complete listing. And if you don't see a User Group near you in that list, that doesn't mean one doesn't exist. Some groups aren't listed on LUGNET, so you have two more options for finding a group:

- Do a search on the Internet with a search engine such as Google (www.google.com). Try beginning with the phrase *LEGO User Group* and going from there.

- Post a question on LUGNET. The best place to post your question is in the http://news.lugnet.com/org/ forum. Specify the state, city, or general area in which you are looking for a group.

After finding a group in your area and the group's web site, search the group's planned events section. If they don't have a robotic sumo event planned, write them and suggest they get one started. Tell them what they'll be missing out on if they don't have a robotic sumo event!

Various Organization's Robotic Sumo Events

Several organizations hold annual (or biannual) LEGO events, which are *large* gatherings. They aren't official; just like the LEGO User Groups, they're organized by people like you and me. But they're different from LEGO User Group's events in that they're held once or twice a year and are usually at a different location each time. They do LEGO on a large scale!

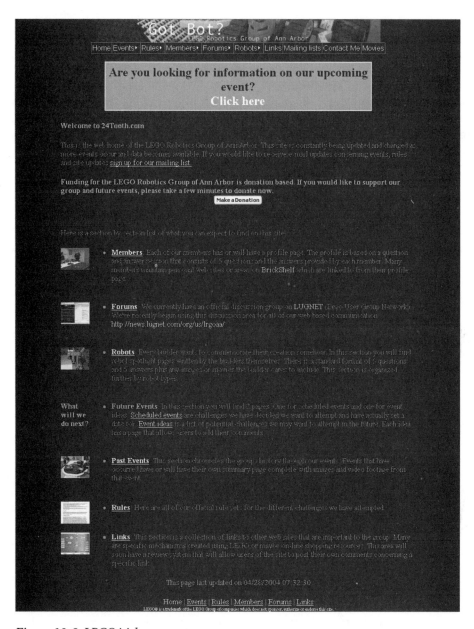

Figure 10-6. LRGOAA home page

One example of this type of event is BrickFest. BrickFest has its own web site (www.brickfest.com), shown in Figure 10-7, and the event is so large it has even gotten the LEGO Company's attention. Do these types of events have anything to do with robotic sumo? You bet! Part of the festivities at BrickFest 2003, held in Richmond, Virginia, was a robotic sumo event. BrickFest is for AFOL (Adult Fans of LEGO) participants only, but as with other events of this type, anyone can attend to watch the fun.

Once you've found an event you would like to participate in, you're ready to move on to the next topic of this chapter.

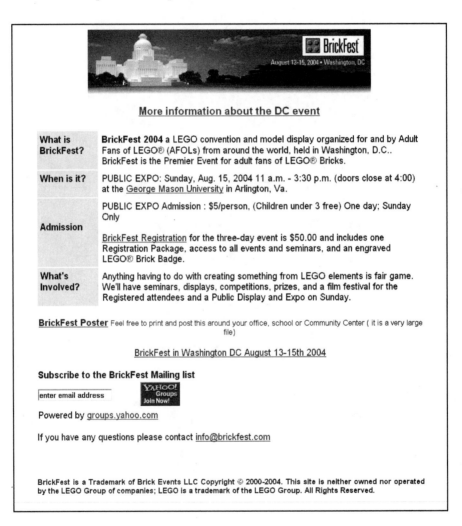

Figure 10-7. BrickFest's home page

Understanding the Rules and Restrictions

I'm not going to gripe about rules and regulations. Instead, I'll give you some very important tips. Back in Chapter 1, I mentioned one of the foremost tips: when you have the rule set for an event, *carefully* read *all* the rules. You don't want to miss or misunderstand something that prevents you from entering the competition once you get to the event.

> **TIP** *One of the most successful strategies in any LEGO competition is coming up with a strategy different from everyone else's. This is done by carefully analyzing the rule set and making a strategy for your robot that is unique and yet stays within the rules.*

Within a rule set for a competition, you need to look for several particularly important rules, which will affect your sumo-bot's design, programming, and what you will do at the event:

Classes, sizes, and weight of participating sumo-bots: Some events allow several different classes of sumo-bots; others allow only one class. In some events, all the robots compete against each other; in others, the different classes compete separately. Determine which type of sumo-bot will be the best one to build. What type of sumo-bot will have the best chance against all the others? Carefully scrutinize the size and weight allowed. Check for limitations on the number of sensors, motors, RCXs, and any other pieces. Events will always differ on this point.

Programming languages: Most events will pick a language or languages that all participating sumo-bots must use. Some allow only one programming language (for instance, RCX Code); others allow multiple languages; and still others place no limit on languages. Additionally, some events allow you to place and use multiple programs in your sumo-bot; others prohibit multiple programs.

> **TIP** *If allowed, you might consider creating multiple programs. Each program could be for combating a certain approach taken against your sumo-bot. And by the way, if the rule set doesn't mention the use of multiple programs, you can use multiple programs (that's what you call a loophole).*

Custom sensors: Some robotic sumo events strictly forbid custom sensors (and anything non-LEGO, for that matter); others allow and encourage using them. If you are a custom sensors freak, make sure you understand the event's view on them before bringing some.

The robotic sumo arena: Every rule set will (or *should*) give a detailed description of the robotic sumo arena. Take particular notice of the colors on the arena: is the line black and the surface area white, or vice-versa? That's one place where you don't want to be mistaken! Also, notice the size of the arena (sizes can be anywhere from 3 to 5 feet in diameter and possibly even larger), because this could affect how you design and/or program your sumo-bot.

Registration and event times: Some events—usually, but not always, larger events—will have strict rules on registering for the event on time and being at the event on time. This might seem a little unfair at first, but consider this: if there are 100 competitors, and 99 are present with all their equipment, will they wait half an hour for one person before getting started? In addition, if you are going to be making a trip to an event that is some distance from where you live, be sure to carefully plan so that you can arrive on time.

The allotted break time: Everyone needs to take a break, and everyone also needs to take a break *at the right time*. In the event in which you will be participating, make sure you know how much time you will have in between rounds for a break.

The time permitted for each round and the scoring system: Most events will give each round 3 minutes. However, what happens (concerning extra time given) if there is a deadlock, suicide (a sumo-bot accidentally falling off the edge), or no winner will vary. And thoroughly understanding the scoring system can be helpful. Who doesn't want to know who's ahead?

How many sumo-bots you can bring: An event's rules may state that each participant can bring only one sumo-bot. However, if the rules say that you can bring more than one sumo-bot or don't mention the topic at all (a loophole), feel free to bring multiple sumo-bots—provided you have the pieces to make them, of course!

Unique rules: Every event will have its own unique rules. These can be defined as slightly odd, not often seen, or an addition to the robotic sumo game. It's in your best interest to recognize these unique rules, because, whether you like them or not, you're going to need to follow them.

Once you've found the competition's rules and carefully read them, you need to make appropriate decisions and be ready to do what is expected of you at the event.

> **NOTE** *There are some points I didn't list here because they are assumed. For instance, you can't harm the opposing sumo-bot or the arena in any way. Every event will have a rule like this one, because this is the essence of robotic sumo. If you could harm the opponent, and use flamethrowers and chainsaws, it wouldn't be robotic sumo. Robotic sumo is a game of pushing and wits, not destruction and mayhem!*

Once you've gotten this far, there's nothing left except actually participating in the event.

Participating in the Event

At this point in the book, you know how to find an event in your area, fully understand the rules, and, of course, build and program efficient and successful sumo-bots. All that's left is for you to actually participate in the event. Here, we'll look at what to bring, how to participate, and what to expect.

To Find the Robotics Event, Just Look for the Crowd

Recently, I attended a LEGO robotics event that was taking place at a huge technical convention. I asked the person handling registration exactly where in the building the event was. She told me the general area, but then smiled and said, "Don't worry—it'll be easy to find. Just look for a crowd." She was right. There were around 50 to 75 other booths at that convention, but almost everyone wanted to see the LEGO robot action. It was as if the robots were powerfully drawing the people in, captivating their minds and imaginations. The audience members, young and old, had their eyes peeled on the bots. LEGO MIND-STORMS is definitely a crowd pleaser!

What You Should Bring

First, what you're bringing (besides your sumo-bot) is important. You never know what might come in handy! Here are a few tips:

Bring extra LEGO pieces. At a robotic sumo event, you never know what can happen. You might lose pieces during the event, so the extra ones you brought can cover that. You might even be able to help someone else out with your extra pieces. I bring a large, plastic storage container (the kind commonly used for storing screws, bolts, and nails—about the size of a large briefcase), filled with axles, pins, liftarms, extra motors, the LEGO remote control, and even a MicroScout.

Bring extra AA alkaline batteries. Some of the sumo-bots at a robotic sumo event can go through a lot of rounds, and that can drain the RCX's battery power *fast*. Bring extra AA alkaline batteries (anywhere from 6 to 24), so that you can change the batteries when necessary. *Do not* bring rechargeable batteries, because they do not provide as much of a voltage (and therefore pushing power) as alkaline batteries.

Bring some snacks and water. Say you've been participating in a robotic sumo event for three hours and have two more hours left to go. You've been fiercely participating—in a LEGO kind of way—and yelling your lungs out for your sumo-bot. The result? You'll be thirsty and probably hungry as well. Unless the information the event you're participating in specifically states that food and drinks will be available for everyone, it would be in your best interest to bring something to drink and eat.

Bring money to pay any participant's or entrance fee. It's not uncommon for the host of an event to charge participants a small entrance fee, which goes toward funding the prize for the winner. Usually, the larger events charge fees, and the majority of smaller events do not. For instance, BrickFest charges a $5 entrance fee. Charges vary, with $1 to $10 as the general range for an entrance or participator's fee for a LEGO MINDSTORMS robotic sumo event.

If allowed by the rules and if possible, bring your IR tower and a laptop. If reprogramming is allowed by the rules, you can bring your laptop and IR tower and make any necessary changes to your program(s) while at the event. I've heard of problems with using the IR tower on some laptops, so test yours before bringing it.

How to Properly and Successfully Participate

When the event gets going, sumo-bots start pushing, and people get excited, there are several important things to keep in mind. Some of these revolve around what the rules state, and others are universal:

The method of starting up the sumo-bots: Your sumo-bot is finally on the ring, but who starts it and the opposing sumo-bot? That's entirely up to the rules. If they want remote activation, step out of the ring. The person running the event will use a remote control to start the sumo-bots. If they want you to start your sumo-bot, start it up. Some rule sets have the participating sumo-bots started up by their creators using a switch or bumper on the sumo-bot (that's something that needs to be programmed in advance, so take note of this if you see it in a rule set).

The judge's decision: If you look at practically any rule set, you will always find one rule: *the judge's decision is final*. If something unusual happens on the ring, and it is not obvious who is the victor, *the judge will make the final decision*. The judge's decision is absolutely and entirely final, so don't argue, even if you really think your sumo-bot won. The judge will be either the host of the event or a person the host appointed.

Switching programs: Suddenly, you see that the next opponent you're going up against uses a particular approach. Do you have a program that is good for combating that approach? Use it, if you can. Some events don't allow the use of multiple programs; others have specific times that switching programs is allowed.

Sportsmanship: This should go without saying. It really doesn't matter who wins or loses; everyone is there for the fun of it. Put your sumo-bot in the ring, hope it wins, but don't get upset if it loses (or *too* upset, anyway).

After the Event

After the event is over, the fun continues. People will want to look at your sumo-bot, and you will want to check out other people's creations. When observers and other participants want to see your sumo-bot up close, don't be secretive and unrelenting. This is your chance to showcase your sumo-bot. When people want to see your little pusher, take it as a compliment!

You should also look at the other sumo-bots. Don't be afraid to go around and ask questions so that you can learn tips, tricks, strategies, and MINDSTORMS secrets to implement in your own sumo-bots. Perhaps you saw a complex subassembly on a sumo-bot, or maybe you observed how one of the sumo-bots used an interesting substrategy, or possibly you're just curious about another competitor's sumo-bot. Whatever the case, don't be afraid to ask the sumo-bot's creator if you could observe their sumo-bot a little closer. When you go to an event, it's a great opportunity to have fun *and* learn new things. The information you can acquire while participating in a robotic sumo event can be invaluable.

The Champion's Prize

If you won a competition, what would you get? Some events give you a round of applause; in other words, there is no prize. But many other events do have prizes.

In some of the robotic sumo events sponsored by LEGO, the LEGO Company provided prizes for the winners. Perhaps this is incentive to try harder to win, but what you really get out of a robotic sumo event is the enjoyment of participating and being with others who share a common interest.

The Best Expectation

As a final point, keep this in mind when participating in a robotic sumo event: You never know what can happen or who will be the victor.

It's easy to take a look at any particular opponent and think, "He is going to win." The simple fact is that the opponent who looked like he *wouldn't* win just might be the one who does. Despite any amount of preparation and testing, despite anyone's level of skill and knowledge, despite anything, you just can't tell what will happen.

Does this mean you don't need to carefully design your sumo-bot? No, spending plenty of time on building and programming (and I echo this from Chapter 2) is absolutely essential and *will improve your chances of winning*. So, actually I have two points:

- Always build and program your sumo-bots with great care, and expect your hard efforts to show through in their performance.

- But also always be ready for the unexpected to happen during a robotic sumo event.

Conclusion

If you've never been to a robotic sumo event before, I hope this chapter got you excited about going to one. Indeed, participating in an event is a great adventure, but you need to know what to expect and what's expected of you when you're there. As you learned in this chapter, it's really not that hard. Just be sure to bring the right equipment with you, adapt your sumo-bot to certain situations if necessary, have a good attitude, and don't get in the way of those running the event. Remember that this isn't supposed to be a stressful ordeal with grumpy judges; it's an event for LEGO fans to have fun.

And when you go to a LEGO MINDSTORMS robotic sumo event, you don't have to go alone—bring a friend. Something as exciting and interactive as a robotic sumo event is a great way to introduce a friend to the wonderful world of LEGO MINDSTORMS. Bring a friend, have some fun, and watch as a new MINDSTORMS fan is born!

What could be more incredible than going to a robotic sumo event? Try this: *hosting your own event.* You can create your *own* rules and decide the date and place. How do you do all that? Find out in the next chapter.

CHAPTER 11

Organizing a LEGO MINDSTORMS Robotic Sumo Event

Out of all the tasks you can undertake in robotic sumo, organizing your own LEGO MINDSTORMS robotic sumo event is one of the most rewarding. And when you host an event, *you* are in full control. You get to decide the way the game is played by developing your own rule set. You can choose whether the event will revolve around the small-and-fast, M-class, or big-sumo strategies; it could even be an event that allows multiple strategies and has an arena for each strategy!

As you would imagine, hosting an event involves a recognizable amount of work. This chapter will guide you through the many different tasks involved in organizing a robotic sumo event. And when it's all over, you'll find that one thing far outweighs the hard work: a sense of personal accomplishment.

Why, When, and How You Should Organize Your Own Event

Why, when, and how—the three questions that cover all bases for understanding the processes involved in hosting a robotic sumo event.

Why should you host a robotic sumo event? As mentioned in the previous chapter, one reason for hosting your own event is that you cannot find any robotic sumo events in your area. Another reason is simply because you would rather have your own. Maybe the rule set of an event happening in your area calls for a type of sumo-bot you don't feel like building at the moment, or maybe you want to start your own LEGO User Group that focuses on robotic sumo and LEGO MINDSTORMS.

When should you host a robotic sumo event? There's no time like the present. In other words, anytime is the right time. Hosting a robotic sumo event is not something that must be done in certain days, weeks, or months of the year. You can even host one if there's already an event (or several events) planned in your area.

How do you host a robotic sumo event? It takes a whole chapter to answer that question, but to give you an idea of what's involved, here is an overview: Create a rule set; make a robotic sumo arena; announce, prepare, and pick a place for the event (not necessarily in that order); and manage the event.

In the rest of this chapter, we'll be discussing the steps involved in hosting your own robotic sumo event, beginning with creating a rule set.

> **NOTE** *When you host a robotic sumo event, you are, in a sense, starting a LEGO User Group. If you plan on hosting multiple robotic sumo events, you should seriously consider starting your own LEGO User Group. You can plan your own events, get yourself a web site, and start a forum on LUGNET. You can name the group whatever you want, and you can be president, CEO, Head Brick, or whatever you would like to call yourself.*

Making Clear and Concise Rules

In a world saturated with rules, laws, and regulations, you finally get to make some of your *own* rules. These rules will shape the event, affect who participates, and decide the design of all participating sumo-bots. Furthermore, you want to carefully craft your rule set so it doesn't contain *loopholes* that someone could take advantage of.

Before you begin making your own rule set, you should carefully observe other rule sets to get an idea of what kinds of rules you'll want and need to include. The best place to observe other rule sets is on the Internet. A great way to do this is to do a search for LEGO User Groups that host robotic sumo events, as they will have their rule sets posted on their web sites. You should continue to scrutinize rule sets throughout your LEGO MINDSTORMS robotic sumo career, as the information and insights you can gain by doing this are invaluable.

The rules in your rule set will be directed at the sumo-bots, the programming, the robotic sumo arena, and the game itself. You'll also need various other rules to ensure fairness and safety in your event.

Sumo-Bot Rules

A great starting place is with the rules for the sumo-bots in the event. Decide the strategy for your event: small and fast, M-class, or big sumo. Then pick the substrategy. For example, for an M-class sumo-bot event, you might limit the weight to 2.5 pounds and no more than 25 studs wide. The participants can then make a yet further substrategy for each of their sumo-bots (usually reflecting the sumo-bot's approach for attacking the opposing sumo-bots).

Here is an example of sumo-bot rules for an event using the small-and-fast strategy:

The Sumo-Bots: All participating robots, known as sumo-bots, must be constructed out of LEGO pieces only. They must be completely autonomous—that is, acting independently of humans—and not contain anything non-LEGO. This includes custom sensors.

Weight and Size: The maximum weight allowed is 2 pounds and the maximum width is 25 studs. All sumo-bots will be checked for weight and size specifications before being admitted. You will be given one chance to reduce your sumo-bot's weight and/or size if it exceeds the 2-pound weight limit or 25-stud width limit. Sumo-bots that fail to meet these specifications will not be allowed entry.

Classes of Sumo-Bots: There are two distinct classes for this robotic sumo competition, and both revolve around the use of the Robotics Invention System (RIS) and the RCX microcomputer contained in the RIS. Both will be competing together, and both are subject to all the same rules except for the parts specifications. The two classes are:

- **RIS-Only.** All sumo-bots belonging to this class must be built out of the parts provided in *one* RIS *only*. All versions of the RIS are allowed.

- **RIS and EP.** All sumo-bots belonging to this class can be built out of the parts provided in *one* RIS and *one* official MINDSTORMS expansion pack of your choice. All expansion packs, including Ultimate Accessories, are allowed. You are allowed a maximum of *three* motors and *four* sensors.

This is the essence of describing the sumo-bot specifications for a rule set. Be specific, strict, and to the point.

As I warned earlier, you need to watch out for loopholes in your rules. What could happen if the word *autonomous* didn't appear in the first rule? Someone might bring a sumo-bot to the event and pull out a remote control. You immediately object, "Hey! You can't do that! The whole point of robotic sumo is autonomous creations!" But he can simply smile and say, "Sorry, it's not stated in the rules." Other possibilities for loopholes would occur if the rules didn't state "must be built out of LEGO pieces" and "we will check your sumo-bot's weight." And if you said "*x* output ports and *x* input ports allowed" instead of "*x* motors and *x* sensors allowed," participants could take advantage of that loophole as well (as you know, quite a few sensors or motors can go on just one RCX port).

> **CAUTION** *Be sure to state something in your rules about the sumo-bots being autonomous.*

Programming Rules

Next, formulate *programming rules*. You might prefer to allow only one programming language, such as RCX Code, or several languages. For example, the following programming rules allow the RCX Code, NQC, and Visual Basic programming languages. These can all be done on the standard firmware and will make remote-control activation easier (if you're doing remote-control activation).

The Programming: All contestants must use the standard firmware for their RCX; no custom firmware please. Multiple programs on the RCX are allowed. If, during the event, any contestant deems it necessary to change or update his or her program(s), he or she can do so, as long as the contestant's sumo-bot is not currently participating and is not currently needed on the arena. The programming languages, within the RCX's standard firmware, admitted are:

- **RCX Code.** The programming language that comes with the RIS.

- **NQC (Not Quite C).** A textual programming language based on C.

- **Visual Basic.** A textual programming language that can be used on the RCX.

Did you catch some of the places where loopholes could be unwittingly introduced? For example, if the rule didn't say that the participants couldn't reprogram when their sumo-bot is needed on the arena or currently participating on the arena, they could simply get up at any time and start reprogramming. I don't think the majority of people at an event would appreciate waiting for someone to fix a messed up calibration function!

Robotic Sumo Arena Rule

You also should properly describe your arena in a rule set. This example describes the robotic sumo arena you will learn how to build later in this chapter.

The Robotic Sumo Arena: The competition takes place in a circular arena 4 feet in diameter. The surface is painted glossy white and is bordered with a 2-inch-thick black, glossy line. The arena is made out of 3/4-inch, BC-grade plywood, which is plywood that is sanded smooth on one side; the smooth surface will be used for the sumo-bots. During play, the arena will be raised approximately 3 inches above ground.

Make sure you describe all the colors on your arena, the diameter, size of the border, possibly the materials it is constructed from, and the height or how high it will be raised. You can also add additional details—the more the participants know about the arena, the better!

Rules of Play

The actual rules of play are obviously a crucial part of your rule set. The following example should illustrate for you what these rules are all about.

The Play: At the beginning of a round, the sumo-bots will be placed 5 inches apart from each other in a parallel position. They will face in *opposite* directions so that they will not merely run into each other (possibly ending the round immediately); active searching is enforced in this way. The *judge* will start *both* sumo-bots with *remote activation*. The round is exactly 3 minutes. A bout is *over* when the following happens:

- **A sumo-bot is either pushed off or falls off the arena.** A sumo-bot is not considered "out" until it has entirely fallen off the arena. Hanging over the edge does not disqualify a sumo-bot.

- **The 3-minute time permitted for a round has run out and there have been no victories.** A sudden death round will be permitted (see below).

- **The sumo-bots are entangled for 30 seconds.** A replay will follow (see below).

- **One of the sumo-bots becomes disabled for any reason.** The other sumo-bot will be declared winner.

Sudden Death: A *sudden death* is a 1-minute round whose purpose is to resolve which sumo-bot is the winner from a previous, expired 3-minute regular round. In sudden death, both sumo-bots are repositioned and started remotely by the judge as is normally done. If no sumo-bot is found to be a winner at the end of 1 minute, the judge will toss a coin to determine the winner. All sumo-bots declared winner in sudden death will be judged by normal scoring standards, *except* those determined by flipping a coin (see below).

A Replay: A *replay* is always initiated at the end of a bout if the 3-minute round isn't up or if an entanglement has occurred. A replay consists of stopping the clock, repositioning both sumo-bots, starting the sumo-bots, and then turning the clock back on.

The End of the Round: After *three victories*, *3 minutes*, or a *sudden death*, the round is declared over. Both sumo-bots will be awarded points, and the sumo-bot with the most points will be awarded a *win*. Here is the point system:

- 1 point for a victory

- 1/2 point for a victory determined by flipping a coin in sudden death

- 0 points for a loss

The Determination of a Round: *All* rounds will be determined by a *judge*. All of the judge's decisions are *final*. Any participant who argues may be disqualified.

The first paragraph's statement about the placement and direction of the sumo-bots is very important. *Always* have the sumo-bots start in a position in which they are not facing toward each other. Facing the opposing sumo-bots directly at each other makes the game predictable to a degree, and some people can take advantage of this and pull some stunts that will land them in first place. Therefore, this can be considered a loophole.

It is also crucial to properly inform the participant about the method of activation. In this rule set, the judge will take care of all activation. However, many events specify user-activation: the creator of the sumo-bot is responsible for activating the sumo-bot, such as through a bumper on the sumo-bot. A rule set that employs user-activation will always have a time limit that the sumo-bots must wait before starting (such as 4 or 5 seconds). All participants must program their sumo-bots (in advance) to wait for that period of time after the bumper has been activated. The participators are then told to *clear out!*

> **NOTE** *A* round *is a 3-minute time period that can have as many* bouts *as you want in the round. The currently participating sumo-bots can play a number of bouts in a round; if there is a victory within the first minute of play, set up the sumo-bots again. They still have 2 minutes! However, most rule sets have an additional rule: after three victories, the round is over. Although the sumo-bots may be only a minute and a half into their round, if there have been three victories, the round is declared over (this can save the underdog from getting unnecessarily slaughtered).*

The stopping point conditions need to be made clear in the rule set. If a sumo-bot goes off the arena, *that* declares the end of a bout. Sometimes a sumo-bot will teeter on the edge of the arena—some say this is considered off; others don't. Be sure to specify your opinion of this situation in your rule set. Another situation commonly discussed in rule sets is *entanglement,* when both sumo-bots are entangled beyond their ability to untangle. Most rule sets will give 30 seconds before declaring official entanglement. And don't forget the disablement rule! If any of the sumo-bots become disabled for any reason, the other sumo-bot should be declared winner.

The sudden death rule is for resolving an undetermined round, when no one has won throughout the entire 3-minute round. To resolve the round, sudden death steps in with an additional minute. In the (rare) circumstance of no sumo-bot winning in that minute, the winner is decided with a coin flip.

The replay is nothing more than getting the sumo-bots set back up. The only important point to make is that the timer that watches each 3-minute round is stopped until the sumo-bots are ready to begin again.

The next-to-last item defines the *end of a round* and point system. Event point systems can vary widely.

The very last rule here is one of the most important, because leaving it out presents a loophole that can cause many problems. Always *firmly* declare in your rule set that the judge's decision is *final.*

Other Rules

Finally, your rule set needs various rules for dealing with (and preventing) unexpected situations.

Various Rules: In addition to the main set of rules, there are a few other rules that must be recognized for the safety and fairness of all participants:

- **Intentional damage or alteration of the arena's surface is prohibited.** Mechanisms on your sumo-bot that can harm or alter the arena's surface are prohibited; any sumo-bot that the judge deems harmful to the arena will be disqualified.

- **Absolutely all violent actions are prohibited.** Robotic sumo is a game of pushing, not destruction. Everything from flamethrowers, to sharp objects, to liquids, to bombs are absolutely and entirely prohibited. **Only LEGO pieces are allowed in this event.**

- **Your sumo-bot may not intentionally drop any LEGO piece(s) or any other object on the arena's surface.** Anything that may be dropped on the arena, intentionally or unintentionally, will be immediately removed.

- **Only regular alkaline batteries in the standard setup, shown in the *Constructopedia* included with the RIS, are allowed.** Any other type of battery and/or custom battery setup is forbidden.

- **Flooding the arena with IR rays, electromagnetic interference, and using any electronics other than the allowed LEGO electronics are prohibited.** Only LEGO pieces are allowed in this event.

- **All participating sumo-bots must possess a form of mobility and use that mobility during play.** Immobile sumo-bots will not be admitted, and sumo-bots that do not use their mobility during play will be disqualified.

- **If, at any time, the judge decides that a participating sumo-bot should be removed, the judge has the right to disqualify that sumo-bot.** This can be due to harmful violence, disregard for the rules, or any other reason that the judge declares.

As you can see, the rule set is very specific and perhaps repetitive in stressing some rules. Although the first section in this rule set, "The Sumo-Bot" section, says that only LEGO pieces are allowed, the "Various Rules" section disallows flamethrowers, custom sensors, and non-LEGO pieces. You want to make it absolutely clear that this is not one of those shows on TV where machines try to rip each other to shreds. This is robotic sumo!

Notice the rule that says all sumo-bots must possess a form of mobility and *use* that mobility. Who knows—someone might think up of a strategy where the sumo-bot doesn't move. Even if you think there is only the slightest chance of something that you don't want to happen, add a rule about it in your rule set. The more loopholes you can eliminate, the better.

Finally, notice the last of the various rules, which once again underscores and clarifies the sovereignty of the judge.

> **TIP** *This rule set was created for a fairly large event, where many participants might not know the host. Giving the judge enough power is important for this situation. Consider your particular situation in developing your rule set. For example, if your event involves only friends coming to your house, you don't need to be that strict about the judge's power.*

Formatting a Complete Rule Set

Once you've written all the rules for your rule set, you'll want to put them into a completed format. The following shows the sample rule set in a completed format.

....

LEGO Robotic Sumo Event 2004 (LRSE)
Rules Created by David J. Perdue

Description: Robotic sumo is a competition where two robots, known as *sumo-bots*, attempt to push each other out of an arena using mechanisms, cunning, and brute force. The arena for LRSE is a 4-foot diameter circle, and the time given for each round is 3 minutes. Your goal is to create a sumo-bot that can push its opponent out of the arena before being pushed out of the arena by the competing sumo-bot.

The Sumo-Bots: All participating robots, known as sumo-bots, must be constructed out of LEGO pieces only. They must be completely autonomous—that is, acting independently of humans—and not contain anything non-LEGO. This includes custom sensors.

Weight and Size: The maximum weight allowed is 2 pounds and the maximum width is 25 studs. All sumo-bots will be checked for weight and size specifications before being admitted. You will be given one chance to reduce your sumo-bot's weight and/or size if it exceeds the 2-pound weight limit or 25-stud width limit. Sumo-bots that fail to meet these specifications will not be allowed entry.

Classes of Sumo-Bots: There are two distinct classes for this robotic sumo competition, and both revolve around the use of the Robotics Invention System (RIS) and the RCX microcomputer contained in the RIS. Both will be competing together, and both are subject to all the same rules except for the parts specifications. The two classes are:

- **RIS-Only.** All sumo-bots belonging to this class must be built out of the parts provided in *one* RIS *only*. All versions of the RIS are allowed.

- **RIS and EP.** All sumo-bots belonging to this class can be built out of the parts provided in *one* RIS and *one* official MINDSTORMS expansion pack of your choice. All expansion packs, including Ultimate Accessories, are allowed. You are allowed a maximum of *three* motors and *four* sensors.

The Programming: All contestants must use the standard firmware for their RCX; no custom firmware please. Multiple programs on the RCX are allowed. If, during the event, any contestant deems it necessary to change or update his or her program(s), he or she can do so, as long as the contestant's sumo-bot is not currently participating and is not currently needed on the arena. The programming languages, within the RCX's standard firmware, admitted are:

- **RCX Code.** The programming language that comes with the RIS.

- **NQC (Not Quite C).** A textual programming language based on C.

- **Visual Basic.** A textual programming language that can be used on the RCX.

The Robotic Sumo Arena: The competition takes place in a circular arena 4 feet in diameter. The surface is painted glossy white and is bordered with a 2-inch-thick black, glossy line. The arena is made out of 3/4-inch BC-grade plywood, which is plywood that is sanded smooth on one side; the smooth surface will be used for the sumo-bots. During play, the arena will be raised approximately 3 inches above ground.

The Play: At the beginning of a round, the sumo-bots will be placed 5 inches apart from each other in a parallel position. They will face in *opposite* directions so that they will not merely run into each other (possibly ending the round immediately); active searching is enforced in this way. The *judge* will start *both* sumo-bots with *remote activation*. The round is exactly 3 minutes. A bout is *over* when the following happens:

- **A sumo-bot is either pushed off or falls off the arena.** A sumo-bot is not considered "out" until it has entirely fallen off the arena. Hanging over the edge does not disqualify a sumo-bot.

- **The 3-minute time permitted for a round has run out and there have been no victories.** A sudden death round will be permitted (see below).

- **The sumo-bots are entangled for 30 seconds.** A replay will follow (see below).

- **One of the sumo-bots becomes disabled for any reason.** The other sumo-bot will be declared winner.

Sudden Death: A *sudden death* is a 1-minute round whose purpose is to resolve which sumo-bot is the winner from a previous, expired 3-minute regular round. In sudden death, both sumo-bots are repositioned and started remotely by the judge as is normally done. If no sumo-bot is found to be a winner at the end of 1 minute, the judge will toss a coin to determine the winner. All sumo-bots declared winner in sudden death will be judged by normal scoring standards, *except* those determined by flipping a coin (see below).

A Replay: A *replay* is always initiated at the end of a bout if the 3-minute round isn't up or if an entanglement has occurred. A replay consists of stopping the clock, repositioning both sumo-bots, starting the sumo-bots, and then turning the clock back on.

continued

The End of the Round: After *three victories*, *3 minutes*, or a *sudden death*, the round is declared *over*. Both sumo-bots will be awarded points, and the sumo-bot with the most points will be awarded a *win*. Here is the point system:

- 1 point for a victory

- 1/2 point for a victory determined by flipping a coin in sudden death

- 0 points for a loss

The Determination of a Round: *All* rounds will be determined by a *judge*. All of the judge's decisions are *final*. Any participant who argues may be disqualified.

Various Rules: In addition to the main set of rules, there are a few other rules that must be recognized for the safety and fairness of all participants:

- **Intentional damage or alteration of the arena's surface is prohibited.** Mechanisms on your sumo-bot that can harm or alter the arena's surface are prohibited; any sumo-bot that the judge deems harmful to the arena will be disqualified.

- **Absolutely all violent actions are prohibited.** Robotic sumo is a game of pushing, not destruction. Everything from flame-throwers, to sharp objects, to liquids, to bombs are absolutely and entirely prohibited. **Only LEGO pieces are allowed in this event.**

- **Your sumo-bot may not intentionally drop any LEGO piece(s) or any other object on the arena's surface.** Anything that may be dropped on the arena, intentionally or unintentionally, will be immediately removed.

- **Only regular alkaline batteries in the standard setup, shown in the *Constructopedia* included with the RIS, are allowed.** Any other type of battery and/or custom battery setup is forbidden.

- **Flooding the arena with IR rays, electromagnetic interference, and using any electronics other than the allowed LEGO electronics are prohibited.** Only LEGO pieces are allowed in this event.

- **All participating sumo-bots must possess a form of mobility and use that mobility during play.** Immobile sumo-bots will not be admitted, and sumo-bots that do not use their mobility during play will be disqualified.

- **If, at any time, the judge decides that a participating sumo-bot should be removed, the judge has the right to disqualify that sumo-bot.** This can be due to harmful violence, disregard for the rules, or any other reason that the judge declares.

The Champion: Play will be conducted in double-elimination tournament style, guaranteeing that each sumo-bot will participate in two rounds. The sumo-bot with the most *wins* will be declared *champion*. If two sumo-bots have the same number of wins, the sumo-bot with the most *victories* will be declared *champion*.

....

Notice a few additions to what you've seen in the previous sections in this real robotic sumo rule set. I added a quick description of robotic sumo for the uninformed at the top of the rule set, and a rule declaring who is the winner at the bottom. This same rule also describes how the sumo-bots will be competing, which is double-elimination tournament style.

Remember that this isn't all there is to a rule set; there can be *many* more rules in a rule set. You can have everything from an addition to the robotic sumo game to a rule where the participants can switch out subassemblies on their sumo-bots. Don't hesitate to experiment with your rule set, try new things, and introduce new rules.

In your rule set, you also need to include information about the location and time of the event. You should also include your e-mail address in the rule set, so that people can ask you questions about the rules and if their particular sumo-bot would qualify. This is all part of *preparing* for an event, as discussed in the "Announcing, Preparing, and Managing the Event" section later in this chapter. You pick a place, date, and answer people's questions all the way up to the time of the event.

Now that we've discussed creating your rule set, the next task for hosting your own robotic sumo event that we need to discuss is making a robotic sumo arena.

Constructing the Battle Zone

Not only do you need a robotic sumo arena (or two or more arenas) for hosting a robotic sumo event, but you also need one for testing your sumo-bots. Here, I'll present a list of materials and step-by-step instructions for building an arena.

Building Materials for an Arena

Building a robotic sumo arena will cost about $30 to $40 (for the plywood, paint, and primer) and take about two to three hours of physical labor (cutting the plywood, priming it, painting it, and a few other chores). However, taking into account the time for the paint to dry, you'll need several days.

The following is a list of the equipment and materials you will need to make a robotic sumo arena:

- A half-sheet of 3/4-inch BC plywood that is finished smooth (sanded to make it smooth) on one side, which will be used as the actual surface

- Masking tape and some paper (you'll use these when painting the arena)

- A pencil and a yardstick (ever heard of a homemade protractor?)

- One can of primer, for the plywood (such as a spray-can-type primer made by Krylon, of the "Interior & Exterior" and "fast drying" type)

- Two cans of white spray paint, for the arena surface (such as Krylon Glossy White)

- One can of black spray paint, for the perimeter (such as Krylon Glossy Black)

- A power jigsaw, to cut the wood into a circle

- A power sander, to sand away any rough edges

> **TIP** *When you buy your piece of plywood, ask the salesperson to cut it in half; it only takes half a piece (half-sheet) to make your arena. Also, make sure to examine it carefully before taking it home. I got mine home, only to find large cracks in it that were filled with wood putty but still uneven enough to cause the surface to be bumpy. I had to fix all the bumpy spots by filling them with more wood putty and then sanding it flush later. You don't want to need to do this!*

How to Construct the Arena

As with the instructions for building sumo-bots, you'll learn how to build a robotic sumo arena step by step.

In step 1, find the center of your piece of plywood and then draw the circle that will outline your arena. To do this, begin by taking either a piece of string or a measuring tape and stretch it from one corner of your piece of wood to the opposite one (this should separate your arena into two triangles). With a pencil, mark along the measuring tape or string about in the middle. Repeat this for the other two corners; you should now have an *X* in the middle of the arena, pinpointing the exact center of your piece of wood.

Next, tape a nail to the very extreme end of one end of the yardstick. You are building an arena that is 4 feet in diameter, so this means the radius will be 2 feet. Find the 2-foot mark on your yardstick (or 2 feet away from where your nail is) and carefully tape the pencil there. Now place the nail *exactly* where the center of the plywood is (where your *X* is), and carefully begin drawing your circle with the pencil. Go all the way around to complete the first step.

In step 2, use a jigsaw to cut the wooden circle by carefully following the line you just drew. After cutting the wood, sand any rough edges.

> **CAUTION** *Make sure you use the power tools according to the manufacturer's guidelines and wear the proper safety gear while using them.*

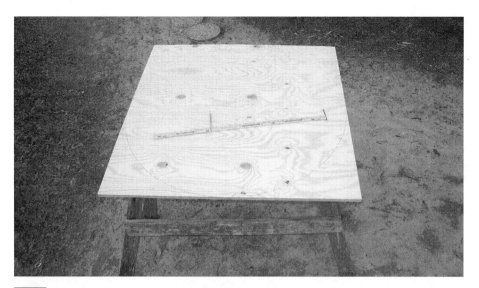

Robotic Sumo Arena Step 1: On a piece of plywood, draw an X, then a circle with a 2-foot radius (notice the homemade protractor sitting on the plywood).

Robotic Sumo Arena Step 2: Using a jigsaw, cut around the circle.

In step 3, you prime the wood. Get your can of primer and spray the entire surface, as well as the sides. I ended up using the *entire* can, so you should probably go over everything lightly first, and then go back later and cover thin spots. You don't want to run out and have just a little spot left! (Actually, even if you did, that would be okay—you can continue with step 4.)

CAUTION *Read the safety precautions and directions before priming or painting. Always paint in a well-ventilated area.*

 Robotic Sumo Arena Step 3: Prime the circular wood surface.

You begin the painting in step 4. With your white paint, cover nearly the entire surface of the arena. You don't need to cover the very outer edge, but try to get most of the surface. Wait for that coat to dry, and apply another coat of paint. Continue applying coats until you are satisfied with a good, uniform white color. Before proceeding to step 5, let the white paint dry completely (it should be completely dry and ready to work with in about a day or two).

 Robotic Sumo Arena Step 4: Apply coats of white paint to most of the surface.

At this point, you need to spray on the black paint, but *without* getting it on the white paint. To do this, use the masking tape and paper to entirely cover the area on which you don't want to get black paint (*mask* that area). First, lay down a circle of masking tape on the arena. You want a 2-inch thick line, so the tape must be 2 inches away from the edge of the board. I got a ruler and went all the way around the arena, making little marks showing where 2 inches away from the edge were. After that, I got the masking tape and followed the lines until I made a complete circle.

Once you've laid down the masking tape, take your paper and entirely cover the area that you want to mask from the black paint. Place one piece of paper, put a piece of masking tape on to hold it in place, and repeat this until you have the entire white surface covered. If you have access to butcher paper or any other large sheets of paper, that will make this part a little easier.

With the black paint, spray the 2-inch thick area and also the edges. Wait for that to dry and apply another coat. Do this until you are satisfied with the results.

 Robotic Sumo Arena Step 5: Spray-paint the edges of the arena with black paint.

NOTE *If you look at the step 5 image, you can see the tape I placed around the perimeter, but you might be wondering where the paper is. Unfortunately, because of the lighting, the paper is virtually invisible in this photo.*

A picture of the completed arena, with all the paper taken off, of course, is shown in Figure 11-1. That's how your arena should look.

Figure 11-1. Completed robotic sumo arena

You are now ready to move onwards in the quest of hosting your own robotic sumo event.

Announcing, Preparing, and Managing the Event

After you have the rule sets defined and the arena constructed, you're ready to concentrate on the event itself.

Announcing and Preparing for the Event

To get the word out about your event, not only tell your friends (and have them tell their friends), but also use LUGNET. Simply put a posting in the proper forum. If you are a LUGNET member, you have the special privilege of being able to place your posting *right up on the front page of LUGNET*. Thousands of people will see your post! This is definitely a good way to get the word out.

To prepare for the event, one important task is picking a place for it. Your place of competition could be your house or garage, but for bigger events, consider places like RadioShack stores, churches, YMCA, country clubs, and so on. After you've picked your place, set a date and time. Also, depending on the number of participating sumo-bots, you may need to have more than one arena for the event. If you're doing a first-time event with some friends at your house, you'll probably need just one arena. On the other hand, if you're hosting a sixth annual event at the center of large city in an Ultimate Electronics store, count on needing more than one arena.

Managing the Event

If there are any problems, any questions, and anything else that needs to be handled, it's up to you, as the host, judge (unless you appointed someone else as judge), and manager of the event. Therefore, you have the following responsibilities:

- Start the event on time (even if you have to stand on a platform and shout through a megaphone).

- Pick out two sumo-bots, place them in the arena as described in the rule set, and activate them (whether by remote or user activation).

- Use a timer to time the sumo-bots for the allotted time given by the rule set for each round. When a replay or sudden death becomes necessary, stop the timer until the sumo-bots are ready again.

- Watch carefully to determine who's out and who's not. Have the sumo-bots been entangled for 30 seconds? That's up to you. Who was the winner of that round? That's up to you, too.

- Keep track of the points. At the end of every bout, mark off the score. You can use paper and a pencil, a handheld computer, or any other method that works for you. Just make sure you're keeping the score *accurately*. Telling someone who just lost by a point, "I must have missed a point or two there. Oh well…," usually doesn't make them too happy.

- When everything is said and done, announce the end of the event and the champion. Hand out any prizes, firmly congratulate the winner, and invite everyone to your *next* robotic sumo event. (After all, you're going to host another one aren't you?)

Conclusion

Since we're at the end of Part Five, it would be a good time to summarize what it was about:

- There are many LEGO User Groups and other organizations that host robotic sumo events.

- Analyzing a rule set and following all the rules carefully is essential when participating in a robotic sumo event.

- Bringing the proper tools—such as batteries and extra pieces—to a robotic sumo event is essential and advantageous.

- Anytime is the right time to host your own LEGO MINDSTORMS robotic sumo event.

- When creating your own rule set, make it as specific as possible and always carefully check for loopholes.

- Creating a robotic sumo arena is a must, and it's a must to make sure you have enough of them for an event.

- The place and time you picked for your event (be sure to include these specifics in your rule set) and how you announced the event will affect the number of people who attend and participate.

- It's your job to take complete control over every aspect at your robotic sumo event. *You* are the host, judge, and manager.

LEGO MINDSTORMS robotic sumo is for people who like to dream big dreams. In other words, robotic sumo can fulfill your LEGO dreams. Go to just one event, or host just one event, and you'll see what I mean. When you combine your favorite hobby, people, competition, and an atmosphere of creativity and LEGO, you get unforgettable excitement. When you start hosting your own events (and I'm confident you will), they start to grow. Over time, and with each event, your events get more exposure and recognition, and more and more people come to attend and participate. Robotic sumo isn't just fun, it's also rewarding.

If you ever get a little discouraged, think of the humble beginnings of the LEGO Company. Ole Kirk Christiansen started out as a carpenter who made some wooden building blocks in his workshop—*that* was the beginnings of LEGO. The LEGO Company, at its earliest stages, was even making wooden model cars. Humble beginnings are common; the worldwide recognition that LEGO now has isn't. The one aspect that all highly successful people and organizations have in common is *big dreams and goals*.

Throughout your quest into LEGO MINDSTORMS robotic sumo, remember the ultimate goal: to play well. But let's not just play well, let's play *well*. Don't be satisfied with going for second place or third place. Always go for first place—the champion's place. Apply this attitude to other areas of robotic sumo as well. Is there a huge, unique, advanced, or particular sumo-bot you dream of building some day? Don't just dream and hope you can build it in the future, make it your goal to build that sumo-bot. Is there a particular type of event you would like to host? Make it your goal to host that event. Think big!

Index

forums.apress.com

FOR PROFESSIONALS BY PROFESSIONALS™

JOIN THE APRESS FORUMS AND BE PART OF OUR COMMUNITY. You'll find discussions that cover topics of interest to IT professionals, programmers, and enthusiasts just like you. If you post a query to one of our forums, you can expect that some of the best minds in the business—especially Apress authors, who all write with *The Expert's Voice*™—will chime in to help you. Why not aim to become one of our most valuable participants (MVPs) and win cool stuff? Here's a sampling of what you'll find:

DATABASES
Data drives everything.

Share information, exchange ideas, and discuss any database programming or administration issues.

PROGRAMMING/BUSINESS
Unfortunately, it is.

Talk about the Apress line of books that cover software methodology, best practices, and how programmers interact with the "suits."

INTERNET TECHNOLOGIES AND NETWORKING
Try living without plumbing (and eventually IPv6).

Talk about networking topics including protocols, design, administration, wireless, wired, storage, backup, certifications, trends, and new technologies.

WEB DEVELOPMENT/DESIGN
Ugly doesn't cut it anymore, and CGI is absurd.

Help is in sight for your site. Find design solutions for your projects and get ideas for building an interactive Web site.

JAVA
We've come a long way from the old Oak tree.

Hang out and discuss Java in whatever flavor you choose: J2SE, J2EE, J2ME, Jakarta, and so on.

SECURITY
Lots of bad guys out there—the good guys need help.

Discuss computer and network security issues here. Just don't let anyone else know the answers!

MAC OS X
All about the Zen of OS X.

OS X is both the present and the future for Mac apps. Make suggestions, offer up ideas, or boast about your new hardware.

TECHNOLOGY IN ACTION
Cool things. Fun things.

It's after hours. It's time to play. Whether you're into LEGO® MINDSTORMS™ or turning an old PC into a DVR, this is where technology turns into fun.

OPEN SOURCE
Source code is good; understanding (open) source is better.

Discuss open source technologies and related topics such as PHP, MySQL, Linux, Perl, Apache, Python, and more.

WINDOWS
No defenestration here.

Ask questions about all aspects of Windows programming, get help on Microsoft technologies covered in Apress books, or provide feedback on any Apress Windows book.

HOW TO PARTICIPATE:
Go to the Apress Forums site at **http://forums.apress.com/**.
Click the New User link.